REBELS FOR THE CAUSE

Also by Jon Spurling

All Guns Blazing: Arsenal In The 1980s
(Aureus Publishing, Cardiff, 2001)

Top Guns: Arsenal In The 1990s
(Aureus Publishing, Cardiff, 2001)

Rebels
for the
Cause

The Alternative History of Arsenal Football Club

JON SPURLING

MAINSTREAM
PUBLISHING

EDINBURGH AND LONDON

THIS BOOK IS DEDICATED TO MY SISTER, HELEN.

Reprinted 2007, 2009

Copyright © Jon Spurling, 2003
All rights reserved
The moral right of the author has been asserted

First published in Great Britain in 2003 by
MAINSTREAM PUBLISHING COMPANY
(EDINBURGH) LTD
7 Albany Street
Edinburgh EH1 3UG

This edition, 2004

ISBN 9781840189001

A catalogue record for this book is available from the British Library

Printed and bound in Great Britain by
Cox & Wyman Ltd

Acknowledgements

It has been almost ten years since I began to gather sources and interview players for this book. I must extend an enormous thank you to the following men who once wore the red-and-white shirt with pride: George Eastham, Bobby Gould, Ian Ure, Terry Neill, Alan Hudson, Malcolm Macdonald, Charlie Nicholas, Stewart Robson, Willie Young, Steve Williams, Brian McDermott, Alan Smith, Anders Limpar, Paul Davis and Perry Groves. Grateful thanks also to Charlie George, who, although unable to grant me a formal interview, was happy to field my and the audience's questions at Sportspages in late 2002. Sadly, Tommy Lawton, Paul Vaessen, Ted Drake and Stoke City's ex-striker Harry Davies died before they had a chance to read their contribution to the text. Thanks also to the two members of recent Arsenal sides, and a current Arsenal star, who were willing to be interviewed but prefer to remain anonymous, and to Claude Anelka, for being so candid during the 'Anelka-gate' saga.

I am also indebted to the following people who helped steer me in the right direction, and offered encouragement along the way: Dilwyn Porter at University College, Worcester, for his assistance on Arsenal's match against the Moscow Dynamos; the understanding staff at the Fulham and Leeds archives for information on Sir Henry Norris and Wilf Copping; Dave at the Newspaper Library branch of the British Library; David Bissmire and Kevin Whitcher from the fanzine stall; Richard Lewis at Sportspages and Ian Trevett from *Highbury High*. Plus, David Scripps at Action Images and Marina Palmer at Professional

Sport, for their trawling of the archives for photographs. To the staff at The Bookcentre, Hoddesdon, for allowing me to pretend I'm a big-shot author for a couple of hours, to Meuryn Hughes at Aureus, for giving me my big writing break and to Linda Durkin for typing the book. Thanks also to the patient folk at Mainstream Publishing. Special thanks to Tina Hudson for the cover design, Deborah Kilpatrick for her careful editing of the text and Graeme Blaikie for his incredibly understanding attitude towards deadlines. And to Bill Campbell for showing faith in the project.

To the Webber boys (Tim and Nick), Brendon, and Stuart ('The Neph') for their company, and opinions, at Arsenal matches, and John Booker for lifts to the games. To my friends, who continue to glaze over whenever I mention the 'A' word – Barry, Phil and Tatiana, Seb and Marnie, Jo and Gareth, Louise, Adam and Nicky, Brummie and Ruth, Ian and Anita, Tim and Lucy, Steve (the best best man) and Lucy, Sarah, Si Williams, Steve Davies, Andrew, Si Barrick, Charlie and Natalie, Louise and Iain, Sam and Simon, and Paul and Vicky.

And finally, thanks to my mum and dad and to my wife – Helen – who were all as encouraging as ever ('Not another bloody book on Arsenal!').

Contents

Introduction

> It doesn't bother me that we're not well liked. It's part of
> our history.
>
> > George Graham, speaking in 1994

Rebels For The Cause takes an alternative look at the history of
Arsenal. Numerous other tomes have dwelt on the club's greatest
triumphs and glorious past. In this book I will focus on the
revolutionaries and rogues who have shaped the Gunners' past
and present and, in the process, baited authority and blazed new
trails. In doing so, I will be venturing beyond the gleaming façade
of Highbury's marble halls and the classic '30s art-deco stands,
and shedding light on the myths, intrigue and controversy which
have surrounded the club since 1886. Rich, southern-based
baddies Arsenal have always been essentially an outsider's club,
mysteriously strengthened by the effective channelling of the
hatred they receive. They remain better than anyone else at
turning a crisis into a triumph.

The Arsenal board, through its mouthpiece, the official
programme, has always tried to underplay – or worse, ignore – the
club's controversial past. They would rather forget about the
bungs, brawls and bust-ups, which fail to fit with the Identikit
image of Arsenal as a traditional, morally upright institution. For
instance, when George Graham was fired in 1995, the club, on
advice from its lawyers, simply did not comment on the affair. In
the official programme, Peter Hill-Wood noted stiffly that while

the club was 'indebted' to the Scot, it was in Arsenal's 'best interests' that he should leave. The official end-of-season video (entitled *What A Season*) was even less forthcoming. King of bland Matthew Lorenzo commented that Graham left the club under 'unfortunate circumstances'. No kidding. The reason given by Hill-Wood for the club's reticence in discussing the Graham case was the possibility of George contesting his year-long ban from football in the law courts. Any public debate on the case would represent a form of *sub judice*. How convenient for the club; it is unlikely that the board would have released the relevant details to fans anyway. It was the same story back in 1977, when, after rebels Alan Hudson and Malcolm Macdonald were sent home from the pre-season tour of Australia and the Far East and the story dominated column inches in the tabloids, official club propaganda had you believe it had never happened.

In the same vein, finding the truth about Arsenal's dim and distant past is as tricky as discovering the whereabouts of the world's most elusive man – and, if tabloid rumour is correct, the club's most infamous fan – Osama Bin Laden. The club's former haunts in Plumstead yield little of interest, and parks and roads now cover the pitches where Royal and Woolwich Arsenal once played. The pubs where players once changed before matches have either been demolished or, in the case of the Royal Oak (situated next to Woolwich Arsenal station), contain no evidence. Most infuriatingly of all, a visit to the site of the Woolwich Armaments factory yields little either. The Ex-Employees Association proves that founding fathers David Danskin and Jack Humble worked there, but there is no information other than brief details on them and a few faded photographs. The factory itself is currently being converted into 'affordable homes'. With its easy access to London and the Thames, a one-bedroom flat will set you back £200,000. There is certainly no plaque commemorating the site of the workers' lunchtime kickabouts. Only testimonies and a selection of old newspapers can reveal the real story behind Arsenal's mutinous origins.

It strikes me as apt that so much information on Arsenal's contentious past is difficult to trace. Several of the chapters in this book are examples of 'hidden history', and the club would rather the stories remained buried. Yet I would argue that without the backstairs intrigue and occasional acts of heresy, the Gunners would probably have remained an insignificant factory team and not moved to Islington or won trophies at all. Part of the Faustian lot of the Arsenal fan is to accept that a combination of downright dodgy behaviour and rebellion has been a principal driving force behind the club during its 118-year existence.

A few years ago, Kate Adie, the erstwhile BBC reporter who was sent to any combat zone which happened to be boiling over at the time, was asked by a member of the *Question Time* audience why only 'bad news' was reported in the media. Unfazed, she replied: 'If you were lying in your garden in the middle of a row of houses, and on one side it was quiet and on the other a fight was going on, which fence would you look over?' Point taken: human nature dictates that we're far more interested in conflict and the psyche of the abrasive (the Liam Gallaghers and the Ollie Reeds) than we are in Mary Poppins-type goody-goodies. Examples: university professors constantly gripe that history undergraduates are keen to study nothing but the machinations of twentieth-century dictators; TV executives make documentaries about hell-raisers Alex Higgins and John McEnroe rather than, say, Steve Davis or Bjorn Borg; and Darth Vader merchandise still outsells all other *Star Wars* gear. It's no surprise, therefore, that Charlie George and Ian Wright are still voted the greatest-ever Gunners on various unofficial club websites.

It is ironic that a club which originally bought the land for Highbury stadium from a college of divinity should have such an excellent reputation for naughtiness. This trait is part of the genetic make-up of the club. Several of the most important officials in the club's history, including David Danskin, Henry Norris, David Dein and George Graham, were prepared to crush existing codes of conduct and behaviour in order to ensure the success of Arsenal. In doing so, they attracted criticism from the national press and, on occasion, Gunners fans and the local community. Many of Arsenal's star players, particularly in recent years, have also made effortless journeys from back to front pages.

Whether it was club captain Tony Adams in the '90s, Charlie Nicholas in the '80s or the booze-fuelled exploits of several of the club's '70s stars, the letters AFC have always sold newspapers.

This book sheds light on why Arsenal remain the club everyone loves to hate. Even in these heady days of Wenger's stylish Continental team, ex-Sports Minister Tony Banks commented in 2002 that it would be 'political suicide' for a high-ranking cabinet minister to profess love for the Gunners. He was probably alluding to the case of New Labour's former Sports Minister, Kate Hoey, whose rapid descent from bright young thing to obscure back-bencher outranks even Martin Hayes' journey from Arsenal star to second-hand car dealer on Highbury Corner. Presumably her dismissal from the Blair cabinet had rather more to do with the Wembley fiasco than supporting Arsenal, or perhaps Tony Banks has hit on a juicy conspiracy theory. Whatever the full truth, most Arsenal fans, and past managers, remain convinced that a media vendetta, dating back to the nineteenth century, has been waged against the club. A case of advanced paranoia, perhaps, or fact? ('You'd be paranoid, if everyone hated you,' Terry Neill wryly commented at a 1980 press conference when he was Arsenal boss.) In reality, from the club's formative days on Kent pitches (Plumstead and Woolwich, now in Greater London, used to be part of Kent), the press has been keen to attach an assortment of derogatory prefixes to the club's name. Those ubiquitous Arsenal tags, 'lucky' and 'boring', originate from nineteenth- and early twentieth-century mud revels with Spurs, who, in the 1890s, claimed to be purveyors of stylish football, in marked contrast to Arsenal's rumbustious approach.

By the time Henry Norris had moved the club to Highbury in 1913 and Arsenal dominated the '30s, the word 'arrogant' had been thrown in by jealous rivals. This was partly because Arsenal were already known to be a club of 'firsts': the first southern side to turn professional, to be run by a football tsar and to push through a share issue. The list is endless. Before and after the Second World War, when other teams struggled to cope with turbulent social and economic conditions, Arsenal, curiously, grew stronger. During the Great Depression in the early '30s, Arsenal's 'Bank of England' status was enhanced, and bizarre encounters with fascist- and communist-controlled sides – Italy's World Cup winners in 1934 and the touring Moscow Dynamos in 1945 respectively – cemented several players' reputations. Some pointed out that only Arsenal, the team with such strong military connections, could prosper in such circumstances. They were probably right.

Throughout the book, I hope you will see that as a collective, Arsenal's rebels, several of whom have agreed to be interviewed, have made massive contributions to the club's success, and that stormy matches, bar-room bother, verbal dust-ups and high-profile brawls have often improved team spirit. Even '90s rebel Nicolas Anelka, whom many believe furthers no cause but his own or his brothers', helped the club to the 1998 Double. It is important to take into account the eras in which many of these characters played and managed. George Eastham and David Danskin – good blokes both – were only considered rebels in their particular time. Eastham's contractual demands, for example, are de rigueur in the twenty-first century, but shocked the class-ridden establishment of the early '60s. On the other hand, Sir Henry Norris's and George Graham's financial dealings would have created tabloid headlines in whatever decade they occurred. And, presumably, Peter Storey will be remembered as arguably football's biggest rogue right through this century and beyond . . .

Jon Spurling, 2003

True story: in early April 2004, as Arsenal's Treble dreams crumbled, and even securing the Premiership title appeared – according to the tabloids – uncertain, the Gunners faced a crucial Good Friday match against Liverpool. At half-time, with Arsenal 2–1 down, the red tops, together with Chelsea fans, could smell blood. Then, Thierry Henry and Robert Pires ruined the script, and secured Arsenal's 4–2 victory with scintillating second-half performances. Two high-profile tabloid journalists were not best pleased. To the astonishment of a gaggle of Arsenal fans filing out of Highbury's East Stand, one said loudly to the other: 'That's fucked my headline for tomorrow.' The other responded: 'My editor has been kicking chairs around. He really thought they'd blown it at half-time.'

Comments that could only add to the conviction of Arsenal fans that the media vendetta against the club never quite disappears.

Since the publication of the hardback edition, I've been able to revise and update several stories, including the ongoing feud with Manchester United, which took another twist during the 2003–04 season. These changes to the text are due to those former Arsenal players, and the member of the current side, who were willing to clarify their versions of events. Thanks also to the generous help of those at the Hammersmith and Fulham archives, and the local historical centre in Islington, and to Tim Webber and Brian Dawes, who pointed out some inaccuracies in the original script.

Enjoy the book.

Jon Spurling,
May 2004

ONE

Freaks from the Factory

> One of the Derby chaps was heard to mutter that: 'A journey to the molten interior of the earth's core would be rather more pleasant and comfortable an experience than our forthcoming visit to the Royal Arsenal.'
>
> *Derby Post*, 15 January 1891

The *Derby Post*'s is a typical view of the time on the Gunners' distant forefathers – and that was in an era when any team south of Watford was invariably dubbed one of the 'southern softies'. Not so Royal Arsenal, the roughest, toughest crew of their time. After 90 minutes of mortal combat against the likes of Morris Bates, John Julian and Jimmy Charteris on Plumstead Common, the battered opposition would limp home, recounting tales of carnage in Kentish fields. Ten years later, perceptions of the newly titled Woolwich Arsenal had barely changed. The entire Second Division was gutted to see the club consistently avoid relegation to Division Three (South) throughout the 1890s, such was the dread engendered by a trip to Woolwich's Manor Ground. To many, it seemed entirely appropriate that the only footballing fatality of 1896 happened to be Woolwich Arsenal's own Joe Powell, whose broken arm became infected after a clash with Kettering Town. The Woolwich boys became everyone's least favourite second team. It was a situation to which those connected with the club quickly became accustomed. Throughout the late 1880s and into the 1890s, the team's infamy grew faster than the club's debts.

The fact that the club were skint, as well as distinctly mediocre and very dirty, was some consolation for their rivals. Years of being exploited by greedy landlords left them staggering from one financial crisis to another, missing out on the gravy train of talent which flowed north to the likes of Wolves and Sunderland. Even when the Royals had attempted to play decent football at their first ground, the crater-ridden surface at Plumstead Common – once used for pig breeding – scuppered their efforts. The Highbury mud-flats, which almost derailed the 1989 title challenge, were like a billiard table compared to the Common's pock-marked surface. Army manoeuvres meant it was littered with holes, ruts and hoof and wheel marks. There were no crossbars – tape was used instead. It was the latest comical instalment in a long-running saga. The 11 workers from the Dial Square workshop had played their first competitive match against the Eastern Wanderers on the Isle of Dogs. Resplendent in a variety of multi-coloured knickerbockers, the boys won 6–0, but were hardly enamoured when the ball kept landing in the open sewer which ran behind the goal. Club secretary Elijah Watkins reported that players had to scrape off the 'mud' – as he tactfully put it – before the game could restart. Little wonder that the local sanitary inspector, the aptly named Mr Fowler, deemed the pitch 'an obvious health hazard'. Heading the old-style football was one thing, being splattered with human excrement was quite another. Ironically, the club's sewer-related problems didn't end there. All this contributed to the fact that, despite their regal name, Royal Arsenal were a rough and ready outfit.

It was hoped, by club officials and opposition alike, that the move to the Manor Ground in 1891 would benefit everyone. The team stood to gain from the improved facilities, the existence of stands and terraces, and cheaper rent. Visiting teams looked forward to parading their skills on a croquet lawn surface and in a generally more pleasant atmosphere. But after a couple of months, the Manor Ground became every inch as inhospitable as Plumstead Common had been. There were several advantages to being regarded, in the words of the *Liverpool Tribune*, as the 'team who played at the end of the earth'. Teams such as Newcastle and

Rotherham dreaded the trek south, especially as rail travel was so slow and unreliable at the time (no change there, then). On top of a seemingly endless journey into London, there was an uncomfortable 40-minute trek from Canon Street Station to Woolwich in an overcrowded steam train, often filled with heckling home fans. Overnight accommodation was also a real pain, particularly as no self-respecting hotelier wanted a bunch of working-class oiks wrecking the joint. So when teams arrived in Woolwich, they were usually knackered, hungry, bad-tempered and in no fit state to play football. Little wonder that during the club's 14-year stay in Division Two, home form was excellent.

The Manor Ground also acquired its own unique notoriety thanks to the tactical deployment of the huge engineering works nearby and the proximity of the southern outfall sewer, the main liquid waste disposal for the whole of south London. The grotesque vision of the factory, belching out noxious compounds, meant that a thick mist and rancid smell hung in the air. The sewer pipe provided opportunists with a chance to watch the team for free, though occasional leaks of raw effluent meant that Arsenal games often stank, literally and metaphorically.

Horrified southern rivals watched in disgust as this bunch of nomads – the bastard offspring of a munitions factory side – rose to become the south's most powerful footballing outfit. Northern opposition, who'd originally invited Woolwich Arsenal to join Division Two on the premise that they could give these Kentish bumpkins a good kicking twice a year, began to regret their decision. The intense dislike aimed at the club wasn't simply due to the team's crude 'kick-and-rush' style of play, the occasionally loutish behaviour of the home crowds or the motley crew of 'soccer mercenaries' within Woolwich Arsenal's side, though of course these factors added to the team's notoriety. The hostility that greeted the team had rather more to do with the actions of Jack Humble and David Danskin. Throughout the latter years of the nineteenth century, the club's bloody-minded founding fathers saw fit to slaughter every sacred cow and destroy virtually all the existing codes of conduct in Victorian football. Humble and Danskin were ruthlessly professional at a time when bumbling amateurism appeared to be the order of the day in southern football. That Dial Square had even got as far as playing their first organised match was down to their rebellious streak and a dash of sheer good fortune. Even in the embryonic stage of AFC's development, those two crucial factors were indelibly imprinted upon the club's DNA. No one liked us and we didn't care; it was a mantra that would ring true throughout the twentieth century, and beyond.

In the mid-1880s, David Danskin came south from Scotland to take up a post at the Woolwich Arsenal. Brought up in the rough end of Kirkcaldy, a town in Fife, he'd taken the brave decision not to work at the Ravenscraig shipyard with his mates and went into the munitions business instead. According to Mrs R.H. Wyatt, one of Danskin's descendants, he was actually forced out of the family home by his parents because they needed the room for his four sisters. He couldn't have timed his move to Kent any better. Europe was already in the grip of a frantic arms race. The in-bred mutants that passed for European royalty flexed their muscles by building gargantuan armies and navies, requiring for both branches of their armed forces powerful guns and a bottomless pit of ammunition. Europe was already well down the road to war, but ironically the French were considered the real enemy at that time, with the Napoleonic wars fresh in the memory.

For Danskin and thousands of other immigrant Scots, the flourishing Woolwich Arsenal offered them jobs, with as much overtime as they wanted. It also gave them the chance to socialise with others who shared their interest in playing football. As he embarked on the long train journey south, Danskin may have steamed past a young Jack Humble, who would arrive at the factory around the same time. Humble, whose poverty-stricken upbringing in Durham was worthy of a *Monty Python* sketch, decided to move south in order to find work. The manner in which he did so made headlines back in the north-east. Known for his stubbornness and unwillingness to accept defeat, Humble, along with his brother Arthur, walked the 400-odd miles to Woolwich and on the way had plenty of time to ponder life in southern England. Like Danskin, he did not suffer fools gladly, and looked forward to getting involved in organising football matches with his new workmates. As the authorities would soon discover, no one was less deserving of his surname than Jack Humble.

Danskin and Humble remain original working-class heroes. Association Football, traditionally the preserve of public schools, was gradually becoming the working man's game. At the turn of the century, southern football was still mired in the game's equivalent of the Jurassic age. Thousands of amateur work teams jostled frantically for position, desperately trying to attract the best local talent. In the future, they could maybe even dream of emulating northern clubs like Blackburn Olympic who'd already turned professional. Roughly 90 per cent of clubs south of Birmingham died out in this atmosphere of social Darwinism, mainly due to a lack of cash and an unfortunate geographical position. Kentish teams appeared to have little going for them. The recently passed Factory Acts gave Danskin and his ilk Saturday afternoons off, and they'd just been given the vote. In these pre-Labour Party and trade union days, workers who campaigned for better housing, health care and leisure activities (including football) were considered gobby upstarts. Unsurprisingly, Humble quickly joined a left-wing political group – the Radicals – and later became a fully fledged member of the emerging Socialist Party. The pair passionately believed that every man should have the right to play Association Football. When Danskin and Humble found that others in their workplace shared their enthusiasm, the boys had a whip-round to pay for a ball, which they kicked about at lunchtimes. After all, there weren't many other appealing distractions during their lunch breaks. The skin and hair of the girls in the nearby TNT section was dyed a sickly yellow by the corrosive chemicals they used, hence the 'Woolwich Canaries' nickname.

Getting beyond a lunchtime kick-about was considered a virtually impossible task. For a start, there were widespread reports across south-east England that migrating Scots were actually being mistaken for French spies on a regular basis, leading to some serious beatings in city alleyways. Victorians weren't too clued up on accents, these being the days when a day-trip to Bognor was the equivalent of travelling across the Australian outback. Not only did Danskin encounter xenophobic attitudes towards Scots, he also ran into class snobbery. Rugby and cricket, he was told, were true Kentish sports, not soccer. Joseph Smith, another worker at the factory, had earlier tried to set up a football team that, he hoped, could share a pitch with the cricketers. Smith had been told to bugger off and his dream had died, but Danskin was more determined, and after a second whip-round, some 'kit' was hastily arranged. The Scot was gaining a deserved reputation among fellow workers for sheer doggedness.

Danskin took the bold step of signing two ex-Nottingham Forest professionals in order to add some experience to this rawest of teams. Morris Bates and Fred Beardsley (a goalkeeper of some repute) taught the lads the tactics of the day and helpfully blagged a full set of red shirts from Forest into the bargain. Bates, a pugnacious full-back, led by example. Nicknamed the 'iron-headed man', he was capable of heading the ball, which in those days was almost the weight of a cannonball, half the length of the pitch. Given the Victorians' obsession for freaks and the bizarre, he could probably have made a fortune in the circus. It's a wonder that he actually had the brain-power left to instil 'tactics' into his teammates. At Forest, both men had become used to exhausting training regimes, which put a special emphasis on building up leg muscles. Little wonder that Bates's and Beardsley's new charges had, in the *Kentish Mercury*'s words, '. . . thighs like oak trees'.

Even in those days, the players had a fine reputation for quaffing ale. Pubs and the history of Arsenal Football Club are intertwined. After a riotous post-match session at the Royal Oak, next to Woolwich station, the boys decided on the 'Royal' Arsenal title, which was a bit of a cheek. There were plenty of other teams from other workshops inside the factory, but Danskin and his Dial Square boys, full of boozy bluster, reckoned they now represented the whole factory. Still, where would the club be today without that special blend of nous and arrogance?

The Royals' early sides, moulded in Danskin's own image, were stuffed with burly, mustachioed Scots, which only increased the team's notoriety and unpopularity. Not for the last time, a Gunners team was accused of being loaded with foreign mercenaries. In such frugal times, the players wore factory boots with strips of wrought iron fixed onto the bottom, making it all the easier to maim the opposition. It was the football equivalent of bare-knuckle boxing. Royals strikers, fully bevvied up after a liquid lunch, hunted in packs and practically assaulted any hapless goalie who was stupid enough to block their path. Opposition defenders, whenever they believed they had control of the ball, would be splattered, with teeth and blood everywhere. Foaming at the mouth, gangs of red-shirted strikers bore down on the opposition's penalty area like rabid extras from *Braveheart*. Bear in mind that the Royals were given further incentive to play well by being taunted for hailing from 'the sinister factory', with its 20-foot-high walls, where workers weren't allowed to discuss with 'outsiders' the nature of their work.

It should be added that the Royals weren't entirely to blame for the on-pitch maiming. Football was a good deal tougher back then and other assorted psychopaths from teams such as Clapton and Thorpe, who later became Norwich City, weren't exactly averse to 'mixing it'. If the other side did try to 'play a bit', one of two things could happen. John Julian, an innocent-looking Royals midfielder, would saunter over to the offender and boot him up towards Mars. Almost always undergoing treatment for blows to his ankles or knees, Julian reckoned the majority of his injuries resulted from his own fouls. Canny Royals defenders were under strict instructions to steer the opposition towards the craters on Plumstead Common. There, the ball would veer off at crazy angles and often the other players would disappear down the nearest hole, spraining their ankles and ripping ligaments in the process. If all else failed, Jimmy Charteris, who appears to have been a Grant Mitchell-like midfielder, would constantly harangue the referee and try to ensure that decisions went the home side's way.

Of all the Royals players, Charteris was the most notorious. His troubled background could be the key to understanding why he played at such a furious tempo. As a child, he'd seen his bigamist father jailed, and the young Jimmy, who'd originally been born illegitimate, was palmed off to various members of the extended family. For opting to move to Royal Arsenal, he was virtually ostracised by his local community. In October 1887, the *Motherwell Times* noted: 'He will find out that he has made a sad mistake. There is little honour playing for some of these English clubs.' To say that Charteris arrived in Kent with fire in his belly is an understatement. This was certainly no haven for southern ponces. Unsurprisingly, the Royals' home record was excellent. At the end of 1886–87 – the first official season – the overall playing record was pretty good, too: Played 10, Won 7, Drawn 1, Lost 2.

But Danskin and Humble were still not satisfied. Any method going was used to recruit better players. Already they had in operation a spy network that would have been the envy of MI5. The spies, who often worked in other munitions factories, would watch games all over the country and if the report on a player was a positive one, the young lad would be 'found a job' in the Woolwich Arsenal (50 shillings a week was the normal going rate) and thrust into the first team. Danskin would stop at nothing to improve the team. Rivals complained about Danskin's and Humble's questionable recruitment methods, but more than that, regarded the boys as cocky young upstarts from south of the river. Just who did the Royals think they were, adopting grand-sounding nomenclature while not even having a permanent ground? Despite the opposition, by 1890 this band of desperados were the best team in the south-east. They'd already secured the Kent Senior and, crucially, the London Senior Cup after defeating St Bartholomew's Hospital 6–0. Though these titles may sound little better than nineteenth-century versions of the Sherpa Van trophy, the club's cult following grew. The disapproving *Kentish Independent* reported that pubs in Woolwich did a roaring trade when the team returned with their rabble-rousing supporters and the silverware: '. . . there was shouting and singing everywhere all evening and, we fear, a good deal of drinking was mingled with the rejoicing and exaltations.'

The Royals' success had also been noted by future rivals north of the Thames. Established London clubs like Tottenham were haemorrhaging support to these upstarts, especially once the Royals secured a 'lucky' (according to the *Weekly Herald*) victory over them in 1887. Keen fans from the capital would frantically 'penny-farthing' it through the Blackwall Tunnel to see the boys play, rather than watch the Totts or Chelsea. The Royals considered themselves so superior, in fact, that as early as 1889 they labelled themselves 'Champions of the South', and there were even whispers that the club was about to turn professional, which appalled high-minded thinkers at the time. After all, to lose the true Corinthian spirit – guts, high tackles and weekly hacking competitions – was as unthinkable as, say, losing the Empire.

Danskin and Humble finally had their minds made up for them after the events of 1890 and 1891. The FA Cup was the only chance the Royals had to pit their wits against the might of the northern professional sides. In 1890, Derby visited the team's new home, the Manor Ground, and narrowly won 1–0 before a then-record crowd of 8,000. Danskin was alarmed that Derby representatives immediately offered professional terms to Connolly and Buist, the Royals' two best players, after the match. The Scot realised that in the grand scheme of things, his team was merely a bit player. An even more alarming game came a year later when crack northern side Swifts arrived for a fourth-round tie. Despite 15,000 Royals' fanatics sweeping the snow off the pitch, and the team's Herculean efforts, the legendary E.C. Bambridge inspired his team to a 5–1 victory. Hack-fests were all well and good, but when it came down to it, the Royals couldn't cut it against the very best from the north.

No one at the club, or the factory, wanted to see the team pootle along in the wilderness, so in 1891 the board – badgered by Jack Humble – unanimously voted to turn Royal Arsenal professional. Humble's vision and determination proved that the club was by far the most forward-thinking and revolutionary in the south-east, but within just four years of being formed they were also the most hated. Retribution, as expected, was swift and decisive. Woolwich Arsenal, as they were now renamed, were made outcasts, branded with the name of 'traitor', for the next two years. The decision to cast the team into the wilderness was taken at an extraordinary general meeting of the London FA, held in Fleet Street's Anderson's Hotel. The dice appeared to be loaded against Woolwich Arsenal from the start.

Mr A. Jackson, who chaired the meeting, vehemently denied having previously labelled professional footballers as 'wretches', although he did later admit he 'despised the little tricks of the game', which non-amateurs appeared to have picked up. Mr J. Farmer – Old Harrovians chairman – pointed out that most amateur sides paid their players 'extremely liberal travel expenses' and that Woolwich Arsenal were, at least, 'up front about it all'. Tellingly, the *Kentish Mercury* reported Mr A. Jackson's comment: 'I wish to pay a high compliment to the press generally for the stand they have taken against Woolwich Arsenal Football Club.' Although the vote to expel the club was close, 76–67, it is little wonder that Humble and Danskin felt aggrieved by the decision.

For a time, Humble's decision looked suicidal. Expelled from all London and Kent cup competitions and leagues by southern clubs anxious to punish the upstarts, the only competitive games the team had were in the FA Cup, where the boys invariably got battered due to a total lack of match practice. Crowds crashed to a hardcore 3,000 and, apart from a few lucrative friendlies, the team hardly played at all.

Within a year, the Woolwich Arsenal board put forward yet another revolutionary idea. Why not form a professional southern league, which, in time, could grow to be as powerful as the northern-dominated First Division? Staggeringly, Woolwich's southern rivals (most of whom wanted to turn professional but didn't dare do so) actually backed the idea, aware it could lead to their coffers being rapidly filled. A selection committee elected Woolwich Arsenal, along with the mighty Chatham, Marlow and West Herts, to the ten-team strong league, ahead of London's most established club, Tottenham, who received only one vote. Known as the 'Marsh-dwellers', the Totts were mightily annoyed, but their fans' habit of throwing mud at their own players was held against them.

Due to a lack of cash, the southern league never took off and by 1893, Woolwich Arsenal had once again alienated themselves from their neighbours. But the club was then invited to join the Second Division. Danskin and Humble realised the enormity of the decision and what could happen if Woolwich Arsenal struggled. There would certainly be no way back, so despised was his club by anyone south of Watford (apart from Woolwich fans, of course). This truly was the point of no return. Danskin and Humble accepted the invitation to join.

Then, as now, the Second Division was tough and brutal – about as welcoming as a wet weekend in Skegness. The Manor Ground did little to add to the ambience. Woolwich Arsenal's crowds, consisting mainly of squaddies and factory workers, were regarded with unmitigated fear by visiting northern teams. The fans had a reputation for hurling ale-fuelled foul-mouthed insults and the opposition would dread having to take throw-ins or corners, as they were likely to be on the end of some fairly rough treatment. A letter of complaint in the *Kentish Independent* noted 'the conduct of fans who spouted foul language and coarse abuse'. On one occasion, the referee actually abandoned a match due to crowd swearing and, in a game against Wolves, a group of squaddies invaded the pitch and beat up the referee, who, incidentally, was a former Wolves player. No wonder the *Newcastle Echo* described the Geordies' trip to the Manor Ground as 'an annual visit to hell'. The *Kentish Independent* also reported that the hooligan element wasn't simply confined to the squaddies: 'These were not weedy uneducated hooligans but well-dressed middle-aged gentlemen,' one journalist wrote. A glance at the Woolwich Arsenal team group from the late-nineteenth century, ten years after that first match on the Isle of Dogs, suggests that the boys remained an intimidating crowd. With their handle-bar moustaches and unsmiling faces, they resembled a group of desperados from a silent movie – the type who'd tie hapless maidens to railway lines and be shot out of a cannon in their spare time.

If the crowd's belligerence continued to bring the club unwanted headlines, the club's officials were also regarded with trepidation by rival clubs and within the local community. That Woolwich Arsenal remained a viable concern for so long was largely due to the brilliant juggling and spivvy methods employed by these men. Shimmying and swerving around innumerable obstacles, with sometimes questionable legality, they dragged the sickly football club behind them. Their novel money-spinning schemes became legendary in Woolwich. Archery competitions, raffles, open days – anything went, as long as it brought much-needed cash flooding into the coffers. On one memorable occasion, with the accounts suffering from scarlet fever and the bailiffs poised to break down the door, Jack Humble was dispatched to Woolwich High Street to see if anyone wished to become a club director. One G.H. Leavey, a prominent outfitter, agreed. In a jiffy, Humble yanked £60 from Leavey's till and ran back to the ground. This covered the boys' wages for the next week and the long train journey to the forthcoming away match. Though Leavey was granted his place on the board, he never saw his cash again.

Jack Humble, in particular, grew to love the club, seeing his mission as more than just a job. He spotted early on that the growth of professionalism – though a necessary 'evil' – threatened to divide players from fans. So players were encouraged to collect gate money prior to games and mix with supporters in various Woolwich hostelries. It was all a far cry from www.icons.com, through which modern players 'communicate' with fans.

To other clubs, Woolwich Arsenal's officials were a militant lot. Southern rivals didn't care much for Danskin's and Humble's 'foreign' accents, much less the heinous practice of professionalism in their midst. Directors of northern clubs simply believed the two had 'sold out' by emigrating south. They remained very much 'hands on' at away games, cajoling the troops and urging the travelling support to 'sing up'. But it was the board's continued discussion of subversive ideas that made them pariahs in the football world. In 1893, the board formed a limited liability company and pressed on with a share issue scheme in order to make the club a more financially viable outfit. The board was by no means unanimous over this decision. Humble protested: 'It is my intention to see it [the club] carried on by working men.' A letter to the *Kentish Independent* questioned the wisdom of mixing football with business: 'The funding of a soccer club should be left to the working men and those who know the game. Surely allowing clerks or accountants to control a football club through buying shares is a retrograde step.' For some it was, and Humble especially would feel uncomfortable with the unwanted interference from shareholders. He continued to object, but admitted that without the share issue, the Manor Ground could not have been refurbished each year. Even as early as 1893 – a century before David Dein pressed ahead with the Bond Scheme – Humble realised that, strictly speaking, football never was the working man's game.

Danskin was far less comfortable with the emergence of commercialism at the club. He left Woolwich Arsenal in the 1890s, to open a bicycle business. The venture flopped, and Danskin's descendant, Mrs R.H. Wyatt, confirms that his family were regular visitors to the pawnbrokers, in a desperate attempt to make ends meet. Despite this, and the tragic death of his son from pneumonia, the Scot lived to see the successes of Chapman's Arsenal sides in the 1930s.

Humble stayed on as a director, and remained a dab hand at dealing with the local press and getting involved in their 'exclusive' stories. Humble and other club officials were canny enough to realise that a couple of crowd pleasers in the side would add 1,000 to the gate. Woolwich fans enjoyed the phenomenal shooting power of 16-stone Charlie Satterthwaite, whose ferocious shots actually smashed the stanchion on one occasion, and goalkeeper Jimmy Ashcroft, who could punch a ball half the length of the pitch. Caesar Llewlyn Jenkyns, the club's first England international, stayed for a season and his mere presence could double the crowd. With his reputation as a boozer during his days at Birmingham, combined with his fearsome wrestling physique, he'd have been a superstar in the modern era, plastered all over young Gooners' walls. So too would Bobby Templeton, a mercurial Scottish left-back. A hairdresser by trade, he had the ability to swerve the ball in a virtual semi-circle. Then there was the prolific Bill Gooing – the Ian Wright of his day – whose thirst for goals almost matched that of his love for brown ale. The local press was fascinated by these star players, particularly as they were high-profile characters who enjoyed the local hostelries and willingly attended Woolwich functions. Normally Templeton and Gooing led the drunken singing, whilst performing the obligatory jig on the bar tables. The *Kentish Independent* reported that on one memorable occasion – to the astonishment of the onlookers and his wife – the 'gruesome twosome' got Woolwich's mayor to join them in their close-harmony hollering. Templeton, considered the bad boy in the team, revelled in his role as small-town anti-hero. Moody, inconsistent and prone to missing training, a journalist wrote of him: 'When he's good, he's very good. When he's bad, he's horrid' – just like Woolwich Arsenal, who began to turn themselves into the meanest of mean machines under the tutelage of gruff, bowler-hatted managers like Phil Kelso and Harry Bradshaw.

By 1904, Jimmy Jackson (half Aussie, half Scot), appointed himself leader for team affairs/tactics. Jackson had trained as an Aussie-rules player, which served him well in the kick-and-rush environs of English football. Jackson introduced zonal marking to the club and was ruthless in his pursuit of points. When the going got tough in a league game, he told a teammate: 'We're not here to show fancy play. We're here to get points. When we can't get two, we can at least make sure of one.' (Was Jackson George Graham's maternal grandfather, perhaps?) In the 18 years since that first match on the Isle of Dogs, the team from 'the factory' had become southern heavyweights. Yet there was always a flip side, which threatened to destroy the club: transfer requests piled up quicker than club debts. Star players, fed up with 'WOOLWICH ARSENAL IN FINANCIAL STRIFE' stories, rarely stayed around for longer than a year and were tempted by the promises of filthy lucre up north. They were fully aware of the tragic ends met by several of the club's earliest stars. Ironically, the two 'hard men' were struck down first. Morris Bates died from tuberculosis at the age of 41. Jimmy Charteris died in poverty from a suspected heart attack at just 28 years of age.

The onset of the Boer War was as damaging for Woolwich Arsenal as it was for the British Government. The club haemorrhaged both players and fans at alarming speed. As the most unfit army in British history travelled to South Africa, the all-consuming need to preserve Britain's empire impacted massively upon the munitions industry. Saturday afternoons at the football were no longer an option for most supporters, as they were forced to do compulsory overtime in the factory. Crowds slumped to a measly average of around 2,000, and only 900 watched the club's record 12–0 win over Loughborough in March 1900. Worse, Tottenham won the FA Cup in 1901, becoming the first non-league club to do so. It was estimated that a jubilant crowd of 20,000 lined the streets to welcome back the Spurs players. Inwardly, Woolwich Arsenal directors seethed, fully aware that in the long term, their bunch of unglamorous Kentish urchins could not compete financially with London poseurs like Spurs or Chelsea. It was a clear sign that Woolwich's title as the south's most cutting edge and progressive club was in danger of being wrestled away. For all their best efforts, the club was sliding towards oblivion. Like Second Division rivals Darwen and Burton Swifts, Woolwich Arsenal could have vanished, if an archetypal Edwardian bounder hadn't injected his unique brand of villainy and panache into the club.

TWO

Sleaze and the Tory MP

My dad knew Henry Norris from the building trade. Dad was a strictly no-nonsense man, who'd fought in the Great War and survived the trenches for four years. But I'll tell you this. He was terrified of Norris. After his meetings with him he'd come home shaking and down a double whisky.

Leslie Anderson – Arsenal fan from the 1920s

Although Sir Henry Norris died nearly 70 years ago, his name continues to provoke controversy. Searching for his full title on the Internet throws up some useful information on him. No less than 20 Spurs-related sites cite him as the prime reason to hate Arsenal and the reasons for his lifelong ban from football in 1928 are graphically recounted. More bizarrely, a sixteenth-century diplomat of precisely the same name was also a Falstaffian rogue of the highest order. Granted unprecedented access to Henry VIII, he was later executed for 'intriguing' with the King's young wife, Anne Boleyn. He was noted for his 'raffish charm' and revelled in his reputation as the 'playboy diplomat' of his era. It seems apt, therefore, that his distant relative was also such a notorious character. As it turned out, both men were destroyed by the Icarus factor: they flew too close to the sun.

The second Sir Henry Norris, after buying Woolwich Arsenal in 1910, controlled his club like a medieval fiefdom. In an era when directors and chairmen tended to sit on boards in order to heighten their exposure in the local community, Norris broke the mould. He sprung a variety of 'questionable' fiscal tricks and used bully-boy tactics that made him powerful enemies within the game. Norris has spawned several imitators, but 'Deadly' Doug Ellis, Ken Bates and the late Robert Maxwell have nothing on him. In transforming Arsenal Football Club forever, Norris remains the original and best, or worst, depending upon your point of view. The game's first 'Soccer Tsar' has become a creature of myth and more stories circulate about him than any other official in Arsenal's history. The amazing thing is, most of them are true.

Born in 1865, Fulham-based Sir Henry (or just plain old Henry, as he was in 1910), was a self-made man who had accumulated his fortune through the property market. His company, Allen & Norris, was responsible for transforming Fulham from a semi-rural area into an urban jungle. In the process of constructing, renovating and selling houses, he'd built up a formidable network of contacts in the building and banking professions, many of whom owed him 'favours'. This proved invaluable in future years, particularly when the time came to build a new football stadium. Norris loved to mingle with the hoi polloi, and his 'networking' skills were legion. *Who's Who* from 1910 lists his interests as 'wine societies', 'dining clubs' and 'vintage car rallies'. As a member of the Junior Carlton Club, Mayor of Fulham, leading light in the local Conservative Party and eminent Freemason, his name was well known throughout the capital. Being a God-fearing Tory, he believed it his duty to perform philanthropic acts in the local community. For several years, he worked closely with the Battersea vestry and the local orphanage. Yet political opponents believed him to be a self-serving fraud who'd used his position simply to befriend, amongst others, the Archbishop of Canterbury. Norris, who had a reputation for banging out libel writs faster than Ken Bates, always refuted these allegations, but the Archbishop certainly proved to be a useful ally for him in 1913. Returning 'favours' was the preserve of this particular social circle, after all.

Photographs and written accounts prove that Norris was a terrifying man, bearing an uncanny resemblance to Dr Crippen, notorious wife murderer of the day. Standing at well over six feet tall, invariably with a pipe stuffed into his mouth, he dwarfed his rivals both literally and metaphorically. Immaculately turned out in a trench-coat, crisply starched white shirt and bowler hat, he would glare demoniacally at them through his pince-nez. The lenses of the pince-nez were so strong that his gaze was totally distorted. This proved to be useful in board meetings, where he could make his directors uncomfortable by bawling at one while apparently looking at another.

Norris's accent, upper-class wannabe with a cockney twang, betrayed his working-class roots. His parents had sent him to a minor public school, but on his own admission, 'school was not for me'. Aged just 14, he was articled to a solicitor's firm and made rapid strides. A year later he left, tempted by the cut-throat world of building. He had several chips on his shoulders, admitting that he disliked 'authority figures' and 'time-wasters'. Norris was a man in a hurry and he wanted to run things his way. One of his chief gripes was that northern sides had always dominated professional football. He firmly believed that a London team should be in command.

Scaring the shit out of his rivals was all very well, but Norris was also a master at charming potential opponents and getting them onside with sheer enthusiasm and gusto. As a successful estate agent, he knew only too well how to smarm when appropriate. When he branched into the building trade, he honed his skills further. If he liked you, a quick word with the local council would bypass the official channels one had to go through in order to extend a house. If it came to constructing houses in a 'tricky' area of London (for example, Wimbledon was notorious for having a fearsome NIMBY regiment even then) he could chat to 'buddies' in the local community and, in a jiffy, a new housing complex would go up. One of his rivals in the building trade dared to suggest that Norris ran a protection racket in order to preserve the status of his construction company. He retracted the accusation when Norris threatened to let loose his lawyer on him.

So even before he became connected with Woolwich Arsenal, Norris was well versed in sharp practice. Where better than the world of football to become a grand-master of such chicanery?

In the early years of last century, with Norris already a director of Fulham, he decided to expand his business interests in the sport. He wanted to buy a football club and surveyed the leading teams in southern England: Chelsea, Spurs, Orient and Woolwich Arsenal. The first three clubs were fairly secure financially at that time. The boys from Woolwich, on the other hand, remained in an awful mess. Even in Division One, Manor Ground crowds averaged out at around 10,000, four times less than those at Chelsea or Spurs. In addition, a touch of the farcical always surrounded the club. Woolwich Arsenal reached the 1905 FA Cup semi-final, but lost 1–3 to Sheffield Wednesday. The match, played on a mound-like pitch, was memorable because neither goalkeeper could see each other and, bizarrely, neither could the linesmen. As with all dictators, Norris made his move when matters were at their lowest ebb. Woolwich Arsenal's misfortunes turned out to be his gain and in the manner of other twentieth-century autocrats, he injected new life into the club, stopping at nothing to enforce his beliefs.

The board welcomed him with open arms, having heard of his political 'skills', when he negotiated Fulham's frankly unbelievable rise through the southern league up to Division Two. That this meteoric rise took place in just four years led furious directors from other clubs to suggest that substantial amounts of cash had been handed over to the Football League, but no firm evidence of backhanders was ever found. Norris was already the undisputed master of covering his tracks. On buying his majority stake in Woolwich Arsenal, he proposed a merger with Fulham in order to create a London 'super-club', and a permanent move to Craven Cottage. This was possibly the first proven case of a member of the Conservative Party being involved in 'cottaging' activities. The merger plan bore an uncanny resemblance to Robert Maxwell's attempt to unify Reading and Oxford in the mid-1980s. Fortunately, the fat crook failed in his attempt, as did Norris with his proposal. He was blocked by the Football League (the only time they stopped him getting his way), but they couldn't prevent him staying as director of Fulham, whilst also serving as Arsenal chairman. From that, you can guess that the Monopolies and Mergers Commission did not yet exist.

Foiled in his plan to merge the two clubs, Norris set about rejuvenating the ailing Woolwich Arsenal. Together with his business partner, William Hall, Norris controlled 57 per cent of the club shares, and he spent the rest of the decade buying a greater stake in the club. In 1912, he realised that the club had to move elsewhere after an embarrassing catalogue of disasters at the Manor Ground, which, like many of the club's old haunts, flooded regularly. A match with Spurs, which Arsenal won 3–1, was described as a 'mud revel' by *The Sportsman*. Another local newspaper described the ground as: 'a perfect quagmire, as water lay in a pool along the touchline'. On that day, the weather was so appalling that factions of the crowd refused to pay the shilling entrance fee, preferring instead to stand on the sewer pipe and watch the game. At least they got wet for free. The press claimed there had been a near riot between the law-abiding fans and the refuseniks. That wasn't quite true, but it was a fact that opposition teams often failed to reach the ground on time, due to heavy traffic and poor accessibility. These embarrassments reflected poorly on Norris, and he wasn't one to suffer fools gladly. The club was relegated in 1913 with the (at that time) worst-ever record in Division One: P38 W3 D12 L23. For Norris, there was only one option.

In early 1913, *Kentish Independent* readers were gobsmacked to read the following front-page headline: 'ARSENAL TO MOVE TO THE OTHER SIDE OF LONDON'. In an official statement, Norris pointed out the benefits to the club of moving to a district that had a population of 500,000. The relocated club could tap into the huge reservoir of supporters in Finsbury, Hackney, Islington and Holborn. Through his contacts in the church, he found that six acres of land at St John's College of Divinity at Highbury were available. Where better to move than a spot that was only ten minutes away by Tube from London's West End? Norris required all his arrogance and political skill to negotiate the minefield of red tape, pressure groups and NIMBYs blocking his path.

He didn't figure on the furious reaction from Woolwich Arsenal's hard-core supporters. Norris mentioned the 'push' factor from Woolwich; that people from the region simply did not turn up at games in large enough numbers. Many reckoned Norris was using dirty tricks. In the relegation season, they believed he'd deliberately leaked news about the proposed move and under-invested in the team, which he knew would drive down crowds and make the case for relocation even stronger. Letters to the local press accused him of being a heartless capitalist and of selling the club's soul. One letter, sent to the *Kentish Gazette* by Mr Paul Donaldson, would ring true for Wimbledon fans today. It said:

> Mr Norris has decided that financial gain is more important than protecting our local club. He is making a mistake. You cannot 'franchise' a football club – Woolwich Arsenal must stay near Woolwich. Would Norris advocate moving Liverpool to Manchester? People like him have no place in Association football.

Mr Walter Bailey's letter, published in the *Kentish Independent*, went further. He wrote:

> There is, and has been, sufficient support to run the team on a business basis . . . Many clubs in different parts of the country would be glad of such support. Woolwich has been found guilty of apathy . . . because it cannot furnish the huge gates that Tottenham and Chelsea get. The most distant part of London to which they intend moving will effectively prevent those who helped to make the club, and can morally claim it as their birthright, from having anything further to do with it. Is this right?

The local press ran a series of cartoons, one of which, in the *Woolwich Gazette*, claimed Norris was kidnapping Kent's 'only son'. He countered, and further fanned the flames, by claiming that he'd always regarded Woolwich as part of London anyway, not Kent, and that it was about time the club enjoyed the capital's spoils. It was alleged that he received death threats after proposing the move, yet he pressed on regardless. If the reaction from the Woolwich public was extreme, it was tame compared with the lynch mob that awaited him in London.

Representatives from Orient, Spurs and Chelsea were quick to spit out their proverbial dummies and protest, 'in the strongest possible terms', about the move. They were terrified that another London club could erode their traditional fan bases. The *Tottenham Herald* described Norris as an 'interloper', and a cartoon portrayed him as being the equivalent of the Hound of the Baskervilles, prowling around farmyards in an enormous spiked collar, ready to rip apart the Tottenham cockerel and steal its food. An FA inquiry was set up to investigate the whole affair. Norris successfully packed the committee with his buddies and furnished them with some useful facts. Birmingham, with a population of 400,000, and Sheffield with 250,000, housed two top-flight teams each. Why couldn't an ever-expanding London – population two million – house four? Unsurprisingly, the committee ruled that the opposition had 'no right to interfere'. The *Tottenham Herald* placed an advertisement begging its fans '. . . not to go and support Norris's Woolwich interlopers. They have no right to be here.'

The next hurdles to be overcome were the formidable Highbury residents, quivering with righteous indignation about 'undesirable elements of professional football' and 'a vulgar project' on their doorstep. The Islington Borough Council minutes recorded Highbury Park resident Mr Coventon's comments: 'I ask whether it is open to the Borough Council to protect the district from what, in my opinion, will be its utter ruin.' Mr A. Bailey of Avenell Road wrote: 'There will be considerable annoyance and inconvenience suffered by the residents in Avenell Road as a result of the erection of lofty stands by the Woolwich Arsenal Football Club. Can the Council please help us on this matter?'

Norris knew only too well the power of the NIMBY brigade,

being so well versed in local politics. He launched a charm offensive on the group, assuring them that they'd barely notice a football club in their midst, and, in any case, that 30,000-plus fans in the district every other Saturday would be excellent for local business. This was enough to convince several members of the opposition, many of whom stood to gain from the construction process. Those who continued to moan were effectively silenced by Norris's contacts in the local press. Highbury residents discovered that their vocal anti-Woolwich Arsenal meetings had never taken place and that local protest groups simply didn't exist, in the Orwellian sense of the word. With censorship skills worthy of Nazi propaganda chief Goebbels, Norris's buddies starved protesters of the oxygen of publicity and their efforts to prevent the move failed.

The final group that Norris needed to deal with, and one which certainly could not be silenced, was the Church of England. Many on the ecclesiastical committee believed football to be 'ungodly'. Local residents believed that the thought of the Church of England agreeing to a football club buying the land was inconceivable. But Norris's contacts went right to the top. After waving a £20,000 cheque under their noses, the Church committee virtually bit his hand off and his old buddy, the Archbishop of Canterbury, personally signed the deed. Of course, Norris agreed that no games would be played at Highbury on holy days and no 'intoxicating liquor' would be sold at the stadium. Yet within a year, in the manner of most dictators, he had quickly reneged on his promise. In the early twentieth century, football began to replace organised religion as the main passion amongst the working classes. How apt, therefore, that the devilishly cunning chairman of the nation's least saintly club should begin constructing Highbury stadium on land where would-be priests once played bowls and tennis.

By 1913, Norris's Arsenal ('Woolwich' was permanently dropped) had indeed moved to their new home and offended virtually everyone in the process. In a bitter parting shot, a fan from Kent, who decided not to make the regular one-hour trip to Highbury, wrote in the *Kentish Independent*: 'Henry Norris has gambled away the club's soul. He is a Mammon worshipper. We've not heard the last of this bounder, you may be sure of that.' He had no idea. But Norris's dream of turning Arsenal into a 'super club' had begun to take shape.

Sir Henry's ability to galvanise others was never better demonstrated than during the building work on the new stadium. He summoned the world-renowned Archibald Leitch, foremost ground builder of the day. In order to do his bit for the club in the community, Norris employed local roofers, tilers and carpenters, as he'd originally promised. Traders were invited to dump their rubbish into holes in order to build up the terraces. Problems remained, though. An assortment of rules and regulations were broken during construction, mainly relating to heights and lengths of walls and stands. The old geezers on the Parish Council in Holloway Road threatened to get heavy, but Norris knew that, in reality, they did not know the difference 'between a retaining wall and a retaining fee'. He urged his assistant to 'forget them'. Norris realised that a bit of cunning, and a willingness to gamble, paid rich dividends in Edwardian Britain, a time when Dickensian-type parish beadles still made the rules. Despite a ferocious argument between Norris and Leitch (the latter actually 'disappeared' for a week in fear), the work was finished on time. Whenever workers got stroppy about toiling at weekends, Norris would take the foreman out to a superb Italian restaurant, where, over veal and champagne, he was 'persuaded' to get his men to change their minds. Arsenal played their first competitive match at Highbury against Leicester Fosse on 6 September 1913, in a Second Division match.

Five years later, Norris's dreams for the club appeared to be in tatters. Due to the First World War, a ball hadn't been kicked in anger since 1915, and several promising members of the youth team lay dead on French battlefields. In the season before play was suspended, Arsenal finished a miserable sixth in the Second Division. Norris, having pumped a massive £125,000 into the club, faced the grim prospect, like the rest of the country, of a painful rebuilding process. The thought of a tortuous trek back into the First Division would have made lesser men quit and he'd need all his cunning to turn the situation around. He was about to pull off the most audacious, and dodgy, deal in football history.

Bearing in mind all the skulduggery and under-the-counter payments that have been rumoured to be going on in professional football since its inception, it says something for Norris that his 1919 scam remains more infamous than the Graham affair of 1995. When the FA reconvened in 1919, Norris had every reason to feel confident in his powers of persuasion. He'd just been knighted for his work as a recruitment officer during the war. Through sheer willpower, he'd managed to assemble three artillery brigades from the Fulham area that played a prominent role in the Battle of the Somme. As a reward for his efforts, Norris was granted the title of Colonel. More importantly for him, he'd recently been elected as Tory MP for Fulham East, winning over the electorate with his pledge for 'common decency', 'family values', and 'moral strength'. Nowadays, if a male Conservative candidate mounted his high horse in such a manner, *News of the World* journalists would automatically quiver, sensing double standards and a juicy Sunday scoop on the horizon, à la Neil Hamilton or Jeffrey Archer. Back then, MPs remained beyond reproach, supposedly incorruptible figures. No chance of them spawning illegitimate children or handing over cash in brown paper bags. Norris was about to demonstrate that sleaze and (alleged) under-the-counter payments were already de rigueur over 80 years ago.

An FA management committee, anxious to get football back on its feet, and headed by 'honest' John McKenna, proposed that Division One be expanded from 20 to 21 clubs. This seemed irrelevant information to Arsenal Football Club, who'd finished fifth in Division Two in the 1914–15 season. Birmingham and Wolves finished third and fourth respectively, and it was widely believed that Division One's relegated clubs, Chelsea and Spurs, would obtain a reprieve. But Norris got to work on his contacts within the committee. He secretly 'canvassed' every single member of the committee (bar Spurs directors) and suggested that Arsenal deserved an unlikely promotion. Norris informed them that Arsenal had massive potential support – useful in the days when gate receipts were split between clubs – and that Highbury's proximity to the capital's delights represented a fun weekend jaunt for other clubs and their directors. Grey weekends in Wolverhampton and Birmingham just didn't seem as attractive to those chairmen who enjoyed the high life.

Norris was smart enough to get pally with Chelsea's chairman and assure him that Chelsea would get their reprieve, as long as Arsenal got promotion. Spurs directors, on the other hand, were blissfully ignorant of Norris's dodgy tactics and gambolled along innocently, unaware of what was about to hit them. Norris also maintained that the Gunners should be rewarded 'for their long service to league football', neglecting to mention that Wolves had actually been league members for longer. Even by Norris's standards, this line of argument was obscure. Since when have clubs ever earned promotion on the grounds of longevity of service? He did absolutely everything in his power to ensure the vote went Arsenal's way. Leslie Knighton, Arsenal's manager, commented that Norris corresponded with 'a few financiers here and there', in order to guarantee the vote went his way. When the vote was taken, Chelsea got their reprieve and Arsenal, staggeringly, were promoted – by eighteen votes to Spurs's eight. Even Tottenham's parrot, presented to the club on a voyage home from their 1908 South American tour, was unable to cope with the news. It dropped dead, thus giving rise to the footballing cliché 'sick as a parrot'.

It was rumoured that committee chairman McKenna, whose club Liverpool had been involved in a bribery scandal before the First World War, was immediately offered a plush house on the cheap in the Wimbledon area by Norris's estate agency, although this was never proved. Nor were allegations that brown paper bags stuffed with cash were handed to other compliant club directors. Norris had once more covered his tracks. 'Lucky Arsenal', and 'Cheating Arsenal' were two of the more complimentary titles bestowed upon the club at the time, but that was nothing compared with the number of enemies Norris was making, especially down Seven Sisters Road. Ironically, in 1919, Stanley

Baldwin described the House of Commons as 'a lot of hard-faced men who have done well out of the war'. He probably had the MP for Fulham East in mind more than anyone else. Norris enjoyed his day of triumph, but his rivals would eventually enjoy theirs.

By the early '20s, with Arsenal treading water in the First Division, Norris appointed Leslie Knighton, former boss of Manchester City, as Arsenal manager. He was respected for his encyclopaedic knowledge of players around the country. Knighton was a laid-back gentleman but, with the club still in debt, he was forced to work under increasingly difficult conditions. Norris and Knighton enjoyed a General Melchett/Captain Blackadder-type relationship, in which the walrus-moustached chairman dreamt up imaginative ways for his hapless manager to risk his life for Arsenal. In the early '20s, Knighton unwisely mentioned to his chairman that he'd heard glowing reports on Alec Mackie, a young Irishman who plied his trade in the rough end of Belfast.

Immediately, Knighton was dispatched to the civil-war-torn city, where he tip-toed through segregated streets, dodged sniper fire, tripped over a corpse and witnessed a brutal match between Catholics and Protestants. Staggeringly, he persuaded Mackie to sign for Arsenal, despite the player demanding a pet monkey as an interesting alternative to a signing-on fee. Norris's contacts in international trade meant the player's request posed no problem.

Knighton also had an army of scouting spies in Wales. The problem was, Welsh supporters didn't take too kindly to English managers pinching their best players and regularly beat them up as they left the ground after having completed the deal. Sir Henry (as he became in 1922) provided Knighton with a ridiculous Clouseau-eque false moustache, and glasses, in order that he wouldn't be recognised on such trips. Yet again, his absurd gamble paid off, as Knighton was able to pinch Caerphilly's Bob John from under Cardiff's noses in 1924.

In Knighton's autobiography, he confirms that Sir Henry constantly bullied him during board meetings, for which there are few minutes remaining. Norris felt the evidence they might provide could undermine him. He treated meetings as his personal soapbox, sounding off about matters he found distasteful; Germans, Tottenham . . . anything. As his petrified directors and manager cowered in the corner, Norris would turn to Knighton and bawl: 'Well, man. We pay you a great deal of money to advise us and all you do is sit there as if you were dumb. Can't you talk?' Just as his manager was about to hand in a resignation letter, Norris would smile at him and let Knighton know, as if he didn't already, that he'd stop at nothing to further Arsenal's cause.

By 1922, the mutual dislike between Arsenal and Spurs reached a climax. Ever since Norris's stunt in 1919, officials from both clubs used the local press to spit poison at each other. Sir Henry, of course, was the worst culprit for anti-Spurs jibes, firing stray bullets around town and not much caring if his comments were overheard. As General Manager Bob Wall later commented: 'The roads and pubs outside Highbury and White Hart Lane could be dangerous places back then. Often the knives were out – quite literally – between fans before and after the match.' In a disgustingly dirty match at White Hart Lane in September 1922, the simmering contempt boiled over. Reg Boreham's cracking double pinched the points for Arsenal in a 2–1 win, but the behaviour of fans and players shocked the tabloid press of that era. Gunners defenders Frank Bradshaw and Arthur Hutchins shoulder-charged any Spurs player who moved and as a result two Spurs players went off injured, after which Bradshaw and Hutchins were pelted with missiles from the crowd. It's a wonder that the game continued, yet *The Sportsman* reported: 'The Spurs . . . were the finer artists as a whole . . . but Tottenham lost because they had nearly all the bad luck that was going . . . one could not help feeling impressed by the sledge-hammer opposition of the Arsenal.' Here was another example of Spurs's artistes being bullied out of it by 'grim Arsenal', according to *The Herald*. The outraged reporter from the *Sunday Evening Telegraph* reported that the game contained 'the most disgusting scenes I have witnessed on any ground at any time. Players pulled the referee . . . fists were exchanged.' In the event, the Commission of Enquiry found Spurs' Bert Smith guilty of 'filthy language' and Arsenal's Alec Graham of retaliation. Norris allowed Knighton to face the music alone while, in Melchett style, he stayed miles away from the trouble. Knighton recalled that whenever a major problem arose, Norris disappeared to his bolthole on the French Riviera. On this occasion, others suffered as a direct result of his actions. But his time was running out.

By 1924, Norris was becoming a desperate man. He had opted not to stand again as Tory candidate for Fulham East at the general election after becoming embroiled in a damaging libel case. A rival Conservative MP, Charles Walmer, who took exception to Norris's support for tariff reform, described him as, amongst other things, having a 'minuscule intellect'. Sir Henry was furious, believing his rival had 'slurred my name and character in the most offensive manner possible'. Touchy. Norris won his case at the High Court, but there was far more to it than met the eye. Like Norris, his rival was a leading light in the Masonic lodge and was distraught when Sir Henry became Grand Deacon of the Grand Lodge of England rather than him. Norris was now amongst the elite. As he commented, he'd 'made it'. Being notoriously boastful, he couldn't resist winding up his fellow MP at every opportunity. Both men sniped at one another in committee meetings and, to the astonishment of onlookers, in the corridors of power outside the House of Commons. Norris's rival eventually snapped, but came to regret the 'idiot' jibe, as it cost him a small fortune in damages and he was forced to resign his seat as a result. Internal Tory bickering? Whatever next? Although Norris felt vindicated by his victory, at this point he virtually withdrew from public life, putting all his energies into the Masonic lodge and Arsenal Football Club. Now in his late 60s, his behaviour grew more eccentric by the week, which piled further pressure on poor Knighton. Norris had owned the club for nigh on 15 years, yet still no trophies were forthcoming. Convinced that the team was too soft, out-shoulder-charged in most matches, he announced in a board meeting that his manager must sign 'no more small players. We must have big men.' Knighton was also warned by his chairman that the FA Cup of 1925 represented his final chance of glory. A Harley Street specialist (one of Norris's acquaintances) approached Knighton and offered him a box of 'courage pills', which would 'tone up the nerves'. When the boys popped the pills, it was akin to stuffing wodges of pure tobacco up the bums of 11 Grand National horses. At Upton Park, in a third-round clash with West Ham, the lads tore around like 'Olympic sprinters' and were unlucky to draw 2–2. After four replays, the boys eventually lost, partly because they'd stopped taking the medicine which gave them a 'red-hot thirst' and made hearts practically burst at over 160 beats per minute.

That defeat, and Knighton's unwillingness to abide by Norris's 'no short-arse' rule, cost him his job. 'Midget' Moffatt, an impish winger, arrived from Workington – all five feet four of him. He looked a good prospect too, but Norris, furious at his arrival, barked at Knighton: 'What is that dwarf doing here?' Moffatt quickly disappeared to Everton and Knighton, who was dismissed shortly before he was due a £4,000 golden handshake from Norris, vanished too. Knighton later claimed that Sir Henry's eccentricities had cost the club dear. One of his gripes was that he had been forbidden from spending over the £1,000 limit for a player imposed by his chairman. In Norris's advertisement for a new manager, he wrote: 'Those who pay exorbitant fees in players' transfers need not apply.' Slowly, though, 'Tight-wad' Norris would begin to turn Arsenal into 'the Bank of England club'. In reneging on his beliefs, he achieved the ultimate pyrrhic victory.

When he appointed Huddersfield Town's treble championship-winning boss Herbert Chapman as manager in 1925, he finally met his match. The rotund, five-feet-six Chapman, already dubbed 'Yorkshire's Napoleon' by *The Examiner* newspaper, would, in time, clash headlong with Arsenal's tsar. Chapman was an extremely self-assured figure, who'd defied convention all his life. Like Norris, he was part of the new literate working class and was also a self-made man, having successfully managed a munitions factory in the First World War. Somehow he had quadrupled the factory's shell output and halved costs over a four-year period. *The Examiner*, in 1910, labelled him a 'sharp figure, well versed in political intrigue'.

He needed to be. As boss of the ultimately doomed Leeds City, he'd impressed his board of directors with his 'impressive canvassing techniques' after they'd successfully gained re-election to the Second Division. No wonder Norris was impressed with what he heard. Chapman appeared to be an astute political animal as well.

Like his new chairman, Chapman was a man of many contradictions. On one occasion, he commented: 'I do not believe any man would choose to be a professional if the question of earning a living did not arise.' Yet he stood accused of producing over-pampered footballers at Huddersfield, with his emphasis on sea-baths and golfing breaks. In the mid-'20s, a time when Huddersfield's heavy industry was already in decline, he bought the likes of Clem Stephenson for a whopping £4,000. Many locals believed it obscene to pay that kind of money during such hard times for the town and Chapman was even accused of having betrayed his working-class roots. Horror of horrors, he introduced team meetings, where players could raise concerns about their performances, or those of others. This shocked the establishment at a time when players were treated as ignorant serfs. But in becoming Arsenal boss in 1925, he was about to show yet another side to his nature. This most committed of Yorkshiremen would wrench the balance of power away from his homeland and, over the next ten years, shift it to London N5.

Chapman informed Norris that if he really wanted to see Arsenal win a trophy during his lifetime, he'd have to splash the cash. Norris was horrified, but firing Chapman after only a few months wouldn't be prudent. Herb told Norris that Sunderland's brilliant striker, Charlie Buchan, was the catalyst needed to turn Arsenal into a championship-winning outfit. Buchan, however, was officially worth £5,000, so Sir Henry eked out a deal where he would pay £2,000 to Sunderland up front and £100 for every goal Buchan scored during the season. Buchan came to Highbury, but crucially, there was an unexplained, month-long delay in the deal. No one appeared to notice – except an inquisitive journalist on the *Daily Mail*, who fished around for exclusives and clung to his story for two years.

In the late '20s, Chapman continued to build his team with Norris's money, signing the likes of Joe Hulme for £3,500. He spent a tricky few years introducing new tactics and new players. Chapman insisted that central defenders remain deep in defence (acting as 'stoppers'), rather than moving forward in cavalier fashion. He also played a 'link-man' between defence and attack, in order to encourage counter-attacking from his team. Critics reckoned this would leave other midfielders redundant and destroy football as a spectacle. After an early 0–7 reverse at Newcastle and years of mid-table finishes, Chapman's team-building finally took shape, but as publicity about the club grew, journalists – ever eager to affix simple labels to teams – began to refer to the team as 'boring Arsenal'. The *Daily Mail*, for some reason, was particularly keen on that term and would often make snide comments about Norris in their match reports. They seemed to be hinting at something. As anti-Arsenal feelings grew, whispers about the chairman's 'creative accounting' grew louder in the football world. In 1927, the *Daily Mail* finally ran a series of articles alleging that Norris was guilty of making illegal payments to Charlie Buchan. Norris, they claimed, had given 'under-the-counter' sums to Buchan, due to the loss of income (the player had to give up his business interests and buy an expensive house in London) he would incur from his move south. To the *Mail*'s middle-class readership, this was disgusting, immoral behaviour. The FA was strict about payments made to players, even though everyone in football knew that the use of 'sweeteners' regularly lured players to big clubs. Payments on club houses, new cookers and washing machines, and private schools for the kids were all likely to tempt players to move on. Norris, typically, was simply too brazen about the whole thing, virtually shoving Buchan's money into a brown envelope and handing it over.

Norris had also personally 'overseen' the sale of the team bus in 1927, which raised a princely £125. The proceeds from this somehow found their way into his wife's bank account. It was also well known that Sir Henry liked to be chauffeured around London while he puffed on a cigar and drank brandy. But latterly, he'd decided to pay for the cost of this through an Arsenal

Football Club expense account. The revelations were sensational. Embezzlement? Brown envelopes? Getting Arsenal Football Club to fund his lavish lifestyle? How could a high-profile member of the Conservative Party indulge in such financial malpractice? Norris challenged the *Daily Mail*'s allegations in court two years later, but the charges were upheld by the judge. Not without justification, Norris had argued that because of the £125,000 plus he'd pumped into the club, surely he was entitled to recoup a measly £125. And why should he not treat himself to the occasional glass of Courvoisier every so often? As far as the 'under-the-counter' payments to Buchan went, he said that without them 'we should not have got the player'. Logical thinking and refreshingly straight talking there, but during his spell as Arsenal chairman, Norris had trampled upon so many that he had no real allies left in the game who could save him.

When the FA inquiry questioned Norris in 1928 about the illegal payments, he seemed set to drag down Herbert Chapman with him. Arsenal's manager, Norris maintained, was fully aware of payments made to Buchan and had 'begged' his chairman to do 'whatever it takes' to retain the player's services. Not only was Chapman an accomplice, he claimed, but Norris now also reckoned he'd made 'a grave error sacking Knighton'. During that fraught period, when his whole career and reputation was clearly on the line, Chapman's mind must have shot back to 1919, when he and fellow Leeds City directors were accused of making illegal payments to keep players at the club during the First World War. Lord Kitchener's beckoning finger had decimated City of players and Leeds directors decided to pay existing players an extra two months' wages in order to induce them to stay at the club once the war ended.

Heading the investigation had been Norris's buddy, 'honest' John McKenna, whose claim that 'We just can't have this sort of thing going on' is fairly amusing, bearing in mind his reputation for dodgy deals. The result was that Leeds City were expelled from the Football League and their players put up for auction. Chapman was found not guilty of financial malpractice. Though he remained a director, he was not party to executive decisions because of his work in the munitions factory during the war. But the fact that he suddenly resigned his post at City in 1918 aroused suspicion anyway and for a period, although he was technically innocent, there was a stigma attached to his name. Ten years on, Norris narrowly failed to drag down Chapman with him. The FA ruled that he was 'not an accomplice' and was 'not involved in Norris's financial dealings'. Jack Humble, one of Arsenal's founding fathers, fared less well. He was suspended from football for 'not having discovered the improper transactions'.

With the old tyrant finally out of the way, Chapman was free to break all traditional managerial moulds. The days of club bosses being seen simply as glorified office boys were over. Chapman was fortunate that Samuel Hill-Wood was now the main mover and shaker on the Arsenal board. The Hill-Wood family's motto, which rang true until grandson Peter oversaw the Graham affair in 1995, was: 'Why interfere when you've got experts to do the job?' No manager had ever wielded as much power as Chapman. He oversaw player sales and administration, and controlled training procedures. In short, his power was virtually absolute. One dictator had replaced another – but the new boss was more benevolent.

Like any affair in which Norris was involved there were even murkier stories doing the rounds. With Spurs fighting relegation in 1928, he was accused of telling the Arsenal team to 'take it easy' against struggling Portsmouth and Manchester United in order that the Totts be relegated. Such allegations were common during the 1920s and the maximum wage was virtually an inducement for players to cheat. Nothing was proved, but the committee believed they finally had enough dirt on Norris anyway. He was banned 'indefinitely' from football and never returned to the game.

When Arsenal finally won their major honours under Chapman in the 1930s, Norris could only watch in frustration from the stands. He was proud of their achievements, but without the daily aggro of being Arsenal chairman, he was also a broken man. He felt increasingly bitter about being labelled as 'selfish' and a 'bully' throughout his business, political and football careers. As his lawyer mentioned in the 1928 court case, Norris was a public figure who'd worked 20-hour days in order to solve the housing problems of Belgian refugees after the First World War, grabbing a short nap in the mayor's parlour before beginning another exhausting day's work. His QC also pointed out: 'Thirty years ago Colonel Norris deliberately kept the property prices down on his houses, in order that they be affordable for as many of the population of Fulham as possible. This is hardly the behaviour of a self-serving individual. And did not Lord Kitchener personally thank Colonel Norris for his sterling efforts for king and country during the Great War?' Indeed he did, but all that had been a long time ago. The biggest rogue in the club's history had brought Arsenal to Highbury amid a storm of opposition, bribed their way back into the First Division and enticed Buchan and Chapman to the club.

Norris was doggedly committed to the club's cause and his rabid hatred of Tottenham was something with which all Arsenal fans can identify. In 1934, his hectic lifestyle finally caught up with him and he died from a massive heart attack. He remains a Highbury legend, proof indeed that even the most villainous will be remembered if they give their heart and soul to the club. Upon his death, Norris's estate was valued at a whopping £71,000, the equivalent of over £4 million these days. Despite his 'difficult' reputation, he ensured that his family – a widow, three daughters and two sisters – were 'taken care of'. Leslie Knighton was staggered to receive a cheque for £100 from the Norris estate, especially after the pair had parted so acrimoniously. The sum enabled Knighton to take a well-deserved early retirement and prompted him to comment that Norris was a man of 'many multitudes'. Arsenal trainer George Hardy and groundsman Alec Rae were given £50 each, over a year's wage for the pair. Rae was similarly dumbfounded, as Norris was 'always on to me if the pitch wasn't quite like the croquet lawn he wanted'.

Norris rewarded those who'd worked for his building firm and was also rumoured to have sent a sum for £500 to the Tory rival he'd sued in 1922, precisely the amount Norris had won from him in damages. As one of his former constituents commented: 'Many of his battles seemed serious at the time, but to him, they were often simply a form of good sport.' The Fulham chapel at which his funeral took place overflowed with well-wishers and friends. The vicar who conducted the service summed up: 'Of the dead speak nothing but good.' Rivals from within the football world, especially those from White Hart Lane, would probably disagree. The final word on Norris must stay with Knighton, who commented that his activities as Arsenal chairman were 'merely a bagatelle compared with some of his other business deals'. The mind boggles.

THREE

The Iron Man

I soon learned not to push Wilf Copping too far. Before
Wilf's first game for the club I was busy chatting to him
in the dressing-room and he kept ignoring me. So I
tapped him on the shoulder. Big mistake! He grabbed me
by the collar and shouted right in my face: 'I want quiet!
Is that clear?' You could say I got the message.

Ted Drake, speaking in 1992

While '70s hard-man Peter Storey may be the baddest Gunner
ever to stomp the Highbury turf, his reputation is built partly on
'off-field' activities after his retirement. Confined to on-field
psychotic tendencies, Arsenal's '30s legend Wilf Copping wins
the award as the meanest, toughest player Highbury has ever
seen. Nicknamed the 'Iron Man', he prowled First Division
grounds for nigh on 15 years, seeking prey. Nervous opposition
strikers and midfielders would skulk about like frightened
wildebeest before Wilf devoured them, employing his famous
'shoulder charge' and, when necessary, a 'two-footed lunge'.
Copping's motto was: 'First man into a tackle never gets hurt'.
His detractors labelled him a 'two-trick pony', but perhaps
comparing him with a rutting rhino would have been more
accurate.

Signed by new Gunners boss George Allison in the close
season of 1934, it was hoped he would add more steel to a team
that, despite winning consecutive titles, had appeared to be going

soft over the previous 18 months. The players, it seemed, never quite got over the shock of losing a third-round FA Cup clash with Third Division Walsall in 1933 – arguably the greatest giant-killing of all time. Chapman had been forced to introduce rookies like Norman Sidey, Charlie Walsh and left-back Tommy Black due to a spate of injuries. The atmosphere at the game has gone down in folklore. The Gunners trotted out onto the Fellows Park pitch to a cacophony of booing from the Midlands fans. On a terrible surface, Walsall niggled, punched and kicked their way to a historic 2–0 win. The denouement came when Tommy Black, who'd had a running battle with an opposition striker all afternoon, hacked him down and conceded a penalty, which confirmed Walsall's victory.

In public, Chapman was magnanimous about the defeat, telling his players: 'Never mind boys, these things do happen.' Cliff Bastin later commented: 'Napoleon must have felt like that in Russia, 120 years before.' Privately, Chapman spent the rest of the weekend seething and, on Monday, Black was summoned to his office. 'You'll never play for Arsenal again,' he was told. Within six months, all of those reserves who'd played against Walsall were sold to lower-division clubs. Chapman informed his assistant: 'Mr Allison, it is time to rebuild,' and earmarked a number of potential signings, one of whom was an infamous Leeds United right-half. Chapman's death from pneumonia in 1934 prevented him from beginning the rebuilding process, but his successor, George Allison, knew exactly what to do. The Gunners desperately needed The Terminator. It was time to bring Wilf Copping to Highbury.

Standing at 5 ft 8 in., he was built like a middleweight boxer. Petrified opponents probably reckoned that his pugilistic technique would have been better employed inside the ring. Although Copping played at right-half, it never stopped him wandering over to the left-hand side of the pitch to wreak havoc. Ironically, Copping's background was not dissimilar to that of the late Herbert Chapman. It partly explains the furious intensity with which he played. He was raised in a tight-knit mining community in Middlecliffe, near Barnsley. Life was tough for young Wilf and his brothers; the little information we have about his background tells us that his family 'suffered greatly' during the First World War, though there are no further details.

Wilf worked down the mine from the age of 14, in one of the country's most dangerous shafts. Cave-ins, floods and noxious gases were everyday occurrences, but this didn't stop him from gaining a Stakhanovite reputation for hard work and sheer enthusiasm. Then, after an exhausting 12-hour shift, he would return home for his evening meal and, after a short break, proceed to knock seven bells out of the opposition on the pitch in the local Yorkshire League during the evening. No wonder, then, that he had little time for 'fancy-dan' footballers in London whom, he believed, led too easy a life. Even after turning professional with Leeds, his sense of duty forced him to do the occasional shift in the mine.

Copping was just the kind of dynamic, all-action right-half who would complement the laid-back, aristocratic Jack Crayston on the left. The pair were to become known as 'Beauty and the Beast' and Copping's reputation had already made him a cult hero at Leeds. His dedication to the line of duty knew no bounds. On one occasion, when the team bus failed to collect him at his house, he jogged five miles across Leeds in the sleet to get to Elland Road on time. Wilf still played a blinder and was man of the match by some distance, according to the local press.

But Copping's fearsome attitude, even to training, didn't always endear him to the Leeds secretary/manager. In 1932, Dickie Ray decided to add three new players to his squad. Keen to impress, they unwisely tried to run rings around Copping during pre-season exercises. Forty minutes later, two of the three had already been ruled out of action until Christmas. 'Iron Man' Wilf, having taken exception to the newcomers' fripperies, removed them from the equation, via shoulder and boot.

When he headed for Highbury in the summer of 1934, his arrival coincided with the growth in popular demand for visual images in football. Cigarette companies like Wills rushed to include cards showing footballers, knowing full well that entire families would smoke themselves to death in order to get a rare glimpse of their heroes. In Wilf's case, carefully employed airbrushing techniques disguised many of his distinctive features, but fortunately the black and white photos that now regularly appeared in tabloids did not.

His face was instantly recognisable. Wilf's piercing stare, made even meaner when he narrowed his eyes Clint Eastwood-style, terrified opponents and his wonky, tight-lipped mouth rarely betrayed a smile. This crooked grimace was due to a twice-broken jaw, sustained at Leeds, and he would receive that particular injury again at Highbury. His misshapen nose was testimony to the number of headers he contested. Wilf was famed for his amazing 'spring', although it's a wonder he wasn't put off from aerial combat after he saw its effects on his new Arsenal colleagues. Cliff Bastin and David Jack succumbed to premature deafness from heading the heavy ball, and Eddie Hapgood and Joe Hulme suffered from severe headaches after each game. Not that Copping seemed overly bothered by serious injuries. On the occasion he shattered his jaw again, in four places, he finished the game anyway . . .

Trainer Tom Whittaker was given the task of 'restraining' him on match days – and that was just in the dressing-room. It wasn't easy; Wilf was notoriously tense before kick-off and insisted on 'total silence' around him, something that the chatty Ted Drake often seemed to forget. Copping would then proceed, in Whittaker's own words, to 'blow his top', presumably like Mount Etna spewing out molten lava. Wilf had three match-day rituals. Two of them were considered bog-standard amongst the footballing fraternity. He insisted that he put on his right boot first and that he emerge sixth in line from the tunnel. Dressing-room joker Ted Drake, who sometimes enjoyed messing up the order, did so at his peril. Drake later recalled: 'Once I decided to have a bit of fun at Wilf's expense. He insisted on coming out sixth in line, I think it was. I found that slightly annoying. So one day, I pushed in front of him, which meant he wasn't in the right place. It was like the Second World War had come early. He grabbed me by the neck and yelled: "Do that again and I'll knock your block off." He would have done, too!' His third superstition was the one which gained him notoriety. He did not shave on match-days. In Bob Wall's words, this gave him a 'satanic appearance'. Wilf reckoned it added to his 'iron man' image. He delighted in staring out his opponents before a game.

Ex-Stoke City striker Harry Davies recalled the occasion when he came face to face with Wilf: 'There was a hold-up on the pitch, so we ended up having to queue alongside the Arsenal team in the tunnel, which was unusual back then. I looked in awe at James and Bastin and Drake. They looked so confident and classy. This was '30s Arsenal and I was stood next to their legends. Then I glanced at the man behind Drake, whom, I realised, had been glaring at me for about a minute. It was Wilf Copping, and his ice-blue eyes sliced through the gloom, through me and into the wall behind. I realised that this tough, stubbly figure would be marking me. With his hair greased back, he reminded me of a Chicago mobster. As we ran onto the pitch, he said: "It's going to be rough out here today – watch yourself." For the first time in my career, I'd been intimidated, and I hardly got a kick all afternoon. He was simply the toughest opponent I ever came across. He never gave me a second to settle on the ball, and he pushed and shoved me all the time. His tackles were ferociously hard – overly hard – but strictly within the rules. After the whistle, he ran across, playfully punched me in the ribs and shook my hand. "How was that, then?" he asked. I didn't reply, I was too shell-shocked. After we'd got changed, we joined the Arsenal players for a pint. Wilf was there drinking his Guinness, which I believe was his favourite tipple. He bought me a drink, but he still had that satisfied smirk on his face. I was the opposition's main threat and he'd snuffed me out. Job done.'

Arsenal cruised to the title in Wilf's first season at Highbury. One reason for this was their exceptional away form at hostile northern outposts, where they were hardly the most welcome of visitors. 'Arrogant, rich, southern bastards,' was how Joe Mercer recalled the Manchester City crowd's reaction to the visiting Gunners, now nicknamed 'The Bank of England Club', in 1935. In *Up The*

'Boro, Middlesbrough In The '30s, George Scott comments: 'I saw thousands of men climb over the barriers and thrust past the police and pour onto the field . . . intending to do damage to the Arsenal team, wearing their pristine red-and-white kit. This was the final explosion of hatred. I still remember the spectacle with feelings of fear and horror.' Arsenal's '30s star George Male later said: 'We were hated all right. They came in their thousands to watch us get hammered – that was all the enjoyment they got out of it.'

At a time of the Great Depression and declining heavy industry, London's reliance on light industry and its vibrant building trade meant that many Londoners did not suffer the same hardships as those who lived elsewhere. With its growing suburbs, Tube network, dance halls and department stores, London was the flagship of the 'soft south', as a north-eastern journalist wrote at the time. Arsenal's enormous crowds remained steady in the early '30s and it was well known that the Gunners were one of the few teams to actually make an annual profit, somewhere in the region of £27,000 a year. Like his predecessor, George Allison invested this capital in new talent and on ensuring that his players enjoyed luxury travel and accommodation on away visits. It was common knowledge that on away trips, the team travelled to games in a private rail carriage, where they would quaff champagne and eat smoked salmon while the home side scoffed fish 'n' chips and downed brown ale. Off would float the aristocratic-looking David Jack, the handsome Eddie Hapgood and the jazz-clubber Alex James. With a taste for expensive designer suits and nightclubs, James, who mixed socially with the likes of Wimbledon champion Suzanne Lenglen and transatlantic flyer Amy Johnson, added to the perception of Arsenal as ostentatiously wealthy.

On the face of it, Wilf Copping had more in common with those on the terraces than with his teammates on the field. Yet when it came to the crunch, Wilf always put the team first. The Copping legend was cemented at Everton just a few weeks into his Highbury career. As the *Examiner* put it, he 'became rather over-zealous in the tackle' and 'swapped words with local fans'.

The Goodison Park crowd was always regarded as the most hostile by Arsenal players. Match reports of the time were notoriously dull and understated, but corroborated evidence via Ted Drake and David Winger, an Everton fan from the '30s, reveal the full truth of what happened that day. A section of the crowd had been goading the Gunners by calling them 'southern poofs' all afternoon. The chanting happened to be directed towards Wilf. They'd got the wrong man, in more ways than one. For a start, he hailed from Yorkshire and he also didn't like to hear his teammates being verbally abused. Five minutes into the second half, something inside him snapped. First of all, the Toffees' Jack Coulter, who'd been laughing at the crowd's antics, was 'taken out' with a Copping assault. To the crowd's fury, the referee deemed that Copping had tackled within the rules and waved play on. Coulter's buddy, Will Cresswell, then decided to get revenge. He believed he'd done so in the 70th minute, when, as Copping charged towards him, the ball seemed to be 60–40 in the Everton player's favour. He left his foot in and split open Copping's shinguard. But, worryingly for Cresswell, he didn't split open the Arsenal man's leg. Wilf ran off his injury and, unsurprisingly, five minutes later Cresswell was bundled over the perimeter fencing and ended up spread-eagled and semi-conscious on the terrace. Again, the 'tackle' was judged to be within the laws of the game. At that juncture, four spectators threatened to get hold of Copping after the contest. Wilf surveyed the four and informed them that if they really 'wanted some', he'd be more than happy to indulge their foolish fantasy afterwards. When the whistle went, the four had scarpered and Arsenal had won the match.

Ironically, Copping's finest hour at Highbury came in an international match. The game became known as the infamous 'Battle of Highbury' and it was fought out between the England team – including seven Arsenal players – and World Champions Italy, who'd recently won the Jules Rimet trophy. Unsurprisingly, the FA still had their heads in the sand, claiming that England were the best in the world and that Italy's title meant nothing. Rivalry aside, there was far more to the clash than just a football match. By the mid-'30s, Italian football was ruthlessly exploited by Benito Mussolini's Fascist dictatorship. He had a unique view on football, claiming 'good kicking is good politics'. Perhaps he should have warned his national team that England's right-half Wilf Copping could kick better than anyone.

Aside from getting the trains to run on time, Mussolini, economically and militarily, was a disaster for Italy. Obsessed with a desire to make Italy great, he focused on flashy ways of achieving his goals. He instructed architects to design monuments to him and, with his own money, ensured that Major de Bernardi smashed the water-speed record. Mussolini was a poseur of the highest order and he was determined to enjoy the kind of cult status Hitler had in Germany. The Führer called Mussolini 'my Italian *gauleiter*' (or wannabe, in layman's terms). Mussolini believed that football would 'further the glory of Fascism' and Italy's 1934 World Cup win was immediately acclaimed as a 'triumph for Fascism'. In effect, his team was a collection of 11 sporting soldiers.

Despite their World Cup victory, a FIFA survey proved that England, Austria and Scotland were considered to belong to the 'super class' of European international sides. The FA continued to remain in isolation and had decided not to send a team to the 1934 World Cup. At the same time, a quote by a Yugoslav diplomat of the time confirmed the Gunners' reputation as the most famous club side in the world: 'Ask any schoolboy in Belgrade: "Who is Bastin?" and he will reply at once: "Outside-left for the Arsenal, the greatest club side in the world." But ask him: "Who is Winston Churchill?" and he will say: "I am sorry, I do not know that player."'

In November 1934, Mussolini's '*azzuri*' faced the sternest test yet to their superiority – an England team at Highbury, whose backbone comprised of Copping, Bowden, Male, Moss, Drake, Hapgood and Bastin. The *Daily Express* called it 'This Highbury occasion' and the *Daily Mirror* claimed that an 'Arsenal Armada' was about to set sail. The game's popular title of 'The Battle of Highbury' was apt, considering Mussolini's belief that 'the only beautiful thing in life is war'. It was rumoured that he'd already heard of Wilf Copping's reputation on the international stage. After a stormy clash with Bill Shankly in an England v. Scotland game, Shanks had said of him: 'Copping had done me down the front of my leg. He had burst the stocking – the shin pad was out – and cut my leg . . . he would have kicked you in your own backyard or in your own chair.'

Before the contest began, the England players also got wind of the fabulous bonuses that were on offer to the Italians if they won the match at Highbury. A press leak revealed that the Italians stood to win £150 a man, a brand new Alfa Romeo car and, most importantly, exemption from the dreaded national service. When Wilf and the other England players heard about this, they were furious. For a start, the Italians were supposedly amateurs, and the professional England players only received a £2 appearance fee. Copping always believed that three lions on the shirt was motivation enough.

The *Daily Mirror*, with its usual detachment from reality, said that a 'ten-goal victory must be our aim', but the 54,000-strong crowd, boosted by a huge Italian contingent, realised that the match would be a red-hot battle. The Italian team was snapped at Victoria Station, glamorously suited and booted, with the following message from Mussolini ringing in their ears: 'You must make use of all your energy and willpower in order to obtain supremacy in all struggles on earth.' (And don't forget the wodges of cash either, lads.) The game began in sensational style. With scarcely a minute on the clock, Manchester City's Eric Brook put England 1–0 up and he added another two minutes later. After 15 minutes, Ted Drake scored England's third. Maybe the *Mirror*'s prediction wasn't quite so ridiculous after all. But the trouble on the pitch had already erupted. Just a minute after Brook had cracked England's opener, the Italian centre-half and captain Monti broke his foot in an 'accidental' clash with Wilf Copping. The legend goes that Wilf deliberately removed him from the equation, but no photos verify this claim and the radio commentator on the game just happened to be Copping's manager, George Allison, who conveniently glossed over the incident.

The Italians promptly went ballistic and England captain Eddie Hapgood bore the brunt of their fury. Italy's right-half scuttled over to him, thumped him in the face and broke his nose. Hapgood carried on playing, but later wrote in his book, *Football Ambassador*: 'It's a bit hard to play when somebody resembling an enthusiastic member of the mafia is scraping his studs down your leg.' True enough, and Hapgood's book is a clear reflection of European hostilities of the time. Even without Monti, Italy continued to fight, literally and metaphorically. Through Meazzi, they'd pulled it back to 2–3 by the 60th minute, but Wilf Copping employed Pesciesque methods to ensure that the Italians got no further.

Towards the end of the first half he'd clashed with an Italian centre-forward and, during the interval, Copping enquired of the doctor how he was. The doctor informed him he 'wouldn't be back'. 'Bloody good job. He'd soon be back in the dressing-room anyway,' came the reply. He employed his shoulder-charge in the second half and two other Italians also ended the game limping. He simply terrified the rest of them, his body language suggesting that it wasn't a wise move to venture near England's penalty area. England somehow clung on to win 3–2, in arguably the filthiest football match ever played. Drake recalled, 'By the end of the match Wilf was virtually playing Italy on his own.' The casualty list was extensive. Eric Brook suffered a hairline fracture to his elbow, Hapgood was taken to hospital to have his nose reset and Drake, Bastin and Bowden all needed medical attention from Tom Whittaker.

There is a famous picture taken in the treatment room after the game of all the aforementioned players, plus Copping, being treated. Wilf's expression is Mona Lisa-like. It has an elusive quality, somewhere between a grimace and a smile, which summed up the situation perfectly. He'd emerged from the pitch bruised and bloodied, so he was in obvious pain, but his reputation as football's hard man was confirmed – and against the World Champions too. Though teammates, and the watching Italian ambassador, claimed he'd played 'within the rules', FA officials, disgusted by what they'd seen, threatened to ban all future internationals. In typical FA fashion, they were immediately forced into a humiliating climbdown.

Over the next four years, Copping continued to excel in his role as Arsenal's terminator. He added a further Championship medal to his collection in the 1937–38 season and won several plaudits for his composed passing when, in the 1936 FA Cup final, Arsenal snatched victory from the jaws of defeat against Sheffield United. Yet the press did not seem too keen to give Wilf – or Arsenal for that matter – a break. Due to the fact that Copping and giant centre-half Herbie Roberts were keystones of their success, the Gunners had apparently proved themselves to be mechanised and unadventurous – 'boring Arsenal', in layman's terms. In actual fact, Arsenal were the pioneers of counter-attacking football and Copping often instigated the Gunners' attacks. George Allison insisted that the full-backs remain deep, luring the opposition into the Arsenal area. At that point, the ball would be snaffled from them and the Gunners would set off on a devastating counter-attack. Arsenal became the undisputed masters of the 'ten-second goal'. In an instant, the ball, often via Roberts or Copping, was dispatched to the 'link man' between defence and attack, latterly Alex James, and switched to either a winger or a centre-forward, who invariably scored.

Often in games, the opposition would fart about with the ball on the halfway line for around 60 per cent of the game, before being summarily destroyed. So the 'lucky Arsenal' myth was also perpetuated. George Male thought the Arsenal style was 'twentieth century, tense, exciting, spectacular, economic, devastating'. Others reckoned it was dull. In 1936, Everton visited Highbury and their manager insisted that star striker Dixie Dean be sought out with long punts all afternoon. Their aerial barrage was easily smothered by Roberts and company, and on three occasions the ball was smashed into Everton's net within about ten seconds of it having left the Arsenal penalty area. 'Disgusting,' boomed their boss in a fit of Alex Ferguson-type pique. He added: 'Do Roberts and Copping actually cross the halfway line?' It became de rigueur for the opposition to leave Highbury fuming about their inability to storm the fortress or get past 'Beauty and the Beast'. As a final insult, they'd spit: 'Boring Arsenal.' Yet Stan Matthews and Matt Busby queued up to pay homage to Arsenal's counter-attacking style. Matthews later recalled 'The flying attacking columns of Arsenal . . . the wizardry of Alec James, the bravery of Ted Drake, the competitiveness of Wilf Copping . . . the perfect interlocking machine.' Joe Mercer was even more explicit in his praise of Copping: 'Any player would want him on their team. I reckon he must have set up as many goals as he prevented. What a player.'

By 1938, international relations were reaching crisis point. The England team, captained by Wilf's teammate Eddie Hapgood, was forced to give the Nazi salute before a match in Berlin with Germany. It caused a media outcry, and Copping realised that a second world war was about to break out. It prompted him to demand a transfer. Trainer Tom Whittaker, stunned at first, asked the player if he hadn't enjoyed his time at Highbury: 'Oh sure, but I feel that war is coming, and I want to get my wife and kids back home up north before I join the army,' came the answer. Ironically, his original reason for heading south back in 1934 had been due to the worsening economic climate in Yorkshire, and his belief that his children would enjoy better job prospects in London. The truth about Copping being a decent family man was not revealed in the '30s. It was easier for the press to portray him as an explosive maniac.

Ted Drake also confirmed there was a softer side to his teammate. He recalled: 'Sometimes, Wilf and I would chat about football in general, and he'd say: "Look, Ted, you've got no idea how much playing football for a living means to me. Getting six pounds a week just to kick a ball around is a bloody fortune for me and my family." You could see in his eyes just what it meant. He used to tell me that his family had always been miners. Sometimes, I think he was embarrassed by what he earned, and how comfortable his life was in London.'

Copping, in 1938, returned to former club Leeds, who were grateful to have their old boy back in the fold and delighted that they no longer had to play against him. One of his first games back at Elland Road came against Arsenal, when the *Leeds Evening Post* reported that 'relations between Copping and his former teammates were cordial'. Surely Wilf wasn't becoming sentimental?

Within a year, league football had been suspended and he was drafted into the army, where he excelled himself in organising and motivating others for the common cause, reaching the rank of company sergeant-major. Who, after all, would dare to defy his orders? In the post-war era, he went on to coach abroad before becoming trainer at Southend United. Naturally, he gained a reputation for being the hardest of taskmasters. 'No one ever feigned injury at Southend,' recalled ex-player Andy Halliday, 'because Copping would have you on the bike or doing cross-country running. He used to say, with that crooked smile of his, "I've got no time for slouches or lazy gits." And he meant it. No one pulled the wool over Sergeant-Major Copping's eyes.'

He became a regular at sports dinners. The former Spurs winger Cliff Jones recalls: 'Even in his 50s, he looked a real hard case. He went on about how he'd have had me for breakfast in his day and how I'd never have got a touch if he'd been there. He then asked me to punch him in the stomach, and it was as if he had a bloody sheet of iron under his jacket. I'm so glad I never had to come face to face with him on the pitch.'

Wilf then retired to Southend-on-Sea, where he died in 1981. This tribute to him, written by a Mr Andrews from Watford, appeared in the *Islington Gazette* soon afterwards:

> People no longer call their sons Stan, Alf or Wilf. These names belong to a bygone era of World Wars, heavy industry and rationing. Fittingly, the late Wilf Copping's footballing skills belong to a different age, too. I saw him play a lot in the '30s, but I remember one incident involving him in particular. Middlesbrough had an up-and-coming winger called George Camsell. He was having a good afternoon at Highbury, as were his teammates. He'd gone round Jack Crayston a few times and, these being the '30s, the Arsenal crowd sportingly

applauded him. We knew what would come. It was simply a question of when it arrived. In the second half, Camsell got the ball and prepared to take on Crayston again.

He didn't see Copping coming from the other direction. I distinctly remember the two gentlemen standing next to me saying: 'Oh no, Wilf, he's only a young lad, he surely doesn't deserve this.' Three seconds later, Camsell, and the ball, had literally been smashed into touch. The poor lad didn't touch the ball again. I'll never forget Wilf's clattering boots as he neared his victims, or the sickening thud as his opponents hit the floor. You have to remember that he was never cautioned or sent off in his Highbury career. He never argued with referees either – but he was the hardest competitor I ever saw at Highbury. Some Arsenal fans would chuckle, saying 'There's only one Wilf Copping'. I should imagine opposition strikers thanked their lucky stars for that. What a truly fearsome sight he was!

A fitting tribute to the toughest Gunner there has ever been.

FOUR

Cold War

One of the most exciting games 54,000 people have
never seen.

Daily Mail, November 1945

In the 13 years that elapsed between the end of the Second World
War and the Munich air crash, Arsenal, for the first time in their
history, became popular with neutrals. Previously only those
inside the walls of Fortress Highbury had genuinely loved the
Gunners, but now, in football's golden era, Arsenal went global.
Supporters' clubs sprang up in all sorts of far-flung parts of the
world. As Tom Whittaker and Jack Crayston took over the
managerial reins from George Allison, 'Good Old Arsenal' gained
a reputation for clean-living, morally upstanding 'niceness', far
removed from Norris's dodgy deals and Chapman's 'win at all
costs' stance. It seemed apt that a war-weary populace, anxious for
better health care, education and housing, should also expect the
highest standards both on and off the pitch at Highbury.

Virtually free from the whiff of scandal – apart from
Whittaker's alleged 'tapping up' of Stanley Matthews in the '50s
– journalists lost interest in digging for Arsenal stories, because it
was clearly a waste of their time. Much of this was because the
three aforementioned managers were considered almost beyond
reproach, and in Allison's and Whittaker's case, practically laid
down their lives for Arsenal. Both added a title each to the
Highbury trophy cabinet in 1948 and 1953 respectively, but the

swaggering, cocky Arsenal of the '30s was long gone. The 'Bank of England' club was bust. Herbert Chapman's claim in the early '30s, 'We can afford to pay £2,000 more for a player than any other club', belonged to a bygone age.

In late 1945, a Highbury official admitted: 'We have absolutely no idea when the club will reopen for business.' As the war escalated, Highbury had been turned into a storage depot and a safe house for refugees. It therefore became a legitimate target for the Luftwaffe and, with two decent strikes, Jürgen Klinsmann's kinfolk inflicted more damage on the North Bank and the Clock End than travelling Millwall or West Ham fans were ever to manage during the '80s. The North Bank roof was destroyed – grotesquely concertinaed on the terrace below – and the Clock End deemed 'unsafe to use'. It would cost a small fortune to repair the damage. In the immediate post-war era, White Hart Lane became the club's temporary home, which made Arsenal look like dossers having to rely on their neighbours' goodwill. No wonder Stanley Matthews commented: 'Arsenal, in particular, sustained heavy physical and spiritual damage during the conflict, more than any other London club.'

Players such as Ted Drake, Jack Crayston and Alf Kirchen would never play again, having sustained injuries during wartime matches; most of the team lost their best playing days to the conflict. In late 1945, many of the lads remained stranded in Europe or beyond with the forces. George Male was stuck in Palestine, Bryn Jones in Italy and Leslie Compton in India. Indeed, when these players did finally return from abroad, having had their contracts cancelled in 1939, they received an unpleasant shock. Their wages were around ten per cent lower than they had been six years earlier. No chance of this lot 'larging' it around London. George Allison, who'd steered Arsenal through the choppy waters of the last six years, would now be forced to pay nominal fees for veterans like Joe Mercer and Ronnie Rooke in order to keep Arsenal's head above water. At last, the Gunners, with their collection of war heroes, avuncular veterans and earnest youngsters, were in the same boat as everyone else. In many ways, they were actually worse off.

Something needed to be done in order to lift the gloom. Salvation, such as it was, came from the unlikeliest of sources. An emissary of the Soviet Sports Ministry – Comrade Revenko – made contact with the English FA and mooted the possibility that one of their leading clubs, Moscow Dynamo, tour England in 1945. Arsenal boss George Allison was alerted to the possibility and immediately realised the vast potential of the tour. Media-savvy George, with his journalistic background, realised that a Dynamos–Gunners match would be massive news, plastered all over newspapers and talked about on radio and cinematic newsreels. This was the man who, against the wishes of the establishment, had allowed in a film crew to shoot the low-budget movie *The Arsenal Stadium Mystery*, in which he and several players starred, in the late '30s. He'd also actively encouraged Herbert Chapman to write his *Daily Express* column a decade before and was responsible for ensuring that the world's first live TV game happened to be an Arsenal match. Allison was canny enough to realise the growing power of visual images, particularly as many of the executives responsible for bringing them to the screen were based in London. No matter that several FA officials believed Allison's flirtation with the media to be 'vulgar in the extreme'. Arsenal players, anxious to restore the Gunners to the forefront of sports news, were excited by what they heard about the Russians.

The tour went ahead, and did indeed attract an unprecedented amount of publicity, but along the way something went seriously wrong. It certainly made a mockery of Dynamos' captain Mikhail Semichastny's belief that: 'By clean sport we can strengthen our wartime friendship.' Arsenal's match against Dynamo proved to be the club's last real tango with controversy for 15 years. It remains an almost forgotten episode of the Gunners' history. The world, in 1945, stood on the cusp of the Cold War and the match was played in an atmosphere of mutual suspicion. By the end of the tour, jovial George Allison stood accused by the Russians of villainous capitalism and xenophobia, and several Arsenal players of telling lies about the Dynamo players. Writing in *The Tribune*, George

Orwell claimed that the tour, and the Arsenal match especially, worsened East-West relations, creating 'fresh animosities on both sides'. Judging by his magnum opus, *Nineteen Eighty-Four*, Orwell was a pessimistic kind of guy, but surely he couldn't seriously be suggesting that Arsenal somehow hastened the onset of the Cold War. Being labelled 'Boring Arsenal' was one thing, but this latest slight was quite another matter.

The arrival of the Dynamos' plane at Croydon in late November 1945 instantly sparked a media frenzy. In those far-off days, it was entirely possible for a foreign side to appear and disappear just as quickly, these being the days before the advent of blanket TV coverage. With all manner of wild stories circulating about the Dynamos, British crowds were very keen to see them in action. On arrival in London, Dynamo officials put forward 14 requests to the FA. One of their requests was that they should play Arsenal, still the most famous club side in the world. They also demanded that the Gunners side must be an official Arsenal XI, with no 'guest' players in the team, as had often been the case during the war. The Russians, finally, insisted that their own referee officiate one of their tour matches and that they be allowed to use substitutes, a practice outlawed in Britain at that time. These requests later proved problematic, but in an atmosphere of goodwill, the FA hastily agreed to the demands. Judging from early press releases, the Russians also expected the match against Arsenal to take place at Highbury. Already, there were signs of a chronic lack of communication, mirrored by the respective political leaders' war of words at the time. These small 'misunderstandings' would mar the tour.

Justifiably perhaps, Dynamo officials pointed out that whatever Arsenal's problems were, they were minimal compared with those of their players and the daily threats under which they were living. As it eventually became known, the Dynamos were the adopted team of the NKVD, Josef Stalin's dreaded secret police. Club patron and Stalin's security chief, Comrade Beria, had once been a tenacious full-back in the Lee Dixon mould. Now, in between sending millions to their deaths during Stalin's purges, he set about sculpting a winning side in a manner which would make George Graham's managerial methods appear positively wimpish in comparison. Star players from archrivals Torpedo Moscow were dumped in *gulags*, never to be seen again, and it was acknowledged that underachieving Dynamo players could also expect extended holidays in Siberia. No wonder the Russians had a reputation for marathon training sessions. A poor performance on match day could have truly disastrous consequences for the underachieving players.

The British press displayed its usual blend of ignorance and misplaced arrogance towards the Russians. Despite the fact that the two countries had been wartime allies, Russia was considered to be at the end of the earth. Journalists knew almost nothing about Russian football and after a wartime match in early 1945, a *Times* journalist commented: 'If you did not know they were Russians you would imagine you were watching an England or Scotland team.' The *Evening Standard* claimed: 'We gave football to the Russians', and the *Daily Worker* reckoned that one of the Dynamos' best players, Vassili Trofimov, played with 'vodka in hand' on chilly afternoons. If the same hacks had added, 'We bailed you tossers out in the war,' it would not have been a surprise. British journalists did acknowledge the legendary status of Alexei 'Tiger' Khomich, the Dynamos' invincible goalkeeper and Vsevolod Bobrov, their deadly striker, who also happened to be a crack ice-hockey star.

Once the tour matches got under way, the Dynamos bewitched British crowds with their deft passing and their organisation. However, the clashes also coincided with crucial negotiations over atomic bomb secrets. The *Daily Mail* urged that the Russians be given information by the Americans on designing the bomb, but this view was not universal among the British press and Stalin's duplicity at Potsdam left a bitter taste in several mouths. The growing mistrust of the Russians would soon be reflected in match reports. Playing in a fetching combination of 'Baltic blue' shirts, light blue shorts and bottle green socks, with a large D emblazoned on their tops, they drew 3–3 with Chelsea in front of 80,000 at Stamford Bridge. Writing in the *News Chronicle*, Charlie Buchan commented: 'No team has ever given a better exhibition of class football and failed to win.'

The Dynamos then hammered Cardiff City 10–1 at Ninian Park in front of 45,000. The atmosphere towards the visitors was becoming frosty. The *Daily Mail* reckoned the Dynamos had an almost sinister air: 'Silent Russians with nothing to say.' The *Daily Mirror* claimed they were in the middle of a 'Garbo act', on account of their inability to enjoy the 'entertainment' laid on for them in South Wales – visiting industrial areas. But it was the forthcoming Arsenal match which really occupied the Dynamos' thoughts. Arsenal players were mystified that the Russians spent the train journey from Cardiff to London discussing tactics for the game, not something which British teams generally did. By the time the preparations for the game were complete, the atmosphere would be even chillier.

Russian officials requested a preparatory meeting with Arsenal boss George Allison. For all his media training, George's meeting with the Dynamo officials didn't go too well. Allison reckoned it was like a 'Secret Police quiz', as the Russians subjected him to probing questions about Arsenal players' training methods and diets. He was clearly unhappy about the grilling, but he 'tried to stick it out manfully for the sake of international sport'. The Dynamo officials asked many question during the tour, but none were ever asked of them. If they had been, maybe English coaches would have realised that actually training with footballs would have been useful, rather than an endless grind of cross-country runs. They might also have realised that fresh vegetables and salads were better for footballers than pie and potatoes. As Allison himself commented a few years before: 'Most British players live[d] out of a frying pan.'

His mistrust of the Russians is hard to fathom. Allison had always endorsed Chapman's scathing criticism of the FA for withdrawing from FIFA. 'A ridiculous situation,' he'd blasted. 'We were wrong to laugh at the idea of Europeans mastering football.' Allison was a fierce critic of such isolation, claiming that 'it is tantamount to suicide' and that it 'will damage our national game in the future'. Yet, given the opportunity to swap ideas, George simply griped about Eastern European 'nosiness'. Many accused him of acting in the manner of the pompous FA official figures of whom he'd always disapproved. He ended the meeting in the manner of a true Englishman, by suggesting the party adjourn for lunch.

During the preparations for the match, the biggest cause of ill-will emerged over the selection of Arsenal's team. The Russians received a list of 'official' Arsenal staff when they arrived, but Allison was unable to secure the release from the Forces of seven first-team regulars. So he did what he'd been forced to do over the previous six years – he put out the message that 'guest' players were urgently required. Despite this going against one of the Dynamos' requests, the Russians may have let the matter pass, except that two of these 'guests' happened to be the two Stanleys – Mortensen and Matthews. Tommy Lawton later told me: 'It was a bit like getting Olivier and Gielgud to fill in for you in an amateur dramatics competition. The two Stans would give you a huge advantage over the opposition. The Dynamos probably had a right to feel annoyed. They expected to face genuine Arsenal players. But then, I suppose George wanted to protect the good name of his club. Not an easy situation.'

It has now been proved, once the 'sensitive' documents were released 30 years later, that a 'higher authority', from within the government or the Royal Family, insisted that Matthews play in the match. Stan, and Arsenal Football Club, were informed by anonymous telegram that this was a 'must win' game. Tommy Lawton told me: 'It was fairly common knowledge amongst the players that the King wanted Matthews to play. I don't think I've told anyone that before. But apparently the Palace saw this game as a political opportunity. With so many Arsenal lads abroad, they wanted to avoid Arsenal, and the name of Britain, being humiliated. People say football's big now. But in my career, it was always used for political ends by politicians and leaders.' Matthews did not refer to this episode in his autobiography, but Lawton comments: 'Stan kept a lot of things to himself, but we ribbed him about the Dynamos match. Actually, it's a hell of a compliment, isn't it? The King insisting that you play.' Clear proof that the clash, like the 'Battle of Highbury' a decade before, was of far more importance than just a football match. It also meant that Allison, for one game at least, had fulfilled his dream of seeing Matthews in an Arsenal shirt. Allison also drafted in several other 'guests', including Fulham striker Ronnie Rooke, a good old-fashioned English centre-forward. The final team was: Griffiths (Cardiff), Scott, Bacuzzi (Fulham), Bastin, Joy, Halton (Bury), Matthews (Stoke), Drury, Rooke (Fulham), Mortensen (Blackpool), Cumner.

When the Dynamos learned about Allison's team selection, they were not best pleased, issuing the following statement:

> We were given a list of Arsenal players and the team we have been presented with contains names that are not on the list. We have therefore concluded that we will be playing a representative England team.

There is some truth in that statement, but as Stanley Rous pointed out at the time, the Dynamos may well have been fearful of what Uncle Joe was thinking back at home and losing to a 'representative England team' would be seen as less of a disaster than losing to an Arsenal side. And if they actually won the game, it would be even better.

If George Allison had stirred up trouble with the Russians, it was nothing compared to the anger he'd created among his reserve-team players. He had reckoned that by selecting guest players, he'd saved his 'immature material an ordeal'. Lads who'd plodded away in the war leagues for Arsenal felt badly let down. One youth player commented: 'Many of us have come long distances at great inconvenience to play for the Arsenal on Saturdays and we think it unfair that we should have been left out . . . We wanted badly to play against the Dynamos.' Nice to see that gripes about youth not getting a chance aren't just the preserve of modern Arsenal players. George, on the other hand, stoically maintained that he hadn't received a single complaint.

With the game rapidly approaching, sound bites became more and more politicised. The Dynamos' Bobrov was asked by a British reporter if Stalin was genuinely interested in the fortunes of his 'soccer soldiers'. 'Comrade Stalin is interested in all aspects of our lives,' came the uncannily accurate reply. Frank Coles, in the *Daily Telegraph*, talked of the Dynamos' 'team spirit' and 'collectiveness', compared with Arsenal's 'pronounced individualist merit'. In some circles, the game was portrayed as nothing less than a clash of two political philosophies, capitalism v. communism. Even the Dynamo officials' refusal to give their players a number, on the grounds that they were playing as a 'collective', took on great significance. George Allison was prime material to be projected as an archetypal Western profiteer by the Russian propaganda machine. Various politicians, like President Harry Truman and ex-Prime Minister Winston Churchill, were caricatured in the Russian press as spivs. The Arsenal boss was no different. With his penchant for sharp suits, bowler hats and patent leather shoes, together with a love of good food and fine wines, a number of unscrupulous Russian journalists, among them radio commentator Vadim Sinyavsky, began to concoct stories that Allison had more riding on the game than simply a desire to win a football match . . .

When match day finally arrived, it seemed that the game might not take place after all. As the 50,000-strong crowd discussed the stories about Herman Göring's trial at Nuremberg, the fog descended outside White Hart Lane. Inside the ground, many spectators were unable to see the other side of the pitch. Anxious Russian coach Yukushin, George Allison and Russian referee Nikolai Latyshev (the Dynamos got their way on this appointment) met in the centre circle to decide if the game should proceed. They unanimously voted to play, but that was practically the last thing upon which they did concur.

Reports on what really happened during the match remain suitably hazy. The problem is that, apart from agreement on the weather that day, every piece of evidence – newspaper reports or players' recollections – contradict each other and in any case are loaded with political bias. Player autobiographies, although mainly banal and understated, still reflect the political mood of the time and add to the confusion. In his memoirs, *Cliff Bastin Remembers*, Bastin recalls glancing across as the teams marched onto the pitch and seeing the Dynamos walking 'with military precision', 'unnatural' in their movements. Not quite as 'unnatural' as Chelsea's embarrassed players after they'd been given bouquets at Stamford Bridge by the Dynamos, but mercifully Arsenal players were spared such 'un-macho' pleasantries. The game began in bizarre fashion. Within a minute, the Dynamos took the lead without an Arsenal player having touched the ball. Cliff Bastin and Bernard Joy claimed that Kartsev scored, but then, it may have been Bobrov, as Brian Glanville believed. Either way, the goal came from a sweeping finish after a neat interchange of passes – or possibly from a free kick. Already the thick fog and the absence of shirt numbers made it difficult to judge. Arsenal fought back quickly and the guest players made their mark.

Ronnie Rooke grabbed the equaliser and Stan Mortensen fired two crackers past 'Tiger' Khomich to make it 3–1. Arsenal players quickly became annoyed by the Russians' 'underhand' tactics. Rooke had another goal struck off for handball, but he later commented: 'Handled it – I never had a chance to use my hands, they were both tied behind my back.' Stanley Matthews complained about his shirt being continually pulled and Stanley Mortensen was unhappy with the number of 'obstructions' against him. This was another crucial difference between English and Russian football. The Dynamos were used to employing these tactics in the Russian leagues, although they were unhappy with being regularly shoulder-charged by English defenders, a practice outlawed back home. George Orwell reckoned it was another example of the culture clash and later commented: '. . . every nation has its own style of play which seems unfair to foreigners'.

By half-time, Beskov had hauled the score back to 2–3. During the break, more of the myths that now surround the match were born. According to Cliff Bastin, the Russians sniffed their half-time cuppas suspiciously and, convinced they'd been spiked by Arsenal officials, threw the contents down the sink. Bastin then claimed that the Dynamo players swigged vodka as a pick-me-up. As several writers said at the time, such highly trained athletes as the Dynamos would have been unlikely to indulge in the 'Gazza approach' at half-time. And just how would Bastin have known what went on in the opposition dressing-room anyway?

Nonetheless, his autobiography perpetuates this myth. Dark rumours also circulate about the Dynamos' coach Yakushin, who apparently told the obliging Russian referee that if the score did not take a turn for the better in the second half, then he should abandon the match. Better that minor inconvenience than shaming the nation and incurring the wrath of Comrades Beria and Stalin back in Russia.

The second half was one-way traffic. Kartsev levelled the scores and Bobrov put them 4–3 ahead, even though by this time it was impossible to see further than 30 yards. Only the occasional magnesium flash from a camera enabled the crowd to see any more. A journalist reported that when fans lit cigarettes in the stands, it looked like 'a thousand bonfires'. The Russian referee, with the Dynamos in the ascendancy, played on and the fog did lift enough for a whole section of the crowd to see a piece of magic, as Matthews danced and dazzled his way past four Russians. Several Arsenal players later claimed the fog enabled the Russians to bend the rules regarding substitutions. At one point, maintained Bernard Joy, there were 12 Russians on the pitch: 'A strapping, fair-haired fellow came out of the mist, with no warning that he was entering the fray.'

With 20 minutes left, and the crowd now unable to see anything, anxious Dynamo players encircled the referee, insisting that the game be abandoned. And it was, finishing 4–3, but during the post-match dissection, the British press, aided by sound bites from furious Gunners, implied that through intimidation of officials and sharp practice, the Dynamos had cheated their way to victory. The *Mail* described it as 'the most farcical match that has ever been played'. Cliff Bastin, talking to a journalist, commented: '. . . as long as the Dynamos got the ball into the net, even if they carried it there, the referee was going to award them a goal.'

The war of words continued during the final leg of the Dynamos' tour, when the Russians defeated Rangers in Glasgow. Semichastny pointed to his black eye and described Arsenal's style of play as 'primitive', claiming that several Gunners, especially Ronnie Rooke, had played 'extremely roughly'. Back in Moscow, radio commentator Vadim Sinyavsky agreed with *Izvestia*'s view that the Dynamos' playing style was 'a game of much higher class'. Sinyavsky also claimed that George Allison had 'fainted when the Dynamos' fourth goal went in. He had a large sum of money riding on the game.' This story would seem to prove the point that Allison was a mammon-worshipping capitalist, but the Russian authorities took an unusual stance, accepting that there was no substance to the allegations. Allison was invited to present his side of the story on the Russian airwaves and Sinyavsky was sacked from his job.

In terms of credibility gained from the tour, the Dynamos certainly received a great deal. The official Russian sports paper claimed that their tactics were: 'A triumph for our school of football, which is based on collectivism, organisation, and the unbending will for victory, the characteristic qualities of the Soviet man.' The Dynamos had proved their point and club patron Beria was understandably thrilled. But Arsenal, and English football in general, had missed a golden opportunity to glean new ideas. Ten years later, a *Telegraph* journalist said of the tour: 'We were so bloody insular and bigoted that we couldn't imagine other countries playing the game better than ourselves.' After the games ended, Russian officials were keen to meet with British managers in order to discuss 'the way forward'. The 12 (out of an invited 50) who turned up had the opportunity to glean crucial information on vitamin/calcium intake, masseurs and warm-ups/downs.

George Allison stayed away, having had 'enough of the Dynamos'. Charlie Buchan, in his journalistic capacity, attended and reported: 'All they wanted was our training methods, our technique . . .' God knows why, as theirs was far superior. Buchan also reported: 'When any Britisher asked a question about the Russian ways, they did not understand.' Yet others disagreed with Buchan, claiming that stiff-upper-lipped British bosses observed 'correct behaviour', sat tight and asked no questions. Tommy Lawton later told me: 'I think that George Allison and the English FA were annoyed with the Dynamos from the start. How dare they come here, the country which invented football, and tell us what they wanted and that they did things better than us? It all sounds petty – but that was how we all thought at that time. I often used to wonder whether Herbert Chapman wouldn't have asked a few questions of them. He's probably the only one who would have done. It was a missed opportunity. Of course it was. Even now, some club bosses are only just taking on board what the Dynamos bosses were saying 40 years ago. The Dynamos were a wonderful side, far more technically gifted than any other team you'd come across in England.'

The Gunners did travel to Moscow for a return match eight years later. After a seemingly endless journey, the tired and hungry team slept overnight in the Polish capital of Warsaw, where they were 'protected' by armed guards with bayonets. The team played the Dynamos two days later and lost 5–0. Russian minister Malenkov was an occasional visitor to Highbury over the next few years, attracting attention, as he was flanked by gigantic minders in trench-coats. By 1946, the 'iron curtain', as Winston Churchill put it, descended and contact with Russian football became rarer and rarer. Many of the Dynamo players disappeared – not to Siberia, it must be added, but back to their jobs in factories or sport centres. As true comrades of Socialist Russia, they'd had to maintain a day job in order to do their bit.

Yet rumours about the Arsenal match persisted for years afterwards. The Dynamos' star striker Vsevolod Bobrov, it was proved, had been 'seconded' from the team's bitterest rivals, Central House, another Muscovite side. Central House was controlled by the Red Army, but Beria flexed his muscles and ensured that Bobrov joined the Dynamos for the tour. His legendary standing in Russia was akin to Stanley Matthews' in England, so technically the Dynamos also had 'guest players'. It was also alleged that Stalin presented each player with a whopping £1,000 on return to Moscow, which hardly adhered to Communist beliefs. The Dynamos fired back with further accusations. Bobrov alleged that Arsenal's Reg Drury had been sent off during the second half, but the referee failed to see his face in the fog and Drury ran away and carried on playing. George Orwell concluded in *The Tribune* that the Dynamos match against Arsenal had provoked 'the most savage combative instincts', and it was certainly a precursor to his belief that 'football is war minus the shooting'. A slightly over-the-top reaction perhaps, but the catalogue of rumours/counter-rumours summed up the political situation of the time perfectly. The actions of English and Russian players and officials from Arsenal and the Dynamos left some bitter memories on both sides.

Under Allison's guidance, Arsenal repaired Highbury and, at that point, he retired. Tom Whittaker took over as manager, during English football's golden era, where demob-happy crowds flocked to watch footie matches. The feeling remained that, good chap though Whittaker was, he didn't quite have the cutting edge needed to lay down a Chapmanesque dynasty. Things may have been different if he had managed to secure the services of Stanley Matthews in the summer of 1951. Hugely impressed by his display in the Dynamos match and his regular romps through Arsenal's defence in league football, Whittaker travelled up to Blackpool in a bid to convince Matthews' manager, Joe Shaw, to release him. Stan had convinced Whittaker it was worth the trip, claiming: 'Every actor wants to play in the West End, and I would like to play for Arsenal.'

After protracted negotiations, Joe Shaw still would not budge. Whittaker threw a blank cheque in front of him, telling him to name his price. Still, Shaw would not agree to the deal. Three years later Whittaker tried again. According to Matthews, in his book *The Way It Was*, Whittaker offered him a tempting but illegal 'double your money' deal if he ventured south. The maximum wage level could be bypassed if Arsenal 'declared' that Matthews had done some advertising work for a catering company. Stan was sorely tempted, but he turned the offer down. Despite securing the title in 1953, Arsenal were about to slump into meandering decline and lie semi-dormant for nigh on 15 years. Predictably, in 1953 the Hungarians destroyed the myth of English supremacy by winning 6–3 at Wembley, showing, like the Dynamos, superior tactics throughout the match. Ironically, George Allison, working in the media after his retirement, predicted England's downfall.

The story of Arsenal v. Moscow Dynamo remains resonant.

Modern Arsenal's dreadful playing record in Russia and the Ukraine suggests that visits to clubs which once competed in the old Soviet-controlled leagues fill the team with fear. Detractors will point out that the Gunners' away record in Western Europe isn't much to crow about either, but the glamour parks of France and Italy have traditionally been happier hunting grounds for the lads. On six occasions in the last twenty-odd years, Arsenal have marched on Moscow, Kiev and Donetsk, full of gusto and optimism. In five cases, the team has been destroyed due to a combination of bad luck and inferior tactics – in true Napoleonic style. Arsenal's goalless draw at Lokomotiv Moscow in September 2003 is a statistical anomaly. The Champions League home wins against Lokomotiv and Dynamo Kiev represent, in Arsène Wenger's words: 'the removal of a massive millstone from around this club's neck'. The away clashes have all taken place just as the winter permafrost is descending. Yet with the total aggregate score currently standing at 8–13 against, the fear of playing teams from the 'mysterious East' has its historical origins in the bizarre events that occurred over 50 years ago.

FIVE

Reluctant Rebel

Thanks to George Eastham, footballers finally got the
rights they'd deserved all those years.

Tommy Lawton, speaking in 1991

In 1961, Arsenal's George Eastham was Britain's most
controversial and, in some quarters, least popular footballer.
Receiving copious amounts of hate mail each week, he had been
branded a 'big-headed mercenary' by the chairman of his former
club, Newcastle. When he arrived at Highbury, he was already a
freedom fighter for players' rights and, backed by the PFA, he
pursued High Court action that changed football forever. By his
own admission, Eastham, a mercurial talent with the deadliest left
foot of all '60s footballers, was ill at ease with the furore that often
seemed to surround him. He was arguably the frailest-looking
player ever to pull on an Arsenal shirt, and his delicate skills were
being squeezed out of fashion by '60s bully boys, as football
became hooked on the drug of defensive play. His off-pitch
struggles were mirrored by his battles to stay in the England team,
which was being shorn of flair by Alf Ramsey, and to restore the
glory days to Highbury. These proved to be even tougher
assignments for him than winning his high-profile court case.

Professional footballers in the early '60s remained in a position
similar to that of medieval serfs. Bound to clubs by the outmoded
'retain and transfer' system, they had virtually no rights at all, and
were controlled by their lords and masters like martinets. Two

first-hand accounts, from the late Tommy Lawton and Eastham himself, illustrate perfectly the situation in which footballers of that era found themselves. Lawton, who retired in the '50s, had decided to ask his manager at Everton for a transfer some years before. It was a decision he came to regret. He recalls: 'I'd asked the assistant manager if I could see the boss and he sent me up to his office. I knocked on his door, opened it, and went to walk in. Before I made it into the room, this voice boomed out: "STOP. GO BACK OUT. SHUT THE DOOR. KNOCK AND WAIT UNTIL I SAY 'COME IN'." So I did as he told me and knocked again. He said: "Come in", and as I walked towards his desk, he said: "What do you want Lawton? I haven't got long – make it quick!" So I said to him: "Well, boss, I'm coming to the end of my contract and I think I'm ready to leave. I hear that Chelsea and Arsenal are quite interested in me." Without hesitation, he said: "Don't be stupid, Lawton. I've been offering you around for the last four months and no one's interested in you – not even on a free transfer. What you'll do is go to training today, tomorrow, next week and next month, until I tell you not to come any more. You can forget about Arsenal. Is that clear?" I just said: "Yes, boss", and that was the end of it. I did end up at Arsenal – but not until a few years later.'

Eastham explains the situation even more clearly: 'In the early '60s, players would always address the chairman of a football club as "Sir" and could expect, in return, to be called (in my case) "Eastham". The clubs had you by the proverbials. With the "retain and transfer" system, footballers were not free to change employers at the end of their contracts. In theory, we could be retained at the club's pleasure, and if we argued about it, we could be left to rot in the reserves. The club could also refuse to pay you if that happened.

'Our contract could bind us to a club for life. Most people called it the "slavery contract". We had virtually no rights at all. It was often the case that the guy on the terrace not only earned more than us – though there's nothing wrong with that – he had more freedom of movement than us. People in business or teaching were able to hand in their notice and move on. We weren't. That was wrong.'

This was the system Eastham and his ilk had endured for almost a century and as George wrote, in *Determined To Win*, he'd seen at first hand just what could happen to a footballer at the end of his career. His uncle Harry had been a decent player with Accrington Stanley and Liverpool before a knee injury curtailed his career. Harry did not have a player's pension (not encouraged in those days), and he hadn't played for Accrington long enough to justify a testimonial. He even lived in a club house, which he had to vacate within a week. 'I think that may have sown the seeds of rebellion in me,' George commented. Potless, homeless, jobless . . . a ten-year-old George Eastham, through his uncle's experience, already understood why Len Shackleton once said, 'Old footballers should be shot.'

At around the same time Eastham moved to Highbury, the *Islington Gazette* told the sad tale of Arsenal legend Jimmy Logie. In 1961, Logie wound up in a bankruptcy court after he admitted to 'heavy drinking' to cope with the depression which set in at the end of his playing career. 'Yes, I drank more than I should have, and have done since,' he confessed. As owner of The Greyhound pub, Logie's income was £17 a week, and £10 was spent on alcohol. Happily, the Scot rebuilt his life after this episode, but as the Official Receiver, N. Saddler, commented: 'It seems he was not as good a businessman as he was a professional footballer.' That statement rang true for many a retired footballer.

The poor financial position in which many footballers found themselves was even more absurd considering the amount of money pouring into the game throughout the '40s and '50s. In the post-war era, a relieved population had money to spend and gates around the country rocketed. Crowds of 50,000 plus were almost de rigueur at Highbury. Spectator sports as a whole boomed. Over 30,000 would turn up to watch greyhound racing, or speedway at the White City. The rule was that anything that farted, roared or could be kicked was worth queuing up to watch.

Yet despite the fact that most First Division clubs showed healthy profit margins, footballers remained stuck on poor wages and many were forced to take on extra jobs to supplement their income. Alex James turned to pig-breeding after he retired, and

'20s baseball star Babe Ruth, whilst paying a visit to London in the '30s, labelled Arsenal footballers as 'bloody idiots' for putting up with such conditions. Tommy Lawton comments: 'The whole system was wrong. It was ridiculous. Crowds came into the grounds to see us – the players. Yet we got peanuts, while the board of directors made a fortune. I got increasingly bitter about it later in my career. It's wrong that so many players of my generation made nothing from the game. I don't begrudge modern players a penny of what they earn – I just wish I'd been able to earn the same.' Where the huge amount of gate money went remains open to conjecture. Arsenal were one of the few clubs to invest in supporters' facilities. Many other club's directors certainly made a fat profit. As long as the players 'turned up, shut up, and played on a Saturday' (in Eastham's words), the directors didn't really care, happy in the knowledge that, ultimately, they played God with the lives of their stars. Newcastle United's George Eastham was, in 1959, poised to bring this archaic structure crashing down.

Then, as now, Newcastle were the biggest underachievers in the country, and the similarities with the Geordies' recent past don't end there. Wodges of cash were spent on overrated players and squabbling directors frequently dragged the club's name through the mud. By 1960, Eastham, already a promising Under-23 international, had had enough of life at St James's Park. Messed about over an uninhabitable club house, Newcastle directors then blocked his attempts to travel with the England Under-23 squad on an international tour. Eastham was also unhappy about the job the club had fixed up for him to help supplement his wages. This was common practice among his contemporaries, who were still bound by the maximum wage of £20 a week. The job involved him trawling around working men's clubs and selling glass to customers. A dedicated family man, he was concerned about the effect it would have on his domestic life. The final straw came when the club became stroppy about giving him match-day tickets for his father. So in 1959, as he came to the end of his contract, he dared to ask for a transfer. Over the next two years, Eastham was kept under virtual house arrest by

Newcastle and then lived in self-imposed exile in London. The full truth behind that fraught period was not made public for four years. Arsenal eventually helped him to shake off the manacles of serfdom by signing him for a whopping £47,500 in late 1961. It was easily the most sensational transfer of that decade, not just because Eastham was a star, but because it was the first transfer to be conducted through the tabloids.

The *Daily Mirror* blasted the FA's reluctance to discard the 'slavery contract' and sided with Eastham and Arsenal. 'WHAT A WAY TO RUN A SPORT', ran the headline in early 1961. The PFA, of which Eastham was now the highest-profile member, threatened a 'soccer strike' unless Newcastle and the FA backed down and released Eastham. Supported by other trade unions and broadsheet newspapers, they would have carried the threat through. At that point, as Eastham commented: 'The FA shot themselves in the foot. Alan Hardaker, the secretary of the FA, just couldn't understand why other unions lent support to the PFA. He regarded the PFA as anarchists and troublemakers. And he didn't cotton on to the fact that during industrial strife, trade unions tend to support one another. He virtually told the other unions to mind their own business, which just stirred up more trouble. As I recall, the coal-miner's leader was none too happy with Hardaker's views. That showed just how little the FA knew about industrial relations, and how outdated they were!'

Finally, the FA was forced into a humiliating climb-down, and Eastham's protracted transfer to Arsenal went through. Technically, players were now free to move at the end of their contracts, but the PFA realised that until the system was officially outlawed by a court of law there was always the chance of a return to the Dark Ages. Eastham, who 'just wanted to get all that nonsense out of the way and start playing again', realised he must take legal action against Newcastle United in order 'to stop things going backwards'. At the same time, PFA chairman Jimmy Hill, who realised that revolutionary winds were blowing, had just won another epic battle: the abolition of the maximum wage. Footballers would now enjoy, or suffer, the vagaries of market forces. Technically George had nothing to do with Hill's campaign but he was clearly a key figure in these more subversive times. Eastham was now the symbol of a more upwardly mobile generation of footballers. This didn't make him popular in all quarters and he commented at the time: 'According to which side of the fence you are on, I've become a martyr, a big-head, or a rebel . . .' Arsenal fans hoped that this much-hyped new signing would also be a winner.

For Arsenal, the swinging '60s barely swung at all. It was a period unique in post-war club history, as no silverware was added to the trophy cabinet. Signing Eastham represented Arsenal manager George Swindin's final throw of the dice and, after the player's lengthy absence from the game, it was a huge gamble. Swindin, who'd been an Arsenal goalkeeper during the '30s, quickly learned that the new transfer system, as well as bringing Eastham to Highbury, also had a downside. Top scorer David Herd, a guaranteed 25-goal-a-year man, who'd become unsettled after Swindin had tried to use him as a make-weight in the Eastham deal, quickly left for Manchester United. The move put pressure on Arsenal's (then) record signing to deliver immediately. Swindin's team, consisting of players like Tommy Docherty, John Barnwell and Mel Charles, simply could not gel effectively and Eastham felt the pressure.

He was pitched in at the deep end and scored two excellent goals on his debut against Bolton Wanderers. But his early form fluctuated and he felt crushed by the weight of expectation upon his shoulders. He later commented: 'Every expensive Arsenal signing was regarded as a Messiah, who might prove the vital spark to set them alight.' Eastham did have one moment of great satisfaction early in his Highbury career. He was in the Arsenal team that played up at Newcastle. The Geordies, aware that he was taking court action against the club, spent the afternoon screaming 'Judas' and pelting him with apples. He popped in a late equaliser – it was a rare moment of triumph in a turbulent first season at Highbury.

His wildly inconsistent form occasionally led the crowd to get on his back and, in the increasingly physical world of '60s football, his 'butterfly tackling' was sneered at by critics. It didn't help that Spurs were on their way to completing the 1961 Double and 'golden boy' George, with '40s-style Brylcreemed hair, bore the brunt of the North Bank's anger. In late 1961, with the maximum wage formally abolished, Eastham turned down Arsenal's offer of £30 a week and refused to accept a new deal. Hate mail poured in from Gunners fans. Letters to London newspapers accused him of being 'big headed', 'greedy' and a 'symbol of all that's wrong in the British game'.

Eastham, on the other hand, believed he was simply fighting for his rights. As Arsenal's most gifted and creative player, he was directly at odds with the Arsenal chairman's egalitarian view that: 'A team of 11 is a team of 11. And that's the way they'll be treated.' Eastham recalls: 'I was perfectly within my rights to hold out for a better deal. After the way I'd been treated at my old club, I wasn't prepared to tolerate anything other than a fair deal. Johnny Haynes, who played for Fulham, was earning three times what I was getting, and Fulham's gates were far smaller than Arsenal's. The problem was that fans weren't used to "player power" in England. And the prevailing thought was, "You don't mess the Arsenal around." I wasn't messing anyone around, actually. At heart, most people still thought we should put up and shut up. My view was that we'd been slaves for too long and I was just standing up for myself.' After another protracted row and the prospect of him being put into the reserves by the furious Swindin, a compromise was reached and Eastham given a new, improved deal.

For all his bluster, Swindin, who'd stated after his appointment as Arsenal manager in the *Evening Standard*: 'If I've got something to say, I'll say it,' was struggling to control events both on and off the pitch. Eastham won this particular battle, but towards the end of 1963, Arsenal were still no closer to winning a trophy and Eastham's form, according to a letter in the *Islington Gazette*, 'hardly justifies such an inflated salary'. By now, though, he had weightier matters on his mind.

The PFA put up £15,000 of its own money to back him in the Eastham v. Newcastle United case. It was to be fought out at the

High Court in London. The episode mirrored those militant times: Prime Minister Macmillan had said earlier in 1963 that the 'winds of change are blowing across Britain' and he was right. The Profumo scandal and the resulting furore destroyed the image of a morally upright, landed gentry and Conservative MPs being beyond reproach. The late JFK's knightly image was already fading, as details of his alleged Mafia links filtered through, and mods and rockers slugged it out in British seaside resorts, just to show that teenagers were not always the good little boys and girls they were supposed to be. Britain's social climate was changing rapidly and with Beatlemania in full swing, and working-class heroes like Michael Caine and Richard Burton starring on the big screen, the country was more of a meritocracy than ever before. There could be no better time for George Eastham and the PFA to consign football's feudal system to the dustbin of history.

When Eastham and his counsel arrived at the High Court, he could have been forgiven for feeling nervous. Facing him in the dock were all his old Newcastle adversaries. Ex-manager Charlie Mitten, once dubbed the 'Bogota Bandit', after he'd decided to leave Manchester United to play in Colombia for financial reasons, was now part of the establishment. Also in the dock was the despotic Newcastle chairman Alderman McKeag, famed for prying into the private lives of all his players. From the outset, Newcastle FC stood accused of a) applying unlawful restraint of trade to George Eastham and b) unlawfully preventing Eastham from joining another club after his contract expired. Club chairmen around the country shuddered when the case got under way, aware that they could so easily be taken to court by hundreds of bitter ex-players.

Eastham, however, showed few signs of nerves as his big day approached. He recalls: 'I was lucky to have inherited my calmness from my father. I never got nervous on the big occasion, and in this case, I had no need to anyway, as I hadn't done anything wrong. We were quite lucky going into the trial. The press was still obsessed with the Profumo affair. Being honest, Christine Keeler and Mandy Rice-Davies were bigger names, and better looking, than George Eastham! There were still lots of journalists in the vicinity, but not too many, so we could all focus on the trial. If it had been today, the trial would have been enormous, given the exposure football gets now. I felt calm about it, but I also felt a big burden of responsibility. People's reputations and careers were at stake, after all.'

The Newcastle contingent made poor defendants in the dock. Edgy and uneasy, they contradicted each other over when conversations with Eastham had taken place and over the nature of those meetings. When key directors did get their stories straight in the courtroom, they contradicted sound bites issued on local radio and in newspapers three years earlier. McKeag denied that Newcastle ever had a problem about selling Eastham. Clippings from assorted tabloids and broadsheets, including one McKeag comment in *The Times*, categorically stating: 'Eastham will leave this club over my dead body,' proved otherwise.

In sharp contrast with Newcastle's board of directors, the smartly turned out George Eastham gave an excellent account of himself in the witness box. He was well briefed by his legal team, headed by Mr Gerald Gardiner QC. Lucid and unflustered, he put forward his version of events. As a journalist wrote at the time: 'Eastham didn't look like a serf – it was the hapless Newcastle directors who looked like the ignorant ones.' George told the court that in late 1959 he'd requested a transfer and, at first, his pleas were not even acknowledged. When his demands were finally made public, he and his wife were virtually ostracised by other Newcastle players and their families. After a few months, Charlie Mitten finally talked with Eastham, but flatly refused the request, saying: 'You are going nowhere, Eastham. We will not sell.' Mitten's mood subsequently lightened and Eastham was promised that if he stayed, necessary improvements would be made to the player's club house. Eastham remained unimpressed, having heard it all before. With his player still refusing to sign a new contract, Chairman McKeag stepped in, and after labelling him in the press as the guy 'with the shortest arms and longest pockets in football', he informed him that if he still wouldn't comply: 'We'll put you out of football.' 'There were gasps of horror in the public gallery,' Eastham recalls.

At this point, Eastham admitted to feeling at his lowest ebb and said that he'd even considered backing down and signing a new contract with Newcastle, before an old friend stepped in to help him. Down in Surrey, Ernie Clay, who later became Fulham chairman, offered him a job selling cork. He accepted the job, partly to prove to Newcastle that he was no longer dependent upon them, but also because by this time the club had stopped paying his wages. Eastham moved to Surrey and for a whole year worked from a plush office in Guildford. He claimed, 'I enjoyed it', but at heart, he missed playing football and his family remained marooned in the North-east.

Aware that their prize asset was rapidly losing its value, the Newcastle directors eventually accepted a £47,500 bid from Arsenal who, they alleged, had 'tapped Eastham up' while he was in Surrey. This was never proved, and Eastham and Arsenal vehemently denied it had happened. When Eastham finally signed on the dotted line for Arsenal in 1961, he was hugely relieved, but his bank balance had taken a battering. Eastham believed he was owed £400 in unpaid wages by Newcastle. This represented around 20 weeks' worth of pay. His inactivity, he maintained, had been the club's fault. He had also missed out on £650 in win bonuses and other benefits.

The jury retired to consider its verdict and Justice Wilberforce prepared his 15,000-word filibuster. Wilberforce worked up slowly. He stated his belief that football clubs should 'communicate with players' more effectively and that it was just that a player should 'fight for the right to bring about a soccer enlightenment'. These comments alone were damning indictments on English football. Then came the verdict that Eastham wanted. In Wilberforce's opinion, Newcastle United FC was guilty of restraint of trade. In failing to allow Eastham to leave the club at the end of his contract, they'd denied him rights granted to employees in other professions. This, along with the club's option to extend players' employment from year to year, would be abolished forthwith. His judgement was: 'The rules of the FA and the regulations of the Football League relating to the retention and transfer of players in professional football . . . are in unreasonable restraint of trade.' Wilberforce believed: 'Soccer players may now consider themselves to have twentieth-century rights, at last.'

Eastham recalls: 'All those sleepless nights, all that hate mail. I felt an overwhelming sense of satisfaction that we'd won.' He did not, however, receive a penny in compensation from Newcastle. The judge commented: 'As Mr Eastham refused to play for Newcastle United, it shall be left to their discretion whether he should receive back pay and other sundry finances.' Unsurprisingly, the board voted unanimously not to show their former player any sign of goodwill. 'I'd won the war but lost the battle,' Eastham comments wryly. This is the crucial difference between Eastham and the likes of Nicolas Anelka, who wasn't even at the end of his contract. George was genuinely fighting for a cause, a principle, but did not profit financially from the affair. Some say that he was the instigator of 'player power' but, unlike the mammon-worshipping players of the modern era, he did not seek to line his pockets or ignore his responsibilities. Thousands of fellow professionals certainly had cause to thank Eastham during the '60s. Ex-teammate Terry Neill recalled: 'When George returned to Highbury after the case, I looked at him with real admiration. The enormity of his achievement never occurred to you until it came to moving on at the end of your contract or negotiating a better deal. Such a simple thing, and yet it had been denied to footballers for years. It was all down to him and yet you looked at this easygoing, popular guy. Everybody liked him and he was so frail looking. You never thought he'd have had it within him to go through with the case. What a battle to win.'

With George's draining court case finally at an end, he returned to pre-season training at Highbury in the summer of 1963, to discover that new manager Billy Wright had been doing some serious thinking in the close season. A year earlier, the board believed that the appointment as Arsenal manager of England's former captain would usher in a new era of glory. On the face of it, the decision seemed an excellent one. Wright had a squeaky-clean reputation and his marriage to Joy from the Beverley Sisters made them the Posh and Becks of their day. It even brought a faint smattering of glamour to the jaded Gunners. Wright wasted little time in splashing the cash. Striker Joe Baker, nicknamed the 'laughing cavalier', arrived from Torino for a gigantic £70,000. With his Elvis quiff, ready smile and fearless play in and around the box, he instantly became a crowd favourite. Baker scored a classic debut goal at Leyton Orient and, with Eastham alongside him, conventional wisdom held that Arsenal were a team on the move. Over the course of that season, however, it became clear that the two were incompatible as a strike force. Baker's form didn't appear to suffer – he scored 31 goals in his first season – but Eastham's did, with only four goals in total. 'We just kept getting in each other's way,' Baker later commented.

For the opening game of the season, George Eastham, Britain's highest-profile and most talked-about footballer, discovered that he'd been axed from the starting line up by Billy Wright altogether, in favour of playing Baker as a lone striker. After a tetchy exchange between manager and player, Eastham was placed on the transfer list at his own request. George received yet another sack of mail, but this time the mood was different. In the aftermath of the court case, George gained a great deal of public sympathy. He was now officially a good guy. The letters begged him not to leave the club and Billy Wright hit upon a solution. In one of his few successful tactical switches, Wright decided to convert Eastham into an inside-right rather than a striker, which allowed the slick and stylish Baker–Eastham partnership to finally flourish. George came off the transfer list and for the next two years, with Alan Skirton, the 'Highbury Express', providing the bullets, Eastham finally became a firm crowd favourite.

George cemented his status by scoring two goals in a glorious 4–4 draw with Spurs at Highbury in 1964, watched by almost 70,000 fans. His form was so good that he won 19 England caps in Alf Ramsey's emerging England team. In the meantime, yet more big names arrived at Highbury. Blond-haired Ian Ure was signed from Dundee for £62,500, a world-record fee for a centre-half, in order to shore up a leaky defence. Ure himself was no stranger to controversy, after threatening to strike in Scotland when Bob Shankly originally refused to allow him to go to Arsenal. In echoes of the Eastham saga, Ure claimed he was 'a slave' and eventually got his move. For Igor Stepanovs at Old Trafford in 2001, read Ure on his debut against Wolves in 1963. Pacy Wolves forwards nipped around him at will, and though Ure later settled down, Arsenal's defence in the mid-'60s simply wasn't good enough. Leicester's Frank McLintock later arrived for £80,000 and, playing originally in midfield, he also took time to settle.

Darker forces were at work. In Ure's words: 'Billy wasn't a good manager. He wasn't hard enough and he didn't have the willpower to get the players to work together. Forwards played as forwards, and midfielders purely as midfielders. The groups didn't help each other out. Some players simply played for themselves.' Ex-Arsenal pros, while not wanting to criticise their colleagues, confirm that cliques, that most cancerous of growths, were spreading. Frank McLintock, in his book *That's The Way The Ball Bounces*, confirms that Wright relied far too heavily on 'the big names' and that the team was never an interlocking whole, which is the key to all successful Arsenal sides. Haunted by the ghost of Herbert Chapman, Wright would shake his fist at Chapman's marble bust, all too aware that he would never emulate his achievements.

In a bid to rid himself of the Chapman 'millstone', Wright decided to abandon the famous red shirt and white sleeves. For a year or so, Arsenal turned out in all red, for the first time in 50 years. Many years later, Frank McLintock confessed that the change had been his idea, but poor Billy copped all the blame anyway. It was hardly fair, but it was all the proof that traditionalists needed. Wright simply wasn't an Arsenal man. With his four-year reign characterised by mid-table finishes and early cup exits, the crowd's patience was running out. The low point of the Wright era arrived when his team faced Leeds United at Highbury for a league match that attracted just 4,554, Arsenal's record lowest attendance. Admittedly, it was pissing stair-rods and Liverpool were playing in a televised European final that evening, but even so . . . The team could play pretty football and pass the ball crisply, but with no real end product. Something would have to be done. With youth-team graduates Radford, Armstrong and Storey breaking into Arsenal's first team, the clock was also ticking for a number of senior professionals. As George Eastham reached his dreaded 30th birthday in 1966, his career had reached a crossroads. Aware that the World Cup finals represented his last chance to shine on the international stage, he was still expected to teach Arsenal's young lads a trick or two.

After a gutless 0–3 reverse at home to Nottingham Forest, the *Islington Gazette* acknowledged: '. . . football thinker Eastham can hardly be blamed. A star is only as good as the men around him allow.' Frank Taylor, writing in the *Daily Mirror*, reckoned: 'George Best aside, Eastham's soft shoe shuffles mean he is the First Division's most elegant performer.' Yet the Arsenal board, which was coming to realise that Wright's tenure was doomed, started to dismantle the manager's team. Joe Baker, at just 26, was sold to Nottingham Forest. It was a baffling decision, particularly as youngster John Radford was yet to become a first-team regular.

More worrying for Eastham was that his delicate skills seemed to belong to a bygone era. During a clash with Don Revie's resurgent Leeds team, a vicious Bobby Collins booted Eastham all round the park, threatening to snap his matchstick legs at any moment. A disgusted Eastham commented afterwards: 'If that's the way you have to play to get success these days, maybe we should let them [Leeds] have it.' He also admitted publicly that he could tell within the first five minutes of a match whether or not he'd have a good game. No wonder Charlie Nicholas was often compared with Arsenal's '60s maverick.

With World Cup fever about to engulf the nation, Eastham made a few substitute appearances in friendlies leading up to the tournament. He was well aware of Ramsey's thinking, though: 'Alf always said that he wouldn't necessarily pick the best individual club players, he'd pick those who would fit into his system.' For Ramsey, runners, gallopers and tacklers were always favoured, a case of efficiency over flair. There was no place for wingers in his teams and ultimately he decided to ditch the individualistic 'cheeky chappie' Jimmy Greaves for the final, in favour of the solid

Geoff Hurst. George Eastham, even though he made the final squad of 22, did not actually get onto the pitch. Secretly, purists despaired about the victory of 'Ramsey's robots', though to have criticised his England team in the '60s would undoubtedly have led to the reintroduction of capital punishment. Eastham holds no grudges. He comments: 'You can't really criticise Alf for not playing me or other "flair" players. Many people would say that day was one of the best of their lives. I was certainly very proud just to have been in the squad. England won the World Cup and managers have to make tricky decisions like that. It's their job.' Tabloids once again sneered at Eastham, labelling him a 'nearly man'.

By August of 1966, with the country still wallowing in World Cup bliss, Wright and Eastham were booted out of Highbury, during the week when Chris Farlowe's 'Out Of Time' was No. 1 in the charts. Ironically, Georgie Fame's 'Get Away' had been in pole position previously. Was some greater force sending a none-too-subtle message to Billy and George? Both decent men, they'd paid the ultimate price for failing to restore the glory days to London N5. It is ironic that precisely 30 years later, the Arsenal board sacked Bruce Rioch, another 'outsider', after Euro '96, when optimism in the English game again reached 'fever pitch'. Billy Wright was crushed and publicly ridiculed. He later became a successful executive at Central TV, although his family remain convinced that the pressure of being Arsenal boss was the key factor that drove him to alcoholism. George ended up at Stoke City. After four years at the Victoria Ground, he decided to wind down his career in America. But in another bizarre twist, the English authorities, in his absence, clamped down on the 'tackle from behind', which had become the bane of George's life. Stoke manager Tony Waddington persuaded him to return for a second spell at the club during which Eastham played some of the best football of his career.

He finally got the silverware he deserved when Stoke beat Chelsea in the 1972 League Cup final. Thirty-six-year-old George, greying and sporting magnificent sideburns, but still as trim as ever, blasted the winner, just for good measure. He later managed Stoke but, like Billy Wright, was considered 'too nice' to be a manager. Eastham finally found his niche when he emigrated to South Africa and began to coach young black players. A staunch opponent of apartheid, he firmly believed that everyone had the right to learn the art of playing football, extremely apt for a man who had put his career on the line to fight for another principle in which he firmly believed. For his 'services to football', he was later awarded the OBE.

'Gentleman George', as he became known, still lives in South Africa, having subsequently run several successful businesses and soccer schools. Engaging, open and perceptive in interview, he refuses to criticise those who blocked his move from Newcastle to Arsenal: 'They were products of a different era, over 40 years ago. It's not all their fault. As for the court case and me being labelled as some kind of "freedom fighter", I never felt too comfortable about all the fuss. I was just a guy who wanted to do his job.' He's now chairman of the South African branch of the Arsenal Supporters' Club. Far away in time and distance from the furore which once surrounded him, he still follows the club's progress and occasionally expresses his disappointment at the lack of genuine left-footers in the modern English game. I wonder if today's multi-millionaire footballers, who rarely see out the end of their contracts, actually know who he is, or what he once represented?

SIX

The King of Highbury

Charlie George, Superstar,
Walks like a woman
And he wears a bra.
                    Popular terrace chant from the '70s –
                    to the tune of 'Jesus Christ Superstar'

An official Arsenal event at Sportspages bookshop, Charing
Cross Road – not the sort of occasion the author would normally
look forward to. Sue, a rather bossy and over-familiar public
relations girl, informs the expectant crowd that there's plenty of
official Arsenal merchandise on sale and that the star of the show
will be available to sign books and magazines later in the evening.
Around 100 people mill around, ranging from teenagers who are
buying their dad's Christmas present to 50 year olds, many of
whom reek of Brut. They've brought along tatty old copies of
Shoot and *Goal*, and are ready for their heroes to sign them. They
are revisiting their youth.

Based on appearances alone, it would be hard for the unwitting
observer to judge who the ex-Arsenal cult hero is. The clue lies in
the fact that everyone seems to be gravitating towards a
bespectacled, smartly dressed man standing next to the fanzine
stand. It is agreed that he's shorter and stockier than expected, and
his face is rounder than it once was. He smiles a lot too, not
something for which he was renowned in his playing days. His
hair is clearly receding, though it continues to brush his shoulders

– the only visible indication of a rebellious youth. But when he talks, he gives himself away, with 'the Arsenal' slipped in at regular intervals. Everyone knows that only true fanatics call them 'the Arsenal'. Then he's quickly ushered to the front desk by bossy Sue, who's been giving out pens and paper for the official Arsenal quiz. His movements aren't as languid as they used to be, due, as he later tells us, to 'me arthritis, bad back, dodgy knees and dodgy ankles'. But now the evening is about to formally begin. 'Ladies and gentlemen,' announces the owner of Sportspages, 'please give a big hand for Mr Charlie George.'

Charlie's voice is clear and pure Holloway, and the eyes look a bit puffy. His patter is fast and streetwise. In the quiz, he asks the audience who Arsenal beat to win the first leg of the 1971 Double. 'And I'll give you a clue – they're still shit,' he adds helpfully. Then, while he's answering the first tentative questions from the nervous audience after the quiz, he slips into a routine honed through regular evenings such as these. 'Do you play golf, Charlie?' 'Yeah, I'd play a lot better if I hadn't argued with me lawn mower and cut one of me fingers off.' (He holds up his right hand to reveal the stumpy second finger – just in case we didn't believe him.) 'Where did you go to school, Charlie?' ''Olloway, before they decided that my grasp of four-letter words wasn't what they wanted.' 'Anyone you regret not having played under?' 'Mary Stavin.' (Miss World 1976 and George Best's ex-girlfriend.)

As the audience realises that any query will be answered, the questions become more pointed and Charlie displays a more introspective side to his nature. During the next 30 minutes, he fields all sorts of questions on various aspects of his career. His responses are a strange mixture of ruthless honesty and blandness. With club officials present, he has to watch what he says. Sometimes, he says things that contradict comments he's made in the past. At times he deliberately grey-washes some of the more lurid episodes in his colourful life. It's not quite what you expect on such occasions. Even the most rebellious of the '70s mavericks has mellowed over time, it seems. The full truth behind his career is far more interesting than he cares to admit.

That Charlie George made the breakthrough into Arsenal's first team during August 1969 is entirely apt, given it was a month that saw the beginning of the end of '60s innocence. As the 400,000 crowd slipped away from the Woodstock festival, they may have heard news of the Americans stepping up their B52 raids on Vietnam. Information was also filtering through of the horrific murders of actress Sharon Tate and friends at the hands of Charles Manson's 'family'. In Britain, as another huge rock event began on the Isle of Wight, sectarian violence raged in Northern Ireland. Not much peace and harmony in the Summer of Love, was there, man? No wonder Bob Dylan was pestered to sing 'The Times Are A-Changin'' repeatedly at the Isle of Wight festival. There wasn't a more apt anthem for the age. Later in Charlie's first season, Concorde flew for the first time and The Beatles' painful divorce finally went through. Arsenal couldn't wait to bid farewell to the '60s. Thanks to Ian Ure's brains, Arsenal representatives won *Quizball*, a sort of early version of *A Question Of Sport*. It hardly constituted silverware. The biggest Highbury occasion of the '60s was the Cassius Clay v. Henry Cooper rematch in 1964. Something, or someone, was needed to lift the gloom. Salvation arrived in the unlikely form of Charlie, the cocky, swaggering skinhead who'd virtually stepped from the North Bank onto the pitch.

He was perfect for the dawning of the brash, in-yer-face era of colour TV. During the 1970 World Cup, ITV ushered in the new age by pioneering 'the panel'. Between them, the game's loudest 'personalities', Malcolm Allison, Derek Dougan and Pat Crerand, picked apart games and players and bullied poor Bob McNab, another member of the group. With satellite link-ups and breakfast shows, coverage of football was changing. Players, on the other hand, remained stuck largely in the Dark Ages. Alf Ramsey's squad appeared on *Top Of The Pops* to sing 'Back Home' in dickie bows and dinner jackets, at a time when most pop stars appeared to be injecting their eyeballs with acid and composing 15-minute guitar solos. It just went to show that football had not really moved on since the days of serfdom. During the World Cup, the vision of Brazil's golden shirts, shining against the electric green playing surface, poured into viewers' living-rooms. They were transfixed. After Mexico '70, Arsenal also decided to wear golden away shirts. The team hardly grabbed the public imagination like Brazil. But Charlie George did, and his most famous goal celebration matched anything which Jairzinho or Pelé could do.

After the success of 'the panel', and with media intrusion growing, tabloids sought to develop the cult of personality within the game. Two mutually antagonistic groups were identified. There were the hatchet-men, like Nobby Stiles, Norman Hunter and Peter Storey (more on him in a later chapter). Then there was the group of footballers loosely defined as the mavericks. Along with Tony Currie, Peter Osgood, Stan Bowles, Rodney Marsh and Frank Worthington, Charlie George was charged with the task of restoring the glory to Alf Ramsey's recently deposed World Champions. The mavericks, whose off-the-cuff skills and unorthodox approach to the game went against accepted codes of behaviour, instantly became cult heroes on the terraces. In many respects, the obstreperous Charlie George did not even fit comfortably into the maverick genre. Womanising was definitely not his thing after he married his childhood sweetheart, Susan Farge. Charlie later commented: 'I didn't get too many women running after me. It was their fucking husbands who'd be after me.' And though he loved a drink as much as most '70s footballers, it wasn't really his vice. Nor was shooting his mouth off in the press, unlike several of the others. But, like Stan Bowles, he had a distinctly gung-ho attitude to the readies. 'Money is earned, money is spent. I never invested a penny,' he tells the audience at Sportspages. And gambling? 'A fair proportion of it did go on the horses and on the dogs,' he admits. And in terms of 'attitude' on the park, he was every inch the 'cockney rebel' that the press dubbed him. Charlie was clearly born within earshot of the Bow Bells. Both on and off the field, he possessed bucket-loads of attitude, which added a serious intensity to his game and would put him at odds with the establishment. In the late '60s, Charlie, along with the golden girl of English athletics, Lilian Board, was tipped by the *Evening Standard* as being a key player in British sport during the next decade. Within a year of that prophecy, Board, who began to complain of falling energy levels and chest pains after she'd won the European Athletics 400-metre title, tragically died from cancer. 'You can control lots of things,' Board commented as she underwent treatment, 'but injuries and sheer bad luck you can do nothing about.' That warning would also ring true for Charlie George during the '70s.

It is fair to say that the teenage Charlie represented every teacher's worst nightmare. Even at school, he was attracting attention due to his spiky attitude as much as his footballing prowess. 'It's fair to say, I spent more time in the corridor than in the classroom,' he says. He certainly wasn't stupid, but as several contemporaries at his Holloway school stated, he was 'unteachable'. Academic subjects simply didn't interest him and when, in desperation, the school sent a careers officer to speak with him, George informed him: 'Don't look at me, I'm off to the Arsenal.' In the playground, Charlie and friends would discuss their hopes for the future. George's aim was simple; to play for the Gunners and score the winning goal in the FA Cup final. Rather like many boys at his school, in fact. Maybe a gambler like Charlie should have put a few bob on it there and then. During the early '60s, he loyally followed the Gunners around the country. Whether it was looking for trouble on the North Bank or throwing cream cakes at opposition fans – which he did once at Peterborough before an FA Cup tie – he was already classed in the 'mad, bad and dangerous to know' category. There was no logic behind many of Charlie's actions: 'I just felt like it.'

Bucking against school discipline, he was later expelled, but not before meeting future Arsenal teammate, Bob Wilson. Wilson, who'd trained as a schoolteacher, still helped out in local schools in the afternoons, and young Charlie was one of his students. Wilson later recalled that, unlike the other lads, who addressed him as 'Sir' or 'Mr Wilson', Charlie would saunter impudently across to him and say: 'How yer doin', Bob?' He has always insisted that he wasn't deliberately antagonistic at school: 'I did what I thought was right.' Wilson recalled that George was clearly a cut above his contemporaries at the school, and even back then, there was 'nothing I could teach him about football'. Charlie, already confident in his talents and abilities, was showing signs of genius, but accepted advice from no one. He recalls: 'I was brash. I used to take the piss out of other players. Like I'd sit on the ball, kneel on it, whatever. It annoyed people and they'd try and kick me. I accepted that, but I could always hit back if I needed to. As a kid, I'd always mixed with people who were older than me because, in a football environment, you just have to. But I was never in awe of any other player. I always believed that I could do anything I wanted to do on the pitch.' The seeds of his success and, some would say, of his underachievement, were already sown.

Charlie ended up at Highbury, just as he told his careers adviser he would, and quickly made strides through the youth system. Ray Kennedy reckons that he was loudmouthed even then. In his book, *Ray Of Hope*, Kennedy recalls that he thumped Charlie 'because he called me an effing so and so'. The two were actually good friends, but Kennedy, with some annoyance, noticed that George was given a freer leash in training than other young hopefuls. When he trained with the first team, he quickly turned people's heads. Frank McLintock noted that he thought nothing of calling established professionals 'wankers' and 'tossers', and was willing to parade his skills with 'total confidence'. Bob Wilson would boot the ball high into the sky and invite Charlie to 'kill' the ball. He always did.

George's favourite training ground trick was to rip through the defence and prepare to take the ball around Bob Wilson. On several occasions, George stopped and shouted to him: 'Which way do you want it Bob? Left? Right? Between the legs?' Wilson rarely saved the shot. By August 1969, Bertie Mee and Don Howe reckoned that Charlie was ready for the first team. Howe informed him that with work and dedication, he could be 'as good as Di Stefano'. Writers have romanticised Charlie's progression from Arsenal supporter to Arsenal player, talking mistakenly of his 'destiny'. What does he make of that view? 'I don't agree at all. I knew I had a great gift, and that I was with the Arsenal, which was where I wanted to be. I thought I could make it as pro, but I never took it for granted. I always practised and worked hard. Don Howe would never let you get away with getting above yourself in training.' Much less Charlie's friends, who were also his fiercest critics: 'I could walk into a pub, and they'd say, "Oi, you played shit today – now get the beers in!" No one around me was ever gonna let me get a big head. They kept me grounded.'

As mods and rockers fought pitched battles on Britain's beaches, Highbury's very own skinhead-cum-mod attracted headlines in the London press. The Arsenal crowd immediately took him to their hearts and gasped at his exquisite control and vision. In the 1969–70 season, his goals against Dinamo Bacau and Ajax, en route to the Fairs Cup final, drew plaudits from luminaries like Johann Cruyff, who admired Charlie's impudence. He began to receive abuse from the terraces and on the pitch. On his full debut against Everton, travelling fans had yelled at him: 'Hope you die before you get old,' a twisting of the words of 'My Generation' by London mods The Who. He would suffer worse abuse than that over the coming years. The North Bank regulars picked up on his ability to 'look after himself'. In an early interview with the *Daily Express*, he confided: 'If they [defenders] kick me, well, I just nut them.' Such a vigilante attitude was virtually unheard of inside the marble halls and Charlie George was immediately granted the title of being London's coolest footballer. 'I love Charlie George' badges sold like hotcakes on the memorabilia stalls around Highbury.

Arsenal stood on the cusp of a great achievement. Buoyed by the Fairs Cup final win over Anderlecht, the team's prospects looked good for the 1970–71 season. By the time the season began, Charlie's hair was spilling over his collar. In the space of just a few months, he'd become, along with George Best, the most striking and attention-grabbing footballer of the day. The nearest analogy to Charlie's startling image change would be to picture a modish, suited David Bowie mutating into the garish Ziggy Stardust. The establishment looked at Charlie as if he'd come from Mars, too. As was the case with Charlie Nicholas 13 years later, Arsenal fans copied their hero's 'barnet' styles. North Bank regular Dave Mitchell recalls: 'No one, and I include Ian Wright and Tony Adams, inspired the same kind of feeling in the crowd as Charlie George. Me and my mates loved him. He was one of us. He'd been an Arsenal fan and now he was an Arsenal player. He was living our dreams. But he also had the attitude, didn't he? Over the summer of 1970, it was rumoured he was growing his hair. So we all followed suit. We were like sheep, I suppose. He'd gone from being a nasty skinhead to a hippy in a matter of months. He was a fashion leader. I reckon loads of barbers must have gone bust in north London that summer, as everyone was growing their hair like Charlie George.'

One would assume that Charlie, anxious to preserve his status as a '70s cult hero, would accept the credit for being a guru in the fashion stakes. But you'd be wrong. 'A fashion icon,' he snorts. 'Bollocks. First I was the "original" skinhead, then I was the "original" long-haired footballer. Then I had me perm. People used to go on about me hair. What that had to do with me playing football, I don't know. I played football with me head, not me hair. I just had it like people had it at the time and that's it.' But his audience remain fascinated with the subject of his barnet. 'Did Bertie Mee ever ask you to get it cut?' 'No, although it's true that I'd rebel against almost anything. Even if he'd asked me to get it cut, I'd have ignored him. But then it never came to that.'

In the opening away game of the season at Everton, George was picked to play up front alongside John Radford. Charlie's goal pinched Arsenal a point in a 2–2 draw, but while scoring, he clashed with Everton goalkeeper Gordon West, breaking two bones in his foot. Did he attach any blame to West? 'Well, I suppose not. But then, he did come flying out with his feet. If he'd done so with his hands, I'd not have got the injury, would I?' Ruled out for five months, young Charlie could only stand and watch as Arsenal made steady progress in the league. For a while it appeared as if he'd be out for the whole season, but endless running exercises up and down the North Bank strengthened his legs. Already, he was discovering that 'nothing was ever straightforward on the injury front where I was concerned'. Between August and January, the Gunners found themselves damned for being 'boring' once more. George Graham aside, critics lambasted the team's 'functional' image. With January kicking in and '70s pitches getting even stickier, the Gunners legs grew wearier. Arsenal seemed to be running out of steam. Something special was needed to unlock those obdurate ten-man defences that barred Arsenal's path every week. Charlie was straining at the leash, raring to go. Bertie Mee and Don Howe made the shrewd move of converting him into an attacking midfielder, allowing Ray Kennedy to continue flourishing up front alongside John Radford. Charlie became Arsenal's X-factor, a loose cannon in a side that purists considered too predictable. The move was befitting for someone of George's ability and it gave him licence to roam, a role granted only to the likes of George Best and Johann Cruyff in world football. Charlie's impact on the team from January onwards was nothing short of incredible.

Action shots from the time prove just what a sensation he was. Forest defenders back off in total fear as George, hair flying out behind him, prepares to smack home his goal. He literally pulverised Nottingham Forest's defence at the City ground to help Arsenal secure a vital 3–0 league win. Forest's boss described it as 'the finest display from a visiting player I have seen this season'. At home to Leicester in the FA Cup sixth-round replay, he out-jumped Peter Shilton to head the Gunners into the next round. In doing so, he appeared to defy gravity, hanging in the air for what seemed a good ten seconds. But colour TV really established the George legend that year. At a quagmatic Maine Road in the previous round, Bell, Lee and company had largely dominated the game, before Charlie destroyed Manchester City with two cracking strikes. In full view of the heaving Kippax terrace, he drilled a scorching free kick right through their defensive wall to give Arsenal the lead, before later roaming forward from the halfway line to plunder the winner.

George's exceptional performance was partly due to the fact that Frank McLintock had told him that City coach Malcolm Allison '. . . doesn't rate you at all'. It was all a bluff, but George fell for it. For the first time, Arsenal fans saw Charlie's unique goal celebration; he lay down on his back in the mud. Any reason why? 'I felt like it, I suppose. Mind you, it wasn't too clever. It was pissing down with rain and I got soaked to the skin doing it.' And he didn't smile, either. Within a few months, the unique celebration was to be repeated in far grander, and dryer, circumstances. The following day, when the team arrived back at Euston station, Charlie, the *Daily Express* reported, was mobbed by 'a gaggle of teenage girls'. No Arsenal player since 'Brylcreem Boy' Denis Compton had worked women into a frisson. His social impact was gathering pace.

As the title heat was turned up, Arsenal faced Newcastle in mid-April 1971. During the match, Charlie seemed to be roaring around like an out-of-control fire engine. Spatting with Geordie defenders, especially his marker Bobby Moncur, he was starting to show the other side to his nature. Late on in the game, he picked up Moncur by the throat and informed him of what would happen if he tried to smash him off the park again. As several observers noticed, this was not simply a fit of pique, it was an obvious dash of hard-man menace. With the game petering out into a goalless draw, George seized the moment. Playing a one-two off a defender's leg, he scorched in the winner, which brought the title a step closer and enabled Arsenal to gain yet another vital 1–0 win. Charlie, poker-faced, didn't seem too bothered by the mayhem on the North Bank, but inside he was thrilled. 'The title seemed so much nearer after that,' he later commented. Four days later against Leeds, Jack Charlton's winner at Elland Road sparked mass protests from Arsenal players, who were convinced that Charlton was offside. Replays later proved that he wasn't. Charlie's measured response was to grab the ball and boot it into the stand, which earned him a booking and an ear-bashing from Bertie Mee afterwards. This was to be a regular ocurrence over the next few years. When Ray Kennedy's late header at White Hart Lane brought the title to Highbury after 18 years, the rest of the team hit the pub. Charlie went home to bed. He just felt like it.

His finest hour (or two, after extra-time) arrived three days later in the 1971 FA Cup final against Liverpool. On a swelteringly hot day, both sides were slowly roasted to a turn in the sun and failed to score in normal time. Charlie struggled to make any kind of impact. Save for a couple of raking passes and a screaming 30-yarder which whistled over the bar, he did precious little. In extra time, Eddie Kelly and Steve Heighway scored to tie the game at 1–1, but George seemed to be little more than a passenger. In these modern times of multiple substitutions, he would have been hoiked off. As it was, Don Howe virtually told him to keep out of the way, such was his exhaustion. Charlie, as usual, chose not to listen. With five minutes left of extra time, a neat passing interchange with John Radford gave him a yard of space and he belted a coruscating shot past Clemence, to put Arsenal 2–1 up and bring the Double to Highbury. His celebration was the most unorthodox ever seen at the old dump. Lying outstretched on the turf – still poker-faced – he waited fully ten seconds until delighted teammates rushed to pick him up. The Jesus Christ Superstar pose didn't go unnoticed and opposition fans would taunt him about it for years to come. Over the years, he's contradicted his own interpretation of the celebration. At the Sportspages event, he claims it was 'purely spontaneous'. He adds: 'If I'd run back to the halfway line and showed no emotion, I'd have cheated the Arsenal fans.' In previous interviews he has claimed he did it because he was 'knackered' and on another occasion, because 'I wanted to waste time'. In truth, he can't remember, so we can interpret it in whatever way we choose. He does, however, recall John Radford telling him to 'get up, you silly bugger'. Charlie also reckoned it was 'probably the best celebration Wembley's ever seen. People like to see that sort of thing. I gave them something to remember.'

That night, Charlie and fiancée Susan Farge, along with the rest of the Arsenal team, partied at the Café Royal. Charlie and Susan were snapped in classic '70s garb, and his kipper tie and butterfly collars earned him the title of 'London's best-dressed sportsman'. It seemed that from here, Charlie George and Arsenal would go from strength to strength. But, as several journalists later wrote, it was a case of 'too much, too young'. Ray Kennedy, a year younger than George, asked Bob Wilson: 'Does this happen every year?' and Charlie admitted that it would be impossible to match those intense feelings again. He'd done it all at 21. As it turned out, it would be downhill all the way for Charlie George and '70s Arsenal.

By the following season, there were tell-tale signs of the problems that would hinder the remainder of his career: flashes of temper, bust-ups with Bertie Mee and knee injuries. A cartilage problem kept him out of the first few games of the 1971–72 season, after Sammy Nelson accidentally knocked him in training. 'Sammy never discriminated against who he kicked,' George chuckles. When he returned to the side in October, he found it hard to recapture his form of the previous year. After he headbutted Liverpool's Kevin Keegan in full view of the North Bank, and winked at the crowd after doing so, Mee dropped him from the team.

Charlie's steadily worsening relationship with his manager is a matter for conjecture amongst his former teammates. In public, most of them prefer not to discuss the issue, although Frank McLintock later claimed that George would refer to Mee as 'the little c**t'. Unsurprisingly, Charlie declines to comment, given that Mee died only a few months previously. But when you hear Mee's former players describe him (albeit lovingly) as an 'over-fussy sergeant-major' figure who spoke in 'clipped tones', it's easy to see how he and the off-the-cuff, streetwise Charlie developed a serious personality clash. To the players' dismay, coach Don Howe, whom Charlie tellingly refers to as 'the real architect behind the Double side', had left the club in the close season to go and manage West Bromwich Albion. 'The club declined from then on,' comments Charlie, suggesting he had a great deal more respect for Howe than he did for Mee.

Perhaps the root of the trouble lies within a Mee sound bite from late 1971. After axing Charlie from the first team, he commented: 'I feel that once he superimposes a higher workrate on his outstanding natural ability, he will be back in the first team.' Here in a nutshell was the problem which precocious talents like George faced in English football during the '70s.

Mee's comment is similar to George Graham's opinion on Charlie Nicholas and Anders Limpar 20-odd years later. Ironically, George Graham later said of Charlie George: 'His main problem was that he'd drift out of the game for half an hour – sometimes he'd do nothing in that time.' Even as far back as 1971, Charlie could see that the writing was on the wall. He moaned: 'I'm being pushed back into defence . . . I'm being turned into the marker.' The pro-Charlie George lobby pointed out that the likes of Cruyff and Pelé would not be required to perform such menial tasks.

But not everyone was sympathetic towards Charlie's problems. As John Sadler later commented, 'fancy Dans' like Charlie were liable to get a good kicking if they didn't wise up to the antics of '70s hatchet-men. Ron 'Chopper' Harris, Chelsea's former captain, now makes a fortune from reminiscing about the on-field carnage he once instigated. The bullet-headed midfielder chuckles about the 'gravel burns' his victims would receive and reveals he was under orders to 'sort them [mavericks] out quick' during games. Of that particular genre, Charlie George was arguably the best at taking care of himself, but he could do little about the now-outlawed tackle from behind, and 'Chopper' and friends prided themselves on the efficiency of the terminating service they provided. Still, this didn't stop Charlie mixing it with the hard men when appropriate. 'I always enjoyed the physical side of the game – it's one of the best features of English football,' he recalls. Rumour had it that he even broke the biggest taboo in '70s footie. Liverpool's Tommy Smith had the nickname 'Beans On Toast' due to his pock-marked complexion. Understandably, no one dared call him that to his face. Except for, legend has it, Charlie George, who foolishly reckoned it would be a good way of putting Smith off his game during a heated clash at Anfield.

As the 1971–72 season reached its midway point, there was further evidence that Charlie George had an edge to his personality which rested uneasily within the marble halls. During an FA Cup fifth-round tie at the Baseball Ground, Derby fans goaded him with chants of: 'Where's your handbag, Where's your handbag, Where's your handbag, Charlie George?' George looked increasingly furious and, with Arsenal two goals down, something inside him snapped. Two stunning goals from him brought Arsenal level. His reaction after he'd equalised, when he smashed the ball into the net after a pass from Sammy Nelson ran loose in the box, was captured in all the Sunday tabloids. There was Charlie, running the full length of the Baseball Ground, flicking a two-fingered salute at any Derby fan who cared to watch.

Tabloids reckoned he'd nearly incited a riot and in *Fever Pitch*, Nick Hornby claims George's impudence almost got the budding young author, who'd got trapped on the home terrace, killed. 'GROW UP LAD', howled *The Sun*, rather amusingly, and the *Daily Express*, the sensible mouthpiece of middle England, said the following: 'Has it ever occurred to you that if Charlie George wasn't a brilliant, sensitive, temperamental footballer, he'd be a long, thin, lank-haired, loud-mouthed yob?' Charlie's response was to reiterate the fact that it was just another example of his vigilante sense of justice: 'If they give me abuse, I'll give it them back.' Manager Mee was clearly concerned and in an *Evening Standard* interview that year he told Ken Jones: 'We can no longer protect him from football. He is now a man as far as football is concerned and in that respect he has got to be able to look after himself. It won't be easy for him because he is the type of player who attracts publicity and it's not possible to keep him out of the spotlight.' Arsenal lost a terrible FA Cup final to Leeds later that season. Charlie did only two noteworthy things in 90 dour minutes. Midway through the first half, he rabbit-punched Allan Clarke, who scored the winner, and later on in the game he rattled the cross-bar. It was Arsenal's only decent chance in the game. The hero of the previous year was now the nearly-man. Charlie's luck was on the wane.

If Bertie Mee couldn't get an effective grip on Charlie, the '70s marketing men were even less successful. With his attitude and looks, he was clearly London football's most sought-after commodity. The problem was, he wasn't overly interested in such schemes: 'I was a footballer, not a piece of meat,' he recalls. In an era of fads like the yo-yo, skateboard, stylophone and spacehopper, the first football agents tried to introduce 'novelties' into football. The most famous of these entrepreneurs was Paul Trevillion, who chose – rather unwisely – to call himself 'The Beaver'. Trevillion had persuaded stuffy old Leeds United to wear sock tags and tracksuits with their surnames on the back, so why not do the same with Arsenal? The thought of running onto the pitch with red-and-white tags clearly didn't appeal much, though, and the boys gave the idea the thumbs down. Charlie dabbled with a pair of red boots for a while, but before long he was back in his trusty old black pair.

The marketing men then tried to turn him into a fashion icon-cum-pop star. His presence had been prominent in Arsenal photographs for years. In team line-ups, Charlie always looked bored with such pleasantries, preferring to snarl or glare at the camera rather than smile. It gives a clue as to the trouble he was starting to experience at the club and gives the impression that if a photographer did ask him to say 'cheese', there would be trouble. But sometimes, he did make the effort. Publicity shots from 1972 showed Charlie sitting on a throne with a crown on his head and an orb and sceptre in his hands. Naturally, the caption read 'The King of Highbury'. He later commented: 'The pictures were fun, but I felt a bit of a prat, to be honest.' He opted not to be snapped up by Burton's men's fashion catalogue, well aware that teammate Peter Marinello had become the butt of dressing-room jokes after appearing in a variety of garish, flowery outfits as part of various winter collections. In the 1971 *Fab 208* annual, Marinello claimed that 'Donegal tweed suits, massive kipper ties and maxi-raincoats are my favourites.' Charlie wasn't interested in flaunting himself in such a manner.

Some years later, when glam-rock outfits like Sweet, T Rex and the Glitter Band were all the rage, some wiseacre suggested that with his long hair and general lankiness, Charlie should cut a one-off, novelty glam record. He appeared in a few photos, under the none-too-subtle pseudonym 'Charlie Gorgeous', complete with silver moon boots, velvet zip-up costume and bright make-up. The photo shoot, organised by a *Mirror* photographer, ended slightly embarrassingly for Charlie. The make-up girl 'accidentally' forgot to bring along any cleanser. So a fully made-up Charlie – London's most cutting-edge footballer – had to get on a packed Tube (footballers still used public transport back then) looking like one of the ugly sisters. He received some strange looks. The record 'A Love Song For My Lady' was never released. 'Negotiations have broken down,' commented a publicist at the time. Even Gary Glitter was said to have been interested in the project – unfortunate in hindsight, but it showed that Charlie's profile was indeed high. Ultimately, the reason behind the failure to cut the record was that Charlie wasn't too bothered about getting involved in other projects. He was, after all, a footballer.

Finally, the Egg Marketing Board decided that Charlie should front their new advertising campaign. This was not an opportunity to be sniffed at. Commercial endorsements were a rarity in the days when football was considered to be the pursuit of the unworthy. The campaign was a disaster and flopped within a month. 'E For B and Charlie George,' went the distinctly uncatchy slogan. As he comments: 'No one, myself included, had the foggiest bloody idea what "E For B" actually stood for.' His most successful dabble came with a column in the *Express* the year after the Double. But that, too, petered out. He recalls: 'I could have used my name much more I suppose – like Bestie – but after a game, I was far more interested in getting home to my family.' Yet again, Charlie refused to fit in with or adapt to others' perceptions of him. Unmarketable, unteachable and in Bertie Mee's eyes, increasingly unplayable, Charlie George was starting to face an uncertain future in '70s football.

The next three seasons were dominated by sporadic runs in the team, yet more niggling injuries and further spats with the authorities. On the eve of the 1972–73 season, Charlie, along with fellow youth-team graduates Ray Kennedy and Eddie Kelly, protested about their pay. He recalls: 'Because of our age, we were at the bottom of the loyalty-based bonus system. It wasn't fair that youth-team graduates should get less than players who'd cost a fee. It wasn't fair. It wasn't right. People look amazed when I tell them I barely even got a rise after we'd done the Double. But that's the truth. It was easier to book a restaurant and stuff like that, but that's about it.' Commentator Geoffrey Green then made a thinly disguised personal attack on George, saying: 'As for George, for all his small triumphs that then brought publicity, he never struck me as the type of player to do the name of Arsenal justice.' He was still regarded as a talisman by the fans and as the Double team gradually drifted away (Frank McLintock was sold to QPR and Ray Kennedy's and Eddie Kelly's form declined alarmingly) he was expected to raise the quality. But he couldn't do it alone and on the pitch he got angry, as referees of that era will testify. Then there were behind-the-scenes problems. Charlie was the only first-team player who refused to participate in a study by a sports psychologist at San Jose University, California. Maybe he was wise not to do so. Peter Marinello's results had been so appalling that the psychologist was amazed he could even get onto the pitch. It was another example of George feeling himself to be above such activities. Bertie Mee, on the other hand, suggested that the player had something to hide.

The 1974–75 season proved to be Charlie's last at Highbury. It was a ridiculous state of affairs. While the fans should have enjoyed seeing the new bubble-permed Charlie line up alongside Alan Ball and the young Liam Brady, the press were speculating upon which club was likely to snap him up. By Christmas 1974, he'd been placed on the transfer list for £250,000, which would have made him the country's most expensive player, but no club seemed willing to spend so much on a 'flawed genius'. Frank McLintock blames the prevailing attitude in English football for Charlie's rapid Highbury burn-out: 'We tend to sacrifice skill in favour of work-rate,' he claims. There was an air of tragedy to the whole affair. 'Bert and I seldom speak to each other now,' George told the *News of the World*, 'and we'd both be better off if he sold me.'

His Arsenal career was almost over and in those final few months, as Arsenal plummeted towards the basement, his fall from grace grew ever more mystifying. Detractors within the game reckoned his external cockiness was his biggest downfall. In reality, Charlie was never quite as cocksure of himself as he seemed. Prior to games, observant teammates noticed that Charlie snuck off to the toilet where he'd be violently sick. 'It was nervous tension,' he recalls. 'My stomach used to produce a lot of acid. I suppose that there was a pressure on me because I was the home-grown boy. If the team played well, it was down to me, and if we played badly, it was down to me. The pressure was great.' With the home-boy expected to deliver, the other players often had to boost his confidence at half-time. But Bertie Mee would have needed advanced counselling and psychology qualifications to penetrate Charlie's iron-plated exterior. The fact was, he didn't seem to be open to any kind of guidance.

His market value, by April 1975, had fallen to £100,000. 'No one would want to buy a problem player for that amount,' commented a First Division manager when he was quoted the original £250,000 asking price. At one point, he was linked with a move to Barcelona to partner Cruyff, who'd raved about him six years earlier. 'I don't recall that gossip,' shrugs Charlie, 'and to be honest, I never really saw myself living in Spain anyway.' Shockingly, Charlie seemed set to sign for Tottenham, who spied a chance to kick their neighbours when they were down. He admits he'd have had no qualms about crossing the divide. 'I was desperate to leave Arsenal. The sooner the better. I'd have signed for Spurs, no question. Football is a business. Everyone knows I'd still have loved the Arsenal. I'd probably have got hassle from Arsenal fans over it – maybe they'd have understood. But it wouldn't have bothered me at all. I'd have been tough enough to get through it, like Sol Campbell has.' Arsenal fans were blissfully unaware of Charlie's feelings at the time, believing he refused to go to White Hart Lane because he couldn't bear to play for the enemy. But now we know. Mercifully, Derby boss Dave Mackay made an eleventh-hour bid for him, whisking him up to the Midlands and avoiding the unthinkable. 'Spurs were a bit tight with the "Nelsons" at the time, so I don't think the Arsenal board would have let me go anyway,' he comments.

After 157 games for Arsenal in 6 seasons, Charlie was gone. Dave Mitchell recalls: 'I was totally and utterly pissed off when he left. I actually stopped going to games for a while, because I was so upset. Our most adored player, and we let him go when he wasn't even in his mid-20s. What a waste. He was no angel, but how could we let someone like him, and an Arsenal fan too, leave? It was such a waste of talent.' Those Arsenal fans that continued to endure watching the team over the next two years had only Terry Mancini and relegation battles to look forward to.

Charlie regained his confidence at Derby, playing under a manager who cut him more slack than Bertie Mee. The Rams players, who expected a cocky cockney in their midst, were pleasantly surprised. 'Charlie George was the consummate pro,' recalls Bruce Rioch. 'He was a quiet, dedicated pro, not the flash Harry you'd think he was.' Derby won the title the year before Charlie arrived, but thanks to his touch, enjoyed their European Cup run during the 1975–76 season. He scored four goals in clashes with Real Madrid, but watched in dismay as his team crashed out 5–6 on aggregate. The pre-match vomiting had ended, thanks to a few drags on a cigarette before the game started. His delighted manager, Dave Mackay, claimed he was 'back to his best form with Arsenal'.

Yet bad luck was always around the corner. There was the smashed cheekbone, sustained after the taxi in which he had been travelling crashed into a central reservation on the outskirts of Derby. An accidental collision with former teammate Ray Kennedy destroyed the cartilage in his left knee. He was never the same player again. After three years at Derby, he signed for Lawrie McMenemy's Southampton ('Lawrie only signed players who were old or knackered or both'). During his sojourn on the south coast, he became embroiled in an ugly incident with a photographer who made to keep the ball after it went out of play. At the time, the Saints were a goal down with three minutes to play. Charlie lashed out and was fined £440 for assaulting Jack Spencer, of the *Eastern Daily Press*. He recalls: 'It was the stupidest thing I ever did, but it was totally out of character. Sometimes, I wonder if I'm remembered more for that incident than my goal for Arsenal in the Cup final. I really do wonder.'

The evening draws to a close. The manager of Sportspages checks his watch and asks if anyone has 'one last question for Charlie'. Thus far, comments such as 'football is never more important than life itself', and 'you're a long time dead', suggest that Charlie – the photographer incident aside – has no regrets. He doesn't regret walking out on European Champions Nottingham Forest. Brian Clough ('He'd come in with his squash racket, then after half an hour he'd disappear and walk his dog by the River Trent') had thrown him a lifeline by taking him on loan in 1980. Charlie scored the goal that won Forest the European Super Cup and linked up well with Stan Bowles and Trevor Francis. But Clough wanted to extend his trial period and Charlie balked, feeling he had nothing to prove. Stan Bowles claimed that Charlie simply said 'Bollocks' to Clough and 'that was the end of him'. Charlie also claims, slightly unconvincingly, that he's 'not bothered' about failing to make it as a coach. 'Me injuries would stop me being too mobile anyway,' he tells us. He's always been stoical about his divorce and his garage business going into liquidation some years before. But there is one question no one has yet dared to ask, so I take the plunge.

'Charlie – Geoff Thomas, Brian Stein and Carlton Palmer won plenty of England caps, but you were awarded just one. Would you agree that the world is a strange place?' He grins at me, but seconds later, there is a grimace too. The question has hit the spot. I expect a diatribe on the ills of '70s football, but receive an unexpected response: 'Well, maybe I wasn't good enough. Most likely I didn't fit in with the manager's plans. I look at other players, good players in the '70s. Alan Hudson only got two caps, Peter Osgood only got a few. Steve Perryman and Howard Kendall didn't win any. These things happen.' Another grey-washed answer, but the grimace reveals there's far more to this story. It also demonstrates not simply the bad luck that dogged him, but also his self-destructive side.

Publicly, at least, new England manager Don Revie had sung Charlie's praises. In an *Evening Standard* interview in 1975, Revie claimed that Charlie had the potential to 'become one of the finest forwards this country has ever seen'. A 'Charlie for England' lobby had been around since the 1970 World Cup and

Alf Ramsey was urged to 'give him a go'. Ramsey declined to do so, and so did Don Revie, until 1976. There was always the feeling that Revie didn't much care for Arsenal players, past and present, in light of the heated battles between Leeds and Arsenal in the early '70s. Revie's decision to grant Charlie his only international outing in a meaningless friendly against the Republic of Ireland seems little more than a feeble attempt to silence his critics. Alan Hudson later claimed that 'Revie picked me to fail'. Right-footed Charlie probably felt the same way after Revie made the decision to play him on the left-hand side of midfield. His display ended in 'humiliation', according to Brian Scovell in the *Daily Mail*, as he was subbed after an hour and replaced by Gordon Hill. Revie asked Charlie if he wanted to sit on the bench or have a bath. 'Fuck you,' was the player's measured response to his international boss's question. His occasional propensity to reach for the self-destruct button was never better demonstrated. Needless to say, Revie opted not to select him for any further internationals.

A year later, Ron Greenwood asked Charlie if he'd be so kind as to join the England B squad for a forthcoming match. Charlie was furious, commenting at the time: 'Why should I have to prove what I can do? I should be the one leading the full England team against the World Champions. Maybe that's part of my trouble – I don't believe I'm second best to anybody, I know I'm first class. The best forward in England at the moment.' Charlie asked his new Derby boss, Tommy Docherty, to convey the following message to Greenwood. 'C is for Charlie, C is for class, and I don't play for no fucking B team.' The incident did lead to some feelings of regret directly afterwards. As he said, C actually stood for crucifixion. It was the end of his brief international career. He has since admitted that maybe he should have bitten his tongue and accepted the olive branch. But, as Arsenal fans will testify, it just wasn't his style.

As Sue announces the quiz result, I discover that I've finished third. Rather embarrassingly, Phil, my Spurs supporter mate, had to lend me a hand with one of the questions. As he reminds me, number 8 was Ian Wright's shirt number, not Thierry Henry's, who has number 14 stamped on his back. He finds my mistake quite amusing. He finds it even funnier when my runner-up prize turns out to be an official Arsenal quiz book, bearing in mind my opinion on most official merchandise. It's almost as ironic as Charlie George, once Arsenal's most infamous rebel, now acting as an official representative for the club. Charlie's considered respectable these days. He's a match-day host in the corporate hospitality suite at Highbury. Engaging, thoughtful and reflective, he's finally discovered how to utilise his name. And, just to ease my disappointment at not winning the signed shirt by Arsenal's first-team squad, at least he's signed my book.

SEVEN

Cold Eyes

Being tackled by Peter Storey was like being hit by an
out-of-control juggernaut.
Jimmy Greaves, speaking in 2002

If Charlie George was the nearest thing the English game had to
a total footballer, Gunners' teammate Peter Storey was his
antithesis. Dark, demonic, dangerous and destructive, his
intimidating glare prior to a match – hence the nickname 'Cold
Eyes' – instilled total fear into the opposition. All top sides in the
'70s had a midfield enforcer, a 'hard man' who'd prowl menacingly
around the centre of the park. As has been well documented,
these players simply operated under a different set of rules from
their modern-day counterparts. Storey specialised in the now
outlawed 'tackle from behind', when unsuspecting midfielders or
strikers who dallied on the ball would suddenly have their legs
whipped away from them and crash to the turf at bewildering
speed.

With a snarl and a stabbing challenge, Storey's role was to stop
the other team from playing and allow more subtle colleagues to
do their work. Contrary to popular opinion, he did possess other
qualities: a canny footballing brain and nerves of steel, for
instance, but his image as Arsenal's hatchet-man lives on. He
remains the most vilified footballer of that era, even more so than
Chelsea's Harris, United's Stiles, Leeds' Hunter and Liverpool's
Smith. George Best, in his autobiography, confirmed that Storey

was his most difficult opponent. The latter would threaten to 'break my legs on each occasion we faced each other'. Best got his own back by later describing Storey as 'a joke', and questioned how 'he ever played for England'. But despite his on field misdemeanours, it was Storey's much-publicised problems off the field which captured the headlines. Even now, he's still being voted England's, not just Arsenal's, baddest ever footballer.

His Arsenal career began fairly innocuously. Born in Farnham, he turned professional in 1961 and made his debut four years later against Leicester City. For a time, the young Storey lodged with Terry Neill and his family. Neill recalls: 'He was the model lodger. He always made his bed and his clothes and books and whatever were always neatly put away. Most footballers are scatterbrained, but Peter was totally the opposite.' Originally he was a right full-back and, along with the up-and-coming Bob McNab, gained rave reviews for his performances in Bertie Mee's emerging team. Some believe that it would have been even better for Storey's career if he'd stayed in his original position. Indeed, Alf Ramsey later picked him for his country at right-back. Storey possessed all the necessary attributes required of a modern full-back: good pace, crossing ability and a knack of overlapping with the winger, in order to cause damage down the right-hand side. His consistency meant he quickly became a fixture in the side, but already his fearsome tackling had gained him notoriety in the old First Division.

In Ralph Finn's fairly staid 1967 history of Arsenal, entitled *Arsenal – Chapman to Mee*, even he noted: 'He tackles like a tiger leaving behind a string of devastation, akin to the rampaging of a hungry animal in a flock of sheep.' In a nutshell, he was already well on the way to becoming the big, bad wolf of English football. Storey studied other players in the '60s and would figure out how to get the better of them. Rather like his teammates, he'd learnt the hard way.

The two League Cup finals in which Arsenal appeared during the late '60s represented the steepest of learning curves for Storey. Against Third Division Swindon in 1969 he saw just what could happen if he didn't stick rigidly to his opponents. After the recently staged Horse of the Year Show turned the Wembley pitch into a slushy mixture of straw, mud and equine excrement, Swindon's Don Rogers got away from him several times during the match in their shock 3–1 win. A year earlier, in 1968, Leeds had won their first trophy of the Revie era against the Gunners. Storey saw at first hand how the Yorkshire side put 'contracts' on the opposition. During a match in which Jack Charlton clambered over Arsenal goalkeeper Jim Furnell like 'he was a climbing frame' (in Ian Ure's words), Storey repeatedly clashed with Norman Hunter.

On one occasion, the embarrassed Hunter was sent sprawling after a legal block tackle from Storey. When the Leeds man hauled himself off the floor, he nodded at Giles and Bremner, then at Storey. The Arsenal player was 'targeted' for the rest of the game, but Leeds' contract killers failed to destroy their man and Storey gave as good as he got. Even the Leeds hatchet-men must have been quietly impressed, but they won the game after Terry Cooper's disputed volley. The rest of the Arsenal side looked uncomfortable with these tactics, but Bertie Mee realised that a degree of brute force was required in order to be successful in that era.

Though teammates remarked on how shy and retiring he was off the pitch (Bertie Mee used to give him a lift to training from Cockfosters every morning, and Storey rarely spoke more than half a dozen words), he did make his presence felt during and after team meetings. Bobby Gould, his teammate in the '60s, takes up the story: 'There used to be an old room on the right of the tunnel at Highbury called the "halfway house". On the Monday after a game, the players would meet to discuss the weekend's game. We'd all tell each other, in no uncertain terms, just what we thought of each other's performance. It got pretty savage in there and it wasn't for the faint-hearted. We were all completely honest, but the good thing was that even the quiet ones, like Peter, got their chance to speak. Considering that he was later branded an animal, his contributions were always articulate and thoughtful. I believe that this was one of the keys to Arsenal's early '70s success – people like Peter were forced to examine their own performance. Basically, it was a case of, if you couldn't be honest and open with your teammates, and handle criticism, you could go.

'But there were never any grudges held for long. After the meeting, we'd go to the five-a-side pitch and if anyone had the hump, they'd get it out of their system. We'd often kick lumps out of each other. Peter never shirked in practice either. He'd glare at you if you ever block-tackled him. You couldn't believe it – such a quiet man off the pitch, but so hard on it. We were all mightily relieved he was on our side.'

Arsenal players simply could not work out what made their teammate tick. Alan Hudson played alongside Storey briefly in the mid-'70s. He recalls: 'To look at him, you'd think butter wouldn't melt. But before a game his eyes would become fixated on the walls, or the ceiling. You'd look at the eyes and you'd think: "Oh my God, what's in his head?" His expression was so eerie. It was like looking at Hannibal Lecter in *The Silence Of The Lambs*.'

The quiet man, as well as turning up the ferocity of his challenges, was learning how to enjoy himself away from football. Practically the only thing he was scared of was flying. Teammates commented on how he'd break out in a cold sweat when the aeroplane hit turbulence. Once the team had landed safely, he would indulge himself on foreign trips. He later commented: 'The idea is to give the manager the slip, find a willing bird and settle down for the night. And if there aren't enough birds to go around, we can always share. We're teammates, aren't we?' On his own admission, he had already become a serial womaniser by the early '70s. Some years after he retired, he confessed: 'From the first time I kicked a ball as a pro, I began to learn what the game was all about. It's about the drunken parties that go on for days. The orgies, the birds and the fabulous money. Football is just a distraction, but you're so fit you can carry on with all the high living in secret and still play the game at the highest level.'

These being the carefree days before AIDS, higher fitness requirements and an intrusive British press corps, players could easily get away with this type of hedonistic behaviour. Clearly, it doesn't appear that his manager cottoned on to Storey's 'nocturnal activities' and Arsenal fans never had an inkling. In the match-day programme, he was shown contentedly playing Monopoly at home with his wife and quietly reading a novel on the coach to away games. It was also well known that his father loyally followed him to all his matches. But when Bertie Mee made the decision to convert Storey from full-back to central midfielder, the classic anti-footballer image was born.

Goodison Park, 15 August 1970. Everton captain Alan Ball was not a happy chappie on the opening day of the season. Resplendent in his prissy white boots, his twinkle toes were being trampled upon at regular intervals by Storey. Early in the second half, Ball was crunched to the ground mercilessly by Arsenal's new midfield weapon. 'Squeak' protested loudly to the referee but, strictly speaking, Storey's challenges were within the rules and Arsenal grabbed an encouraging 2–2 draw. He repeated the trick on West Ham's Jimmy Greaves a few days later, then almost triggered off a war when he and Chelsea's Ron 'Chopper' Harris locked horns at Stamford Bridge in late August. This became a familiar sight during the early '70s, as Storey treated Arsenal fans by frequently clashing with other midfield 'enforcers'. Supporters, if they'd looked hard enough, would have seen sulphurous steam rising from the pitch. Storey's battle with Harris prompted watching Brazilian coach, Mario Zagalo, to comment: 'It's no wonder England produces no Pelés.' More observant journalists noticed that once he'd snaffled the ball, he was well capable of chipping an excellent pass forward to Radford and Kennedy, and his 'blind-side' runs showed clear evidence of an intelligent and perceptive player.

In *Seventy-One Guns*, David Tossell's excellent account of the 1970–71 season, Storey confesses he didn't even enjoy the 'enforcer' role. 'I'd far rather have played a more positive type of game,' he recalls. This made it even worse for the opposition, as he was in such a foul mood during most matches. As in the case of Wilf Copping in the '30s, it was simply more convenient for the press to portray Storey as a 'terminator'. Jim Evans, a fan since the '70s, recalls: 'Some friends and I from university used to go to watch Arsenal. We stood on the North Bank. We did English at Surrey and you could say we were pretentious tosspots. In 1971, Stanley Kubrick's *A Clockwork Orange* was released, and we thought we were really cool because we saw it before it was banned. One day, during a game, one of the others observed that with his mop of brown hair and sharply chiselled sideburns, Storey was only a bowler hat and an eyelash extension away from being the spit of Alex – the Malcolm Macdowell character – in the film.

'We wrote something in the college magazine, pointing out that, like Alex and his droogs, Storey was a purveyor of "ultra violence". It always made us laugh that fans would innocently sing "Storey, Storey, hallelujah" when he appeared, just as Alex did his thing to "Singing In The Rain". We used to really annoy people around us. My friend Dave, who was – and still is – a real smart-arse, used to comment, every time Storey got the ball: "Oh, he really shouldn't spend so much time in the Corova Milk Parlour, drinking Drencrum Milk Plus." Dave thought he sounded really cool, using the language of the film. In the end, this bloke in front turned round and threatened to twat him if he even spoke for the rest of the match. Dave stopped going to games for a while after that. What a muppet!'

As well as taking on the midfield berth, Mee and Howe gave him the responsibility for dispatching spot kicks during the Double season. He was ideally suited to the task. Teammates noticed that during the 1970–71 season, his concentration levels were intense. 'Impossible to put off his game,' Bob Wilson later commented. Opposition goalkeepers took one look at him and knew they'd virtually lost the battle of wits. Storey's ice-cool nerves helped to push Arsenal through the early rounds of the FA Cup. At Portsmouth in the fourth round, the home crowd howled with rage when the referee noticed that a Pompey defender's hand had pushed away Radford's header. With the home team's players lobbing mud at Storey's legs as he ran up to take the kick, he crashed the ball past goalie Millington and Arsenal eventually won a tight replay.

He wrote himself into the Highbury hall of fame during the

FA Cup semi-final with Stoke at Hillsborough: 2–0 down after 70 minutes and with their Double dreams seemingly in tatters, Arsenal needed a miracle to save the season. Storey became the unlikeliest of saviours. On 75 minutes, a loose ball bounced out of Stoke's area and Storey blasted the ball past Gordon Banks to give the Gunners a glimmer of hope. A minute into injury time, the Gunners still trailed 1–2. The referee had already checked with his linesman, as McLintock's header was punched off the line by Stoke's defender John Mahoney. The referee immediately signalled for a penalty, and the Arsenal players jumped around with joy.

One Gunner had to remain calm and collected, though. Storey later recalled: 'It was all very well them jumping around with excitement. I still had to take the penalty, and stick it past Gordon Banks too.' Glancing briefly at Banks, he placed the ball on the penalty spot and blasted it straight down the middle. Banks obligingly shifted to his right and Arsenal were off the hook. In his only TV interview after the game, on *The Big Match*, Storey came across as being intelligent – gentle, even. These were hardly adjectives that could be applied to his performance in the replay at Villa Park four days later. Stoke's Jimmy Greenhoff and Terry Conroy were summarily smashed around the park as Storey bullied their playmakers out of the game. His Highbury colleagues now often referred to him as 'Snouty', due to his ability to sniff out the opposition's master tacticians and destroy them by whatever means he saw fit. Arsenal consequently cruised through the replay, with goals by Ray Kennedy and George Graham. Job done.

A thigh injury ruled him out of the title decider at Tottenham and threatened to prevent him from appearing in the FA Cup final, too. Although he made the team, an under-par Storey was eventually substituted by Eddie Kelly, but not before he'd again caused problems with his blind-side runs. Crucially, in the lead up to the final, he'd also diffused the effect of Liverpool boss Bill Shankly's mind games. Shankly was a master of winding up the opposition, portraying his players as a team of world-beaters and Arsenal as a bunch of no-hopers. In the London dailies, Storey sarcastically compared Shankly with Chairman Mao, commenting: 'Shankly's mind games cut no ice with us.' In fact, the Scot was for once outfoxed, as a grinning Storey and company deliberately lined up in the tunnel some four minutes late in order to annoy the opposition. Shankly could only growl in anger. When Frank McLintock lifted the FA Cup that afternoon, no player had played his role more fully in the Double triumph than Storey.

Over the next five years, he remained a permanent fixture in the Arsenal side and, for two years, in the England team. At club level, he lost none of his potency, or his hard-man image. Bob Wilson recalled Storey glaring at him and telling him to get up in the 1972 FA Cup semi-final, while he lay writhing in agony due to a cartilage injury. Frank McLintock remembers it slightly differently. Storey apparently called Wilson a 'c**t' and then spat on him. This, by Storey's standards at least, was not a particularly callous reaction. On an icy pitch at Reading that year, in an FA Cup tie, most of the skin on his right leg had been flayed off, yet Storey somehow played on. He also gained notoriety for his ability to charge down Scud missile free kicks by the early '70s dead-ball specialists. With head, legs, groin, whatever, as soon as the ref peeped his whistle, Storey would hurl himself at the taker. Those who failed to unleash the shot immediately risked decapitation. Teaming up with Alan Ball and, briefly, Liam Brady, Arsenal's midfield remained one of the best and most intimidating in the country. Yet contemporary writers continued to link Storey closely with the ills that affected English football in the '70s – crowd trouble and the decline of the national side.

At a time when Storey's destructive powers were at their height, the amount of terrace aggro at Highbury grew exponentially. Jimmy Evans recalls: 'In the early '70s you'd walk up the steps to the North Bank and in the beer hut, there'd be the chant going up of: "WE'RE GONNA FIGHT, FIGHT, FIGHT FOR THE ARSENAL 'TIL THE DAY THAT WE DIE." Highbury could be a dangerous place at that time. There was trouble in the pubs outside, crowd surges on the terraces, opposition "firms" invading the North Bank and sometimes a

National Front presence outside the ground. Opposition fans would arrive on "Football Specials", trains which consisted of British Rail's crappy old rolling stock, dressed in "official" fan garb: Dr. Martens and donkey jackets. Often the battles on the pitch reflected what was happening on the terraces.' But, I suggested to Evans, this wasn't down to Storey, was it? 'No, but the type of player he was seemed to fit in with the mood in the early '70s. *Foul* magazine, the '70s prototype of the fanzine, certainly believed there was a direct connection between on- and off-pitch trouble.'

Alf Ramsey greatly respected Storey. Between 1970 and 1973 he awarded him 19 England caps, which confirmed, in many people's eyes, that Alf had become hooked on the drug of grim and attritional football. As the 'Cruyff turn' came to symbolise the emergence of Holland's total footballers, the 'Storey Snarl' gave further ammunition to those who felt that England hadn't so much ignored the 'beautiful game' as chewed it up and spat out the pieces. During a poisonous Auld Enemy clash at Hampden Park in 1972, Storey and Billy Bremner clashed repeatedly throughout the match. In fact, they argued for so long that it was a wonder England managed to grind out a 1–0 win.

In the post-match inquest, a journalist wrote: 'Has the beautiful game really come to this?' Storey countered by saying: 'Don't blame me, blame the system.' There was some truth there, perhaps. After all, it was hardly his fault that he won 19 caps while Charlie George got only one. Stiff, regimented managers like Ramsey and Revie remained unwilling to throw off the increasingly defensive straitjacket during the decade. The Auld Enemy clash prompted impersonator Mike Yarwood to comment on *Parkinson*: 'There's only three things wrong with the England side: Sir – Alf – Ramsey.' Purists reckoned there were just two things wrong, and he played for Arsenal.

By the mid-'70s, Storey was clearly giving some thought to his retirement. In those far-off days, when there was no easy route into media punditry, there were two options for ageing players: owning a pub, or football management. He preferred the prospect of the former, and became 'mine host' of the Jolly Farmers pub in

Islington. It is interesting that Ramsey and Revie mistrusted the 'mavericks' because they believed them to be a bunch of boozers and womanisers. They obviously didn't do enough detective work on Storey. With his pub's close proximity to Highbury, it became a favoured post-match watering hole for some of the players. Rumours began to circulate about just what was going on during lock-ins at the Jolly Farmers. Interestingly, there was a photograph of Storey in the Arsenal programme at the time, reading a novel on the coach. Resplendent in his peach silk shirt with butterfly collar and kipper tie, there is a tabloid newspaper open on his table, showing a headline that reads: 'YARD SMASH HIRE-A-GIRL VICE RACKET'. Pure coincidence, but Storey would soon be reading such headlines about himself.

By 1975, he began to pay the price for his combative approach to the game. As Arsenal's Double team broke up, he still remained an important part of the side. With the Gunners now facing annual relegation struggles, a fully functioning Storey became more vital than ever; better that than watching Jeff Blockley farting about in central defence, anyway. Yet a series of niggling knee and groin injuries hampered Storey and even at the comparatively young age of 30, he knew that the end wasn't too far off. After ten years of loyal service, he'd earned a well-deserved testimonial match against Feyenoord, and in December of that year, the Dutch side, including the likes of Rijsbergen, Jansen, de Jong and Van Hanegem, visited Highbury.

In order to prolong the celebrations, Storey generously threw open the doors of the Jolly Farmers to friends, teammates and the Dutch side, then locked the doors and embarked on a two-day bender. At the time, stories circulated which suggested that it had been one hell of a party, but the Arsenal man later confirmed it had gone much further than that. The guest list included a sprinkling of B-grade celebrities: Mary Millington, the now-deceased soft-porn diva and, staggeringly, the squeaky-clean Olivia Newton John, in her pre-*Grease* days. At 5 a.m. 'a famous international Dutch footballer' found himself 'stark naked' after a drinking game and chased a scantily clad girl around the bar, before picking her up and taking her upstairs for a spot of horizontal training. Those total footballers were so dedicated to their art, weren't they?

Storey's place in the Arsenal team became even more perilous after his refusal to train one Sunday during the pre-season tour to Austria in the summer of 1976. It wasn't for religious reasons, either. By now, the Arsenal boss was Terry Neill, an ex-teammate of Storey's and best man at the latter's wedding. Storey wasn't the only established professional who didn't respect Neill's authority, and Storey and Alan Ball decided to go for Sunday lunch and a few glasses of red wine, instead of training with the others. The incident was not widely reported, but Neill never forgot it. By early 1977, Storey had been off-loaded to Fulham, who, at that time, were buying ageing stars like Best, Marsh and Moore. The move never worked out, as the player was every inch an Arsenal man. At the age of just 32, he officially retired.

As Storey had progressed through the youth ranks, he was never one of Highbury's highest earners and, having blown most of his cash on 'birds and booze', he had to assess carefully his career options. The majority of '70s players found it extremely hard to readjust to life outside the game and, aside from the select group who carved out careers in the media and management, many of them fell on hard times. Storey opted against going into management (the football kind, anyway) and became frustrated, always seeking out the chance to earn a quick buck.

The first signs that he was having trouble adjusting to life outside the game came in late 1977, when he was fined £65 after an incident at a pedestrian crossing. He hadn't stopped in his car, a lollipop man had remonstrated with him about it and Storey had headbutted him. Nowadays, the attack would be loosely classified under the heading 'road-rage incident'. The days when he could behave in this way towards the likes of 'Chopper' Harris were over, and when the magistrate accused Storey of behaving like 'a little boy', he realised that life in the fantasy world of professional football and in the real world were poles apart. He later commented: 'When I was at Arsenal, everything was done for you. You wanted to go on holiday? It was all booked up for you. You needed medical attention? You were booked into a private hospital straightaway. It's not like that when you finish in football – life had been too easy in some ways.' Ex-teammates rallied around him and there was genuine surprise in most quarters that he should have behaved in such a manner. Storey was already on the road to ruin.

By the late '70s and early '80s, Storey had cut himself off completely from football and was mixing with some shady company from the London underworld. His convictions began to pile up more quickly than crumpled attackers once had at his feet. In 1979, he was charged with running a brothel from a grotty flat in the East End of London and living off the earnings. Considering it was a run-down area, the name he had chosen for the business was fairly exotic: The Calypso Massage Parlour. He was fined £700, forced to pay £175 costs, and given a six-month suspended jail sentence. His counsel, John Cope, claimed: 'Peter is a man of good character who succumbed to temptation to make some easy money. He is just relieved it was stopped at an early stage.' Dozens of ex-opponents may have disagreed about the character reference, but Storey's brushes with the law did not stop there.

Since his dabble in the sex trade hadn't worked out, he turned his attention to gold – albeit counterfeit sovereigns. At the Old Bailey in 1980, he was given a two-year jail sentence for putting up £4,000 of his own money to finance a sovereign racket. The tabloids had an absolute field day. It had been years since a high-profile player had drifted into big-league crime and most expected a lenient judge and jury to give him a much shorter sentence. Predictably, *The Sun* led the way with their headline 'HORROR STOREY' and the *Daily Mirror* weren't far behind with 'STOREY OF EX-PRO'S SHAME'. As the judge sentenced him, he commented: 'It is tragic that a man who enjoyed such an illustrious career and held such a position in the eyes of the public should have had this kind of downfall.'

In 1982, shortly before his two-year stretch ended, he was given a further shock when he was charged with having stolen two cars back in 1978 and selling them on before the hire-purchase agreement was completed. This time, the judge's summing up was slightly more dramatic: 'For a man who commanded the respect of thousands of people, to find yourself here, believe me, is tragic.' The only good news for Storey was that the judge ordered that the two six-month sentences be served concurrently. Unsurprisingly, he was declared bankrupt in 1983.

Over the next seven years, the trail went cold. Storey lay low in an attempt to rebuild his life and was reported to be running a stall at Leytonstone market. But in 1990, with Arsenal resurgent under the guidance of Storey's former teammate George Graham, he hit the headlines again and was jailed for four weeks for attempting to smuggle 14 hard-porn videos into the country. He'd picked them up in France and stashed them inside the spare wheel of his car. Suspicious customs officials, one of whom recognised him, smelt a rat and rummaged through the boot. Rather aptly, one of the films was entitled *Big Bust* and, rather unnecessarily, the judge who sentenced him to a four-week jail sentence informed him: 'You know what the inside of prisons are like.' A year later, he got an even clearer message that he was a marked man when a judge gave him a 28-day suspended sentence for swearing at a traffic warden. A tad harsh, perhaps, and pretty insignificant compared with the rest of his misdemeanours.

Happily, Storey appears to have rebuilt his life. Now remarried, he works as a chauffeur in Hertfordshire and occasionally reappears for official Arsenal functions and testimonials. Slightly less well groomed than some of his more prosperous teammates like McNab, McLintock and Graham, he tends to drift to the back of the group. But for all his hard living over the years, he still looks trim and athletic and happy to be back with his old mates once more. Several Channel 4 producers have considered including Storey in *All-time Bad Boys XI* documentaries as part of their Football Stories series. The stumbling block has always been his refusal to talk. Ex-teammates, proving just how 'tight' the Arsenal dressing-room is, refuse to do anything other than praise him for being a 'tremendous professional'. Unlike fellow '70s hatchet-men, he has not chosen to publish a warts 'n' all autobiography and, interestingly for someone who often succumbed to the temptation to make an easy buck, he has not cashed in on his bad-boy reputation by joining the after-dinner-speaking circuit.

He remains essentially a mystery.

The only Arsenal player in modern times to have any kind of empathy with Storey is Paul Vaessen. For one night, in May 1980, the bubble-permed 18 year old was on top of the world, after his headed goal defeated Juventus in the Cup-Winners' Cup semi-final. Shortly afterwards he became plagued by knee problems and retired at the age of 21. Speaking in 1994, he recalled: 'The doctor said that if I played professional football any longer, I'd be permanently disabled. For years, I was totally unable to handle what happened. One minute I was on top of the world, the next, finished. My leg was and still is a total mess. On some days the pain is unbearable. I bore a grudge against Arsenal for years, believing they'd basically booted me out on the street and left me to rot.'

Vaessen's fall from grace was even more rapid than Storey's, and he described it to me in graphic detail in a rare interview ten years ago. 'By the age of 23, I was a heroin addict. I was into petty crime to fund my habit. Robbing warehouses, mugging people. I had to raise £100 a day. I did some terrible things, and I'm still amazed I never ended up in prison like Peter Storey. Some of my old teammates like Kenny Sansom helped out. They'd give me a fiver now and again – but no one really knew how low I'd sunk until I got stabbed six times during a drug deal in the Old Kent Road. I "died" twice on the operating table. I should have stayed in intensive care for months but I checked myself out after four days. I needed my fix, and believe me, I was into everything. Cocaine, benzo-diazapan and 'chasing the dragon', where you inhale heroin fumes after you've heated it up. I lost all self-respect, not helped by people saying: "But didn't you used to play for the Arsenal?" Obviously not many people recognised my face, but they knew the name. Once I got clean and found a new meaning in my life through God, I often wondered how I got myself in such a mess. I suppose that football – and Arsenal – had been the one constant in my life. Once that disappeared, I felt that I had nothing. Playing football was all I knew. I don't know if Peter Storey felt like that, and obviously he wasn't a drug addict, but there are some parallels between what happened to him and me.'

Shocked by Vaessen's trembling hands and appearance – I

didn't recognise him at all and he was only 33 – I asked him what he planned to do next. 'I've been clean for six months now,' he told me. 'I'm planning to become a physiotherapist, like my old teammate Gary Lewin. I'm going to try to make sure it's onwards and upwards all the way for me from now on.' In hindsight, his final words take on added significance: 'Most heroin addicts – even those who reckon they've kicked the habit – struggle to make it beyond 40,' he said. Then, like most people, I forgot about him for the next few years.

The journalists who believed that Peter Storey's decline was a tragedy would do well to consider that Vaessen's story had no happy ending. In August 2001, the *Bristol Observer* ran the following story:

> Addict Paul Vaessen was found dead in his Henbury
> home after overdosing. The 40 year old had been battling
> a drug habit and was on methadone therapy, a substitute
> for heroin, when he died on 8 August. A post-mortem
> revealed high levels of drugs in Mr Vaessen's blood.

Now just another victim of heroin, the *Bristol Observer*'s editor and many of Vaessen's associates had no idea that 20 years before he'd been 'on top of the world' with Arsenal. Henbury resident Tracey Claus recalled: 'a guy who was often drunk or "strung out". He used to enjoy a kick-about with the boys in the park when he was "sorted". He used to complain about pains in his leg and how he couldn't straighten it properly. But I had no idea that he'd once played football for a living. You just couldn't picture him as an athlete. What a waste.' Even Storey's personal problems seem tame compared with that. At least he's still alive to tell the tale, if he chooses to.

In these modern times of Arsenal's cavalier football, Peter Storey's style would be considered distasteful by Highbury's current connoisseurs. Even Steve Ashford, aka *The Gooner*'s Highbury Spy, believes that he was 'over-rated. He'd just foul people and pass the ball'. Perhaps Storey's greatest crime is that, despite his love for Arsenal and his impact on the 1971 side, football was never enough for him. It was, as he commented, simply 'a distraction'.

EIGHT

A Trip to Oz

My spell at Arsenal didn't go too well, partly because, in my opinion, the guys who were standing on the North Bank knew more about the game than the manager, Terry Neill.

Alan Hudson, speaking in 2001

By the mid-'70s, footballers were becoming seriously rich – even those who played for Arsenal, a club with a reputation for paying low wages. Naturally, being footballers, they were keen to flaunt their wealth in every way possible. They'd pose cheesily on the bonnets of their flashy motors, eagerly showing off their brand-new MGs, TR7s, Capris and, the '70s motoring equivalent of the Holy Grail, the Triumph Stag. Any player who had one of those parked on his scrunchy gravel drive during that era had truly reached superstar status. In club programmes, Arsenal players were snapped at home, backed by flowery wallpaper, sinking knee-deep in shag-pile carpets, showing off state-of-the-art 'music centres' complete with obligatory ABBA, ELO, New Seekers and 10CC vinyls. Their wives and children didn't escape humiliation, either. Spouses with flouncy dresses and Farrah Fawcett hairdos floated around, looking like extras from *Charlie's Angels*, and embarrassed offspring played with revolutionary 'video games' (which set Dad back a few pounds) for the benefit of the cameras.

Fashion historians would have a field day with the

photographs. Here was irrefutable proof that hemlines lengthened as the '70s progressed, demonstrated by Bertie Mee's daughter's white miniskirt in 1971, and, four years later, Christine Rimmer's 'midi' effort. A year later, Jimmy Rimmer's wife is shown posing in blue satin flares, the bell bottoms of which acted as a carpet for other guests, at the club's Christmas party. Interestingly, Gunners defender Terry Mancini is seen distributing presents to the kids in the background. As North Bank regulars from that era will tell you, it made a change from him handing out gifts to opposition strikers every Saturday afternoon.

Nowadays, footballers guard their privacy far more and would only allow such intrusion if *Hello!* magazine offered them a five-figure sum. On the other hand, '70s players actively paraded themselves at the flashiest casinos and nightclubs in town. Sometimes they would even alert the press to their whereabouts. They were slowly learning how to market themselves, even if the game itself still had much to learn in that area. The vast majority of players still hailed from working-class backgrounds, but now they liked to consider themselves as 'sort of upper-middle class, with a bit of nouveau-riche flash thrown in', as Alan Hudson nicely put it. With new money flooding in, players' egos, naturally, rocketed. The increasingly nosy tabloid press delighted in highlighting the '70s phenomenon of growing player power. Old-fashioned bosses who'd grown up under the 'retain and transfer' system struggled to cope with the atmosphere of freedom of speech among their long-haired stars, and battled desperately to prevent cliques developing within the club. The fussy, stiff-upper-lipped Bertie Mee had little in common with the new breed of player. Not that Terry Neill, who was a 'youthful' 34 year old when he became Arsenal manager, fared much better.

By 1975, huge chasms threatened to split Arsenal Football Club down the middle. The actions of Alan Ball, Alan Hudson and Malcolm Macdonald ensured that scandal spewed forth from the dressing-room for much of the decade. The nadir, or, for the purposes of this book, high point, arrived during the club's 1977 pre-season tour to Australia. Alan Ball had been bombed out of

Highbury by then, but Hudson and Macdonald continued to 'gun for trouble'.

A popular story, confirmed by several witnesses, circulated about Alan Ball in the mid-'70s. It neatly sums up the man and an increasingly moneyed era in football. Peter Storey and Ball joined the Arsenal side late on a pre-season tour in Miami. The two had been on England duty and, after arriving at the lads' hotel, headed to the bar for a drink with the rest of the team. Ball announced his arrival by yanking out a bundle of banknotes from his sock, slamming them down on the bar and informing teammates, in typically grandiose style, that he would retire to bed when the money ran out, or when midnight arrived, whichever happened first. He also informed his troops that if he didn't obey his own rules, one of them should punch him on the nose.

Three hours later, when the clock did strike twelve, the quarrelsome, bevvied-up Ball informed them that he was ready to guzzle beer until dawn. Teammate Bob McNab, ever the reliable pro, had not forgotten Ball's earlier instruction and on the 12th chime, landed a right hook on the World Cup-winner's hooter. Blood gushed everywhere and a very subdued Ball didn't play too well in the friendly match a couple of days later. Admittedly, this was partly reserve goalkeeper Geoff Barnett's fault. Whilst performing warming-up exercises in the dressing-room prior to the match he had 'accidentally' smacked him on the nose again. Still, at least it gave everyone a rest from Ball's falsetto voice.

By 1975, he was not only one of the most talented players in the country, he was arguably the most controversial. The World Cup-winning midfielder advocated setting up an exclusive group called 'The Clan'. It was to consist of England's most talented and talked-about footballers, comprising the likes of Geoff Hurst, Stan Bowles, Alan Hudson and, er, Terry Mancini. Ball believed The Clan would be able to use its collective persona to push its marketing potential and rake in the readies. Early publicity shots of the group portray them as a bunch of James Bond/John Steed (from *The Avengers*) type poseurs, smoking cigars and sipping champagne in Kings Road eateries. Alan Hudson recalls: 'When I walked into the restaurant, I don't think I'd ever seen so much booze in my life. There was as much champagne on offer as you could manage. It was fun while it lasted, but I never saw a penny in earnings.' Hudson believes: 'If Bobby Moore and maybe people from the acting world, like Dennis Waterman, had got involved, it would have taken off. It certainly needed the World Cup-winning captain involved. Bobby would have given it clout.' As yet, the world didn't seem ready for The Clan, or Alan Ball's brand of player power.

Yet his vision on and off the pitch made him a player ahead of his time. Arriving at Highbury for a British record fee of £220,000 from Everton in late 1971, his crisp passing and driving enthusiasm drew plaudits from colleagues. 'One touch, two touch, you'll never see me take a third,' he later told the mightily impressed Malcolm Macdonald in 1976. Despite his input, Ball witnessed the painful decline of Bertie Mee's Arsenal and, coincidentally, Don Revie's England.

His frustration was apparent by the midpoint of the '70s and he became renowned for his ability to sound off in the media, famously labelling one of Revie's England squads 'a bunch of donkeys'. His occasionally listless displays, along with barbed criticisms of colleagues who he felt were underachieving, meant he was sometimes unpopular with elements of the Highbury crowd. When a tearful Bertie Mee announced that he was quitting Arsenal at the end of the 1975–76 season, experienced professionals like Ball, Armstrong and Simpson sensed that a golden opportunity had presented itself. They expressed a desire that chief ally and first-team coach Bobby Campbell be offered the manager's job. Younger players felt Ball and friends were motivated purely by self-interest. David O'Leary was convinced that they were angling for coaching roles at Highbury, a kind of football pensionhood, as their playing careers neared the end. The greatly respected Campbell would be a useful mentor/patron during the formative stage of their managerial careers.

Ball writes in his autobiography that during a team meeting the Arsenal players 'voted unanimously' to back Campbell for the job. Others differ significantly with Ball's version of events. In David O'Leary's book, he notes that younger players like Graham

Rix and Frank Stapleton stayed out of proceedings and Liam Brady went further, revealing in *So Far So Good* that he, Richie Powling and Wilf Rostron actually voted against Ball's motion. Bally was none too happy, accusing Brady of having stabbed him in the back. Ultimately, Ball failed to get his way. The board appointed Terry Neill, fresh from a tricky sojourn as Tottenham boss, as Mee's successor, rather than the popular Campbell, who resigned. This all came after the board had tried to lure Miljan Miljanic, Real Madrid's boss and, not for the last time, Terry Venables. The directors eventually U-turned over the Venables issue, probably believing there were enough 'geezers' at the club already without installing one as boss. Neill's honeymoon period was brief. Gauging that senior professionals were sceptical of being managed by a former teammate and still smarting from defeat over the Campbell issue, Ball made life difficult for Neill. He complained bitterly about the training techniques introduced by Neill and the new first-team coach, Wilf Dixon. In later years, Ball often recounted the infamous 'cowboys and Indians' episode. Terry Neill swept into a team meeting carrying two plastic bags. In front of a group of experienced players, waiting for an informed team talk on the opposition, he delved into the first bag and set up a ring of model cowboys. Then he tipped the bag full of Red Indians at their feet. 'And we'll destroy the opposition – just like that,' Neill claimed, Tommy Cooper style. The sniggering bunch of Arsenal players looked on, realising that, without a respected first-team coach, Neill would struggle to cope. Tempers frayed even further during a strained pre-season tour to Austria in 1976, when Ball broke Neill's 'no-booze' rule by informing his boss that 'Saturday night is an Englishman's drinking night'. With that, the whole team flocked into the nearby town for a mammoth boozing session. It doubled as an early birthday party for Peter Storey, so soft drinks were not high on the agenda. Neill looked on helplessly, but he realised that if such insolence continued, he would become yet another victim of player power. So, at the first opportunity, the still hugely talented Ball was sold to Southampton. Neill believed he'd rid himself of a dangerous enemy and some players were also glad to see the back of the vociferous midfielder. Others, like Brady, were disappointed that such talent had been allowed to disappear.

In fact, Terry Neill's early teething problems at Highbury had only just begun. In a bid to win over the fans, still suspicious of him due to his Tottenham links, he signed Malcolm Macdonald, Newcastle United's cocky and prolific striker, for the eye-catching fee of £333,333 and Stoke City's Alan Hudson for £200,000. By '70s standards, these were whopping sums, the equivalent of a £30 million transfer splash by Arsène Wenger. No sooner had they arrived than the new stars were at loggerheads with their new boss. In Alan Ball's words, the pair 'feared no one, they feared no situation, they feared no institution'. Terry Neill was about to discover just how accurate that comment was.

Macdonald, the hero of St James's Park, was whisked to Highbury from under Tottenham's noses. Neill endured a bollocking from Bill Nicholson for his cheek. The Tott's ex-manager accused Neill of 'kidnapping' the player. It's hard to imagine Macdonald going anywhere against his will, though. Neill hired a private jet to bring him south, which appealed to the player's monumental ego – he was extremely confident in his own ability. His ex-manager, Gordon Lee, decided to sell his star striker after a clash of opinion on the training ground: 'You'll never be a good pro, Macdonald,' he'd claimed after the player had laughed in his face when Lee 'taught' the squad how to take a throw in. Macdonald recalls: 'I never knew what he wanted from me. I always went by the adage that my job was to put the ball in the net as often as possible. Get the ball, turn, shoot. That was my philosophy. That was my only role in the team. Lee wanted something else.' First Division defenders would testify that there was no more fearsome sight in the '70s than the chunky, bandy-legged Macdonald, with false teeth out, scorching down on goal. Lee's loss turned out to be Arsenal's gain.

Nicknamed 'Supermac' – a title he doesn't much care for – his tendency to shout his mouth off meant he frequently hogged the back-page headlines. Before the Geordies' 1974 FA Cup final against Liverpool, he'd told journalists that he'd 'murder'

Liverpool's Tommy Smith and Emlyn Hughes during the game. As it was, he barely got a touch in Liverpool's easy 3–0 win. Yet Macdonald's brashness was a welcome antidote to the monotony of life at mid-'70s Arsenal. As soon as he put pen to paper, he boasted: 'I'll score 30 goals this season.' He freely admits that he heaped pressure on himself, claiming: 'It's the way I operated – often it did work, sometimes it made me look a bit silly.' But Macdonald was virtually as good as his word, hitting 29 goals during an often chaotic 1976–77 season.

Teammates found Macdonald 'interesting'. One of his former colleagues, who chooses to remain anonymous, told me: 'Life at Highbury was so different after Malcolm arrived. I've never met anyone quite like him. He was the most selfish, super-confident player I ever came across. If you thought Ian Wright used to be selfish, you should have seen Malcolm. He'd come off the field really pissed off if he hadn't scored – and that was even if the team had won 4–0. Also, he'd claim everything. The most blatant own goal – it was his. We beat Orient 3–0 in an FA Cup semi-final in 1978. In the dressing-room, everyone was delighted that we'd reached Wembley. Except Malcolm, who had been arguing with the press boys that his shot, which hit about three Orient defenders on its way in, was not an own goal. On and on he went, saying: "It's my goal, it's my goal." I remember he used to call Frank Stapleton "a dog". He had young Frank chasing around everywhere, screaming at him to put chances on a plate for him. Malcolm took himself awfully seriously. For a while, he used to carry piles of high-brow books under his arms, which, he believed, made him appear intelligent. I didn't think any of us actually saw him read any of them. At times, he drove you mad. He didn't tend to chase back in games and, until Don Howe arrived, turned up to training late. But what a striker, and a good bloke too. So powerful and strong, with those sweatbands he used to wear. Nice '70s touch, that. He secured my win bonus on many occasions, so he was fine by me!'

Macdonald's self-centred approach meant he frequently clashed with Neill, but immediately received adoration from the crowd. The word 'swashbuckling' barely does him justice. He proved himself to be an excellent all-round sportsman in

Superstars and, in 1976, became the first-ever winner of Roy Race's Centre-forward of the Year trophy in *Roy of the Rovers* magazine. On top of all that, he was bowled over by the sheer grandeur of Highbury. It was very different from life at St James's Park. He recalls: 'The Newcastle dressing-room was always like an ice box. I remember that after we'd complained about how cold it was for about a year the directors, in their wisdom, put a three-bar electric fire in the dressing-room. How dangerous is that, with water sloshing around all over the place? At Arsenal, the dressing-rooms were immaculate. Under-floor heating and kit laid out for you. Newcastle was a big club, but when it came to style and professionalism, Arsenal was on another planet. As for the Arsenal crowd, they provided the right kind of atmosphere, which enabled me to do my job – score goals.'

Alan Hudson, on the other hand, found it rather more difficult to adapt to life at Highbury. Like Macdonald, he felt let down by his contract, but his main reason for griping was Alan Ball's departure. Originally, Hudson's prime reason for joining was his desire to play alongside his pal. Neill, it seemed, had planned to sign Hudson to replace Ball, but he neglected to tell his transfer target that particular piece of news. The player felt he'd been 'stabbed in the back'. After just 90 minutes of first-team action, in a midfield that wasn't to his liking, Hudson vowed: 'I'll never play for that man [Neill] again.'

Misfortune, and a tendency to be in the wrong place at the wrong time, seemed to follow Hudson around. This was the man who'd been sold by Chelsea to Stoke in the early '70s to ease club debts incurred after the construction of the gargantuan East Stand at Stamford Bridge. In 1976, the roof of Stoke's main stand blew off in a freak storm. 'Being Stoke City, it wasn't insured, of course,' recalls Hudson. The cost of replacing the roof? £200,000. The price of his move to Highbury? £200,000. Hudson's England career was ridiculously brief. He won just two caps. 'Don Revie picked me to fail,' he recalls. 'He'd hated me ever since Chelsea beat Leeds in the Cup final. He just didn't trust players like me and Malcolm. Revie used to make the England players play bingo and carpet bowls on England get-togethers. I wasn't 80 years old, was I? Revie's dossiers? Never used to read them. Going out for a few drinks is the way for a team to bond, not playing carpet bowls. Revie never forgave Bally and me for going out for a few drinks on one of his get-togethers instead of staying at the team hotel. I couldn't see the problem with that. I always gave my best on the park. It never affected my performance. What game did he eventually pick me for? Germany at home. He hoped I'd be a disaster. Then he could say "I told you so". I took great pleasure in proving him wrong, after he'd sent us onto the pitch with the message: "Just remember what they did to our houses in the war, lads," ringing in our ears. People say he was a great manager, but he couldn't manage the likes of me, Bally, Charlie George or Stan Bowles. We were the players who could have made England great again. We could have taken the team forward. Look what happened to the team he stuck with.'

Interestingly, Macdonald's memories of Revie's England are equally as bitter. He once described Revie as a 'walking disaster for the national game' and although nowadays he would 'rather not speak ill of the dead', he cannot find anything positive to say about him. 'Never congratulated me after scoring all five goals against Cyprus in a game. Then, against Germany, he told me that if I didn't score, he'd drop me. I did score, but all he said was, "I suppose I'll have to pick you again."'

In light of Charlie George's fortunes under ex-Leeds boss Revie, it's fair to say that 'the Don' didn't care much for the mavericks – especially those who played for Leeds' arch enemies, Arsenal.

A stomach injury contributed to Alan Hudson's fluctuating form at Highbury, but at the time he appeared to have brought many of the problems upon himself. Shortly before his transfer to Arsenal, he penned an article for the *Daily Mail*, in which he claimed 'BIRDS AND BOOZERS AREN'T FOR ME'. He had a reputation for complex and wayward behaviour, and despite his early promise at Chelsea and glimpses of genius at Stoke, was regarded as an underachiever. The demon drink was said to be the root of many of his problems. Hudson admits that the drinking culture was rife in '70s football: 'It's only right to enjoy yourself when you're young.' He also recalls playing in a north London derby soon after his arrival when 'all 22 players stank of the night before. Even the referee, I reckon!' When he sustained a leg injury early in his Arsenal career, a cynical fan commented to a journalist: 'A brown ale bottle must have fallen out of his pocket.' There was also a bizarre episode when his wife Maureen, an ex-Bunny Girl, claimed in the *Daily Telegraph* that Terry Neill had made their lives 'intolerable', due to their living in a rented house in London Colney, which was 'too far from their friends'. The player chose to stay, but the uneasy peace between Hudson and Neill always threatened to explode. By the end of the season, Hudson was diagnosed as suffering from depression.

Despite the vagaries of his new stars, Neill was sometimes his own worst enemy. He was nothing if not keen to restore the glory days to Highbury, but many believed he was still too young and naive for the job. This view is best illustrated by an incident that occurred a few weeks into his managerial spell at Arsenal. After an unbeaten five-match run at the start of the 1976–77 season, a delighted Neill walked into the chairman's office and said: 'Well, Mr Chairman, how about that?' 'Excellent, Terry,' replied the canny Denis Hill-Wood, 'only 30 more points and we'll have avoided relegation.' His biggest problem remained that he did not have a respected first-team coach. Either he or Wilf Dixon were forced to take sessions themselves. The stars weren't impressed. Malcolm Macdonald recalls that season as being 'a hotch-potch of half-baked ideas, with players coming and going through a revolving door. Terry struggled to mould the team into an effective unit.' Alan Hudson comments: 'I don't think it helped him that he was manager and coach. I think he needed to keep some distance between himself and the players. You can't achieve that if, like Terry, you were playing five-a-sides against your former teammates. It was as if he was still one of the lads.'

Nowadays, Terry Neill is bonhomie personified. Charming, insightful and dryly funny, interviewing him in the relaxed atmosphere of his Sports Café and Brasserie in Holborn is a pleasure. Yet players sometimes felt he wasn't always entirely straight with them. In discussion with him, he stops short of criticising them, a habit I believed was his way of protecting ex-players. 'Oh no,' Malcolm Macdonald argued, 'that's his way of covering his own back. He protects himself by not talking about controversial incidents.' Neill glosses over the time he called his team a 'bunch of morons' to journalists, after a terrible display at Middlesbrough, or that he apparently used to walk away from players whenever they tried to discuss contracts with him. Macdonald originally planned to sue Neill for the 'morons' comment.

Throughout the latter months of the 1976–77 season, Neill talked enthusiastically in the *Islington Gazette* about the forthcoming summer tour of Singapore and Australia, claiming it would 'further cement team spirit'. Perhaps he should have guessed that trouble was brewing. In recent years, these excursions had been strained affairs. As Arsenal's stock on the Continent fell and European football became a distant memory, disgruntled players voiced disgust at having to play some awful sides in dilapidated old grounds. The big guns from Italy and Spain didn't want to know Arsenal any more, and as rickety buses with dodgy suspensions shunted the boys around central and Eastern Europe, it became a standing joke for players to shout: 'Has Alan Whicker ever been here?' On the last pre-season tour to Austria, as well as Neill's problems with Ball, he'd sent home Eddie Kelly for disobeying club rules.

Just to confuse matters, the club decided that in the summer of 1977 the boys should go to Norway on a post-season tour, before going to Oz for the 1977–78 pre-season tour. Club coffers needed to be filled, after all. The players went to Norway without a murmur of protest, but they soon learnt that although the club stood to make between £30,000 and £50,000 from the Australian tour, there was no guarantee that individual players would make a penny. In addition, their valuable sunbathing time in Mediterranean resorts (players didn't go to the Caribbean in those days) would be eaten into, as they had to report back for pre-season training three weeks earlier than usual. A delegation of 16 players, inevitably led by strike-threatening Willie Young, stormed up to Terry Neill's hotel room in protest. The rattled manager promised them they would 'get something' from the Oz tour. Neill was already annoyed that Hudson and Macdonald had refused to take part in a carnival parade in the local town. 'I told

Terry I wasn't a bloody boy scout,' Macdonald recalls. The deadly duo doing as they pleased? It was a portent of things to come.

Nowadays, a trip to Australia is, apparently, 50 per cent of Britons' ideal holiday. But several members of the Arsenal team did their best to avoid going. 'You wouldn't believe the number of players who said they had colds, flu and muscle strains. I don't think even the Arsenal doctor had heard of most of the strains of flu that were around,' laughs Alan Hudson. George Armstrong, in contractual dispute with the club, suddenly developed all manner of aches and pains. Neill made him go on tour. After all, informing the boss that you had a sniffle didn't really hold up in the boiling summers of the late '70s.

Peter Simpson, at least, was more up front, telling Neill: 'I'd rather spend my summer with the family than fly around the world with you.' The veteran defender, who smoked like a chimney and loved champagne, wasn't the best of travellers and wasn't looking forward much to the air journey. There wasn't much that the pessimistic Simpson did look forward to. At the start of the season, he'd informed Terry Neill that he was ready to retire. 'I've lost my enthusiasm and pace,' he announced. Neill recalls: 'I told him he'd never had any great enthusiasm or pace, but that he was a hell of a player. Then I told him to get out of my office.' Neill tried to force the veteran defender to go to Oz. Simpson was fined heavily for his insolence, but it was halved on appeal as he had not been asked in writing to go.

Unsurprisingly, Neill's other problem lay with Malcolm Macdonald, whom he needed on board in order to make the tour a success. 'Supermac's' presence would certainly pull in the crowds. Yet communication problems put in jeopardy his place on the tour. In a bid to boost his fitness, he'd spent the summer playing for Melbourne Chiefs, on the condition that he was back in time to train for the tour. He failed to get back to London in time, though, and suggested to Neill that he could rendezvous with the team in Singapore. Neill refused, insisting that he fly back to London, in order to fly out to Singapore two days later. Macdonald comments: 'He expected me to fly through about two dozen time zones and then be ready to be on top form. Bloody impossible.'

The player arrived back in London with a day to spare, but then he almost missed the Oz trip altogether after he forgot his passport as the team coach travelled to Heathrow. Only Macdonald really knows if that was intentional – he claims it wasn't – but it's as well to remember that footballers are notorious for having no common sense. Charlie Nicholas comments that 'most players would probably forget to wipe their own arses unless a club official reminded them to do so'. Macdonald's passport duly arrived, but the atmosphere grew more tense when Neill announced that the long flight to Singapore would be strictly a 'booze-free zone'. Alan Hudson, for one, was not too happy about that rule.

When the aeroplane finally took off from Heathrow, Terry Neill was relieved to have both his recent signings on board. But his problems had only just begun. The 'three amigos', Hudson, Macdonald and Armstrong, were in no mood to conform with Neill's rules. Hudson recalls: 'The tour was all about taking the piss out of Terry Neill. We were on this tour and the club was doing well out of us, and we were being treated like children by him. The flight to Singapore was a prime example. We weren't even allowed to have a gin and tonic. Why not? It was the close season. I can't see the problem with professionals being allowed to use their judgement. It was as if the more he told us not to do it, the more we thought: "We'll do it anyway." Going on tour to Australia should have been a fantastic event. My old Stoke manager, Tony Waddington, used to say: "You're here to enjoy yourself. Go out and have a few drinks, and I don't want to see you before midnight." Neill should never have made such an issue out of everything.'

Singapore was hot, humid and energy-sapping. The Gunners would play Red Star Belgrade four days after their arrival as a 'warm-up' match, before training throughout the boiling afternoons. This still left the players with plenty of time to kill and although they were only entitled to £6 spending money a day, militant senior professionals asked the management for a whopping £800 per head for the whole tour. It wasn't forthcoming, but Hudson and Macdonald soon discovered a novel way of getting their own back. The players were expected to attend a stuffy evening function with Singapore officials and a delegation from the British embassy on the second night. After half an hour, the two Arsenal men walked out, bored to tears with official protocol and making polite conversation with a bunch of tedious old men. Macdonald recalls: 'We were expected to talk to society bores, who are on permanent autopilot after a lifetime of attending cocktail parties. "And what do you do?" each one would ask in turn. So we walked. We had better things to do with our time. Terry Neill told us that we'd embarrassed the club. I told him we'd actually been ambassadors for the club, because we went and had a few beers with some Arsenal and Celtic fans, who were also on the tour. It was a fantastic night – I'll bet those fans still remember the night they drank with me and Huddy! That's how to be an ambassador for a club. Neill couldn't handle players whose opinion differed from his.'

After the Red Star match a couple of days later, where Hudson starred in Arsenal's narrow defeat, the players had lost somewhere in the region of eight pints of fluid each, since they'd been roasted in the extreme heat. The local doctor, who happened to be an Australian, recommended that, in order to rehydrate, the team should drink water or beer. Only an Aussie doctor could seriously recommend such a procedure to a bunch of English footballers. Some members of the team took his advice a bit too literally, proving that the old adage 'those who think Australian drink Australian' is true among footballers. Alan Hudson took a more flexible approach, drinking a few gin and tonics over lunch. Terry Neill recalled he looked 'slightly unsteady' for the rest of the day. Macdonald, on his own admission, drank 20 pints of beer and, according to him, didn't 'go to the toilet for a leak once during the whole session'. Being an archetypal '70s boy, he still maintains that 'it didn't affect my playing performances one bit'.

By this time, though, he was also taking sleeping pills, as the long-haul flights had disrupted his sleeping pattern. Neill, by this time, had unwisely boasted to his team that Dave Sexton would be joining the Gunners as the new first-team coach. The boys were pleased, but a day later were dismayed to hear that, instead, Sexton had opted to join Manchester United as manager. 'It made Neill look more of a buffoon,' Hudson later commented. Luckily, though, the manager did not heed Arsenal official Tony Wood's advice to 'have a go' at Hudson and Macdonald for the heinous crime of growing beards. But soon he'd have further cause to castigate his two stars.

On the next leg of the tour, the boys jetted into Sydney and stayed at the famous Rushcutters hotel. Malcolm Macdonald immediately threw a tantrum. In his room, he'd been given what he thought was a kid's fold-up bed. Teammates claimed he needed to pull it out first, but amused roommate Hudson reckoned it was 'designed for Ronnie Corbett' and Macdonald claimed he'd 'never been so insulted in his life'. The quality of Arsenal's play remained poor. At Sydney Cricket ground, an Australian National XI beat the Gunners and then Celtic did the same. Neill again imposed a drinking ban but the majority of the team did as they pleased. By now, George Armstrong, still in conflict with Neill, joined Hudson and Macdonald in defiance of the boss's instructions, with the result that on the eve of the team departing to Adelaide, the three of them disappeared into Sydney for a memorable night out.

The three amigos got talking with some gangsters from the Sydney underworld. They were in the middle of a heated rant about Neill, when one of their new acquaintances asked if they would like to arrange for Neill's immediate 'disappearance' and 'departure' from the country. Hudson recalls: 'The three of us just stood there and looked at each other with open mouths. Malcolm wasn't usually stuck for words, but even he was gobsmacked by the suggestion. History proves that we politely declined their offer. I'd heard the expression "giving the manager the bullet", but this was ridiculous.' After an all-nighter, the three finally piled out of a taxi minutes before the team was due to fly to Adelaide for the final leg of the journey.

Hudson, Macdonald, and Armstrong knocked back the bevvies en route to Adelaide and disappeared once more in between landing and getting on the team coach. On arrival at the hotel, Denis Hill-Wood allegedly bought Macdonald a gin and tonic, after which the player took another sleeping pill and prepared for an afternoon nap. Hudson did the same. At this point, club captain Pat Rice banged on their door and told them to prepare for a hastily arranged training session. The pair were about as coherent and lucid as Gazza. Terry Neill finally intervened and, believing that the pair were again under the influence, decided to send them home in disgrace. This was done with the chairman's full backing, of course.

George Armstrong begged to be sent home too, but Neill had made his point through the two others and 'Geordie' stayed. Hudson claims that: 'For Neill to have sent the respectable and dependable George Armstrong home would have proved that something was seriously wrong with his way of running things. It was much easier for him to pick on Malcolm and me. We already had a reputation, didn't we? Put it this way, we were the two scapegoats. There was lots more going on that trip that just hasn't been mentioned.' Previously unreported events indicate widespread discontent amongst the first-team squad with the afternoon training sessions, conducted, on one occasion, in 120-degree heat. Macdonald mutters: 'Only mad dogs and Englishmen go out in the midday sun.' Hudson still feels bitter about Neill attempting to 'break' the 'three amigos' in training. 'Poor man-management,' he recalls. 'Geordie and myself were the best trainers at the club. For all our misdemeanours, we still coped with long-distance running. Terry was the one who ended up with egg on his face. Of course, he suggested that only us three caused him grief over this. That's not the full truth.'

Liam Brady concurs with this view, claiming in his book that 'Neill could just as easily have sent ten others, including me, home'. On their return flight, the distinctly non-contrite Hudson and Macdonald toasted themselves with champagne and ultimately sold their stories to the *Sunday People* and *Sunday Mirror*. Even Terry Neill got in on the circus, his story appearing in the *News of the World*. None of the stories revealed a great deal, but with constant speculation surrounding the pair, Arsenal continued to feature in the type of articles that the club has always sought to avoid. It was something which tabloid readers became used to over the next 20 years. Hudson claims: 'Malcolm and I could have said more about other high-profile Arsenal players, but we didn't want to land others in trouble. We could easily have taken them down with us.'

As journalists fell over themselves for gossip and tittle-tattle from the other Arsenal players, Don Howe slipped, virtually unnoticed, into Highbury as the new first-team coach. In time-honoured tradition, Arsenal miraculously turned a crisis into a triumph. After protracted negotiations, Hudson and Macdonald were convinced to stay at the club. Howe insisted that the latter chase back and defend rather more, and turn up to training on time. Hudson recalls: 'On one occasion, Malcolm was doing his usual thing, gesticulating with the Arsenal crowd after he'd just missed a chance. In the meantime, Everton went down the other end and scored. You should have seen Don Howe afterwards. He gave Malcolm such a bollocking. For the next week in training, he had him running up and down the pitch after the ball as a punishment. It was really funny. Malcolm took it, though. You didn't tend to argue with Don. But for different reasons, our Arsenal careers were nearly over.'

Though inconsistent league performances and a poor display in the 1978 FA Cup final against Ipswich did Hudson few favours, it was during the post-match inquest that he finally pushed the self-destruct button. In a supposedly 'frank' discussion, players were asked to comment on what they thought had gone wrong. Many of the responses were typically bland, along the lines of 'injuries' and 'the heat'. As usual, Hudson chose to be different. He comments: 'Don Howe asked the players one by one what he thought had gone wrong. I looked Terry Neill in the eyes and said: "You picked the wrong team." Neill called me "a disgrace" – he had a point there – but as I said, Don asked me and I gave a straight answer. I'd had it by then. I'd had enough of Neill.' Hudson was immediately bombed out to Seattle Sounders, in the, ahem, burgeoning North American soccer league.

Malcolm Macdonald's performance in the FA Cup final was, if anything, even worse. There were mitigating circumstances, however. His knees were effectively shredded after a career at the sharp end. From the start, he'd never been the perfect physical specimen for a football career. As a teenager, doctors had detected a slight curvature of his spine and a bowing of his legs, which hardly augured well for the future. At Newcastle, he'd damaged lateral ligaments and cartilage in his left knee. 'By the time I was 28, a piece of gristle zigzagged through the joint. It was riddled with osteoarthritis. At Rotherham, in a League Cup match for Arsenal, I was clean through, ready to shoot, when the cartilage just ripped to shreds. I heard it go as I crumpled in a heap. Nightmare.' His right knee was also in a shocking state. The joint regularly locked during games, leaving the embarrassed player to 'waggle it about' before he could continue. In the Cup final, Arsenal effectively played with ten men. Macdonald recalls: 'Liam Brady put the ball through for me three times in that match and each time, I couldn't go.' Such was his wretched performance in the game that his detractors, who remembered his 'no show' for Newcastle in the 1975 FA Cup final, told a cruel joke about him:

Q: What is taken to the FA Cup final each year but never used?
A: Malcolm Macdonald.

One of the most charismatic players in Arsenal history was forced to retire at 30 years of age. He recalls: 'When I walked out of Highbury for the last time and looked down St Thomas's Road, it was an incredibly lonely feeling. The loneliest I'd ever felt.'

Some unforgiving writers have suggested that in later life, the inevitable happened: '70s hubris was followed by '80s and '90s nemesis. For two players who claimed that as youngsters boozing did not affect their performances, the role that alcohol played in their middle-aged lives is grimly ironic. After a chequered managerial career at Fulham and Huddersfield, Macdonald's business interests took him to Milan, where he worked for Audiotel, setting up the equivalent of an 0891 service. After the Italian government made such lines illegal, he fell on hard times, financially and emotionally. He admits that the pain induced by chronic knee problems forced him to seek solace in whisky. 'My life became totally unmanageable. I couldn't function. I couldn't even get up and down stairs any more.'

Alan Hudson enjoyed (though 'endured' may be a better word) brief second spells at Chelsea and Stoke, before settling into a flourishing writing career for the *Sporting Life* and Stoke's *Evening Sentinel*. In 1997, a time when *The Working Man's Ballet*, his autobiography, was selling well, a car knocked him down on London's Mile End Road. For two months he was in a coma. When he finally came round, the doctor informed him that he'd sustained a shattered pelvis and would spend the rest of his life in a wheelchair. His second wife left him while he was in hospital and a couple of years later he was declared bankrupt. After he left hospital, the tabloids portrayed him as a pathetic figure, drowning his sorrows in various London hostelries. Alan Hudson, it seemed, hadn't just hit rock bottom; he'd started drilling.

Inevitably, where Hudson and Macdonald are concerned, there is a dramatic twist in the tale. Displaying the sheer bloody-mindedness that made them '70s rebels, both have miraculously reconstructed their lives. Macdonald has had a plastic kneecap inserted in his left leg ('I can't play squash any more, but I can get around normally at last, without pain'). The PFA, for whom he used to be an uncompromising representative, funded the operation. He continues to use his invective to good effect on Century FM, the Newcastle-based radio station. Alan Hudson has gone under the surgeon's knife 12 times in the last few years. There are more operations to come and the hole in his bladder means he has to wear a bag, but at least he can walk, albeit with the aid of sticks. His writing is back on track and he visits the gym regularly. 'Life's been hard,' he admits, 'but the main thing is, I'm here to tell the tale.'

I wonder whether either man has any regrets. 'None at all,' Macdonald claims. 'I'm very much of the opinion that you should only look forward.' Ex-teammates used to laugh at Macdonald as he strutted away to his 'important business meetings'. It's reassuring to learn that he's had to delay our interview due to 'being tied up in an important meeting'. Hudson has just one regret: 'That I told Ron Greenwood to piss off back in 1978 when he called me late into the England squad to play against Brazil. He told me I'd be in the team, but I reckoned that as I hadn't been in the original squad, it was a case of "no thanks".' As usual, Alan Hudson was too stubborn for his own good. It's been the pattern of his life, with just one exception: 'You won't believe this, but Terry Neill and me are good mates now,' he confesses.

NINE

Big Willie

> When I started out at Aberdeen, the wind used to howl
> into the ground from the North Sea, and almost cut you
> in two on winter afternoons. You could say it was
> character-building.
>
> Willie Young, speaking in 1999

It is impossible to judge how many adjectives were used to describe Willie Young during his playing days. 'Gigantic', 'intimidating', 'hard as nails' and 'whole-hearted' are some of the more complimentary ones. Hapless centre-forwards who'd been bruised and battered after 90 minutes of aerial combat with him may have chosen to add 'brutal', 'thuggish' and 'dirty Scottish bastard' to the list. Willie was arguably the toughest of the tribe of towering centre-halves who roamed First Division grounds in the '70s and early '80s. Like the lumbering giants of the Jurassic era, this breed is now extinct, destroyed by prissy FIFA officials' insistence on turning football into a non-contact sport. Luckily for him, he played in the right era, although he'd probably have relished playing alongside Wilf Copping in the '30s, too.

Apart from a manic desire to get to the ball first, he had other qualities that made him a cult hero at Highbury. Playing a starring role in the 1979 FA Cup final against Manchester United certainly helped his cause and occasionally he popped in vital goals in key matches. But it was his shock of red hair that meant he blazed a distinctive trail in the game. Willie played at a time when many who plied their trade with First Division sides were not like the athletic, sinewy robots we see paraded at Premiership grounds today. Such players live long in the memory because they appeared to have stepped out from a pub team into English football's top tier. Bald players (as opposed to those who've shaved their head), bearded players, fat players, moustached players and midgets: they all turned out for sides in Willie's day. Yet, simply due to the colour of his barnet and his unique 'style', he remains one of the most recognisable players of his vintage. Twenty years on, he's lovingly remembered by his ex-manager, Terry Neill, as a 'big awkward bastard who liked a drink' and by others as the ogre who committed the most cynical of fouls in an FA Cup final. It was all too easy to brand him as a burly Neanderthal, given the fact that his kinfolk, the Tartan Army, wrecked Wembley in 1975, the year in which he first played in England. It didn't require a great deal of imagination to picture him wearing a kilt, swinging on the crossbar, swigging a can of McEwan's and ripping up chunks of turf, after all. Crucially, he was a trier, who literally spilt blood for the team and occasionally showed there was more to his game than simply 'stopping others'. Some observers of football in that era incorrectly bracketed him alongside Peter Storey as an Arsenal villain. Admittedly, both had an ultra-competitive streak, but Young was more of a lovable rogue. He didn't target opposition like Storey and would usually only respond if he'd been provoked. It often appeared that he genuinely didn't realise his own strength, whereas the more vicious Storey certainly did.

Many English fans were already au fait with Young's bad boy reputation before he ventured south of the border. As a promising Scotland Under-23 international, he'd been invited to go on tour with the first team to Denmark. After the team had beaten Denmark 1–0, Young, along with Billy Bremner and three others, decided to make a night of it in Copenhagen. They left a trail of chaos in their wake. A nightclub owner, the amusingly named Bent Dorf, later commented that the Scots had behaved like 'a bunch of animals' in Bonapartes, the grooviest joint in town. The police were called, but after being given a warning the five were allowed to carry on boozing. The night ended with an SFA official having his hotel room trashed, allegedly by Young and friends, and some mutterings about an unpaid nightclub bill at Bonapartes. Within a couple of days, Willie's name was known throughout Britain. *The Sun* reported: 'FIVE GO MAD IN COPENHAGEN' and the *Daily Record* blasted: 'FIVE BANNED FOR LIFE – YOU'LL NEVER PLAY FOR SCOTLAND AGAIN'. Young's international ban was never lifted, either. He comments: 'It was a ridiculously over-the-top reaction. The SFA was swayed by rumour and tabloid hysteria. I can't recall other such incidents meriting such a harsh punishment.' The SFA came to regret its hasty decision, particularly after inept defending cost Scotland dear at the 1978 and 1982 World Cups.

By the mid-'70s, Willie's club, Aberdeen, was starting to stir. In parallel with the situation in which he later found himself at Highbury, he learned his trade next to a smooth practitioner, Martin Buchan. He and Willie had struck up a formidable partnership at the heart of the Dons' defence. If opponents believed they could take advantage of Buchan's questionable aerial ability, the leaping, red-headed monster alongside him would literally blast them out of the skies. With Buchan departing to Old Trafford, Willie was appointed club captain. But Young also fancied a stab at playing in England and became disenchanted with life at Pittodrie. The end came when manager Willie Turnbull substituted him during a game against Dundee. Young reacted in his own inimitable style. He ripped up his shirt, threw the shreds at his manager, ran down the tunnel and put his boot through the dressing-room door. Unsurprisingly, he never played for Aberdeen again. For several years after that, 'Willie's door' remained a shrine to the departed rebel.

As far as Arsenal fans are concerned, the journey Willie took to becoming a Highbury cult hero couldn't have been a more hazardous or treacherous one. One inescapable and glaring feature of his curriculum vitae still burns out from the page. He did indeed leave Scotland for north London – but he travelled to the other end of Seven Sisters Road. In 1975, Willie Young signed for Terry Neill's Tottenham. It was the beginning of their strange patron/apprentice relationship and the Totts desperately needed

Young to shore up their porous defence. Neill recalls whisking Young south in a private jet 'so small we thought he'd have to sit on the wing'. Spurs, like Arsenal in the mid-'70s, were a crap side. Flirting with relegation appeared to have become their *raison d'etre* and Neill realised that blindly following Bill Nicholson's doctrine of 'pure' football was likely to end in disaster. Spurs no longer had the players to even attempt to play in the manner of the 1961 Double winners. Willie got stuck in to help Spurs keep their heads above water in the 1975–76 season, but neither he nor his manager came close to being accepted by Spurs fans.

It was during a fraught north London derby that most Arsenal fans glimpsed Young for the first time. In a frantic 60 minutes, he put Spurs ahead with a glorious diving header after a cute decoy run, scrapped with and goaded Peter Storey all afternoon, and finally got himself sent off after an outrageous tackle on Frank Stapleton. Young launched into a pseudo-Bruce Lee flying kick and his knees crunched into Stapleton's neck. Bearing in mind that a defender would practically have to garrotte the opposition to be dismissed in those days, the fact that the referee immediately reached for his pocket spoke volumes for the ferocity of his challenge. As he trotted off the field to a cacophony of booing from Arsenal fans, no one could have guessed that within a few months 'Typhoon Willie' would blast into Highbury.

As spring of 1977 arrived, the Gunners were in desperate need of a dose of Celtic blood and thunder in central defence. By now, Terry Neill had, in Spurs' fans eyes, done the decent thing and accepted the manager's job at Highbury. It would be an exaggeration to suggest that it was a universally popular appointment. The Ulsterman now had Spurs connections, didn't he? After a bright start to the season, his team had slumped and were in the middle of a terrible six-match losing streak. In recent years, Arsenal's famed central defensive strength had become a laughing stock. Frank McLintock's replacement, Jeff 'The Block' Blockley, would stroll into any Arsenal nightmare 11 and the follically challenged Terry Mancini (nicknamed 'Henry' after the musical director of *The Pink Panther*), for all his boundless enthusiasm, wasn't a whole lot better. With Peter Simpson nearing the end of his distinguished Highbury career and Pat Howard not shaping up as a long-term fixture, a spot of tartan terror in central defence was just the tonic required. After all, it was no use having the silky smooth David O'Leary present without a granite-hewn terminator to operate alongside him.

Many of Neill's Arsenal signings were questionable. Australian John Kosmina was one dud buy: when he was supposed to be on the pitch as a substitute against Red Star Belgrade he went to the toilet instead and ten-man Arsenal lost a goal, and the UEFA Cup tie, because of it. Mark Heeley and the H-Bums, John Hawley and Ray Hankin, also spring to mind, but there is no doubt that Young's arrival from Spurs for £80,000 was one of Neill's shrewdest moves in the transfer market. He joined former teammate Pat Jennings, whom Spurs had also released for a pittance, at Highbury. Originally lined up to sign for Ipswich, Jennings confirms that he signed for Arsenal in order to cause Spurs directors' maximum embarrassment after not one of them had thanked him for his services to the club when they gave him a free transfer in 1977. Willie's Scottish ancestry seemed to have secured him a place on Neill's shortlist from the moment the new manager arrived. Terry appeared determined to stuff his sides with players from all outposts of the British Isles and the Irish Republic. If Sol Campbell's move across north London registered highly on the Richter scale nearly 25 years later, Willie's transfer generated virtually no interest at all. He received no death threats and there were no Samaritans calls from Spurs fans. They were glad to see the back of him, as was manager Keith Burkinshaw. Arsenal fans were not particularly impressed with the club's latest acquisition.

The prospect of Young remaining anything other than a Highbury hate figure seemed remote after his debut at Highbury against Ipswich on 16 March 1977. Willie played abysmally. Neill reckons: 'He tried to play like Pelé, Best and Gerson rolled into one. He should have remembered that he was a 14-stone Scotsman.' Willie, indeed, hadn't read his brief, and proceeded to scare Arsenal supporters, rather than Ipswich's Paul Mariner and Trevor Whymark. On one occasion, he hopelessly misjudged the bounce of the ball, allowing John Wark to sneak in and poach Ipswich's second goal in their 4–1 win. His inclusion in the team seemed to be nothing more than a belated gesture by Neill to embrace the tartan craze which was sweeping the country, due to Bay City Rollers mania. Steve Ashford, aka *The Gooner*'s Highbury Spy, describes it as 'the worst Highbury debut in living memory'.

Willie recalls his debut and its aftermath: 'I was crap. No question. Part of the problem was that I hadn't played for a good few months and I was totally lacking in match fitness. I put two of their goals down to me. Anyway, after the game, I was walking back to my car with my family when this fan walked up to me and started threatening me, telling me, basically, to "fuck off back to Spurs". I thought to myself: "I'm not having this", so I told him exactly what I'd do to him if he dared to touch me. The guy quickly scarpered, but it showed me that I had a big job on my hands to win over the Arsenal supporters.'

Young's reaction in the car park, if nothing else, proved that he was a fighter. Willie proceeded to get stuck in, with both feet and fists. During a clash with Spurs a month after he joined ('I think I became the first player in a London derby to be booed by both sets of fans when I ran on'), he cut his head open and left the field for treatment. Minutes later he returned, head bandaged, to fight on. And fight he did – ex-Spurs teammates lay strewn across the turf like casualties at the Somme after receiving the Young 'treatment'. Just for good measure, Malcolm Macdonald's last-minute goal gave Arsenal the winner. The North Bank finally began to appreciate Young's attitude and bayed in appreciation. His remarkable transformation from arch-villain to cult hero was under way.

With the club now pulling out of the rut, the boys launched a late assault upon a European spot. Benefiting from a tighter 4–4–2 formation, Young and O'Leary began to form a watertight partnership. It didn't hugely matter that in footballing terms the Scot sometimes didn't actually play very well. He was a bit cumbersome and it's true that he often favoured smashing the ball into Row Z of the stand, putting in peril any poor sod in the vicinity. His enthusiasm and attitude, though, were infectious, and enabled Arsenal to finish the season in style, although a UEFA

Cup spot proved to be a bridge too far. He was granted his own chant too. 'Six foot two, eyes of blue, Willie Young is after you', began to boom out whenever he appeared. Yet that mantra was short-lived, partly due to the fact that he was actually six foot three. The rather more simplistic 'Willie, Willie, Willie' caught on, though, as did 'We've got the biggest Willie in the land', sung to the tune of 'The Whole World In Our Hands'.

Throughout the following season, as Don Howe's coaching methods gradually turned the club around, Young's style began to reap dividends. Originally, Pat Jennings reckoned that Howe would quickly bomb Young out, but Howe encouraged the Scot to continue playing in his combative manner. He totally dominated Highbury airspace, and wasn't averse to employing the tackle from behind when the referee wasn't looking. On the occasions when he sliced the ball or fell over, the ever-alert O'Leary was there to sweep up the mess and, on the road to the 1978 FA Cup final, Young played a starring role at the Race Course Ground during a feisty fifth-round clash with Wrexham. With 25,000 Welshmen screaming for Arsenal blood, Young trundled forward like a Panzer tank to plunder two goals and silence the home crowd. And while he made himself a hero on the pitch, the Young legend continued to grow off it.

During pre-season training, Don Howe insisted that the players do plenty of cross-country running through the fields near London Colney. Alan Hudson recalls: 'Players like myself and George Armstrong loved all that long-distance stuff. Willie loathed it with a passion. One day he got so fed up with doing a lap of this field that he crashed right through the middle of it. Straight through all that corn, like a bloody tractor. Just so he could take a short-cut and finish early. I don't think Terry Neill cottoned on, and he was saying things like: "Oh, well done, big man." Willie just gave him that funny grin of his.'

On a pre-season tour of Kuwait, he'd got hungry in the middle of the night and, on the way to raiding the hotel kitchen, fell down a manhole, nearly killing himself in the process. In a Hong Kong bar, Arsenal players were invited to display their musical talents on stage. Irishman John Devine, who had a penchant for strumming his guitar, bravely accepted the challenge. As members of the crowd began to heckle Devine, Willie got stuck in and laid out the offenders. His teammate, oblivious to the fuss, won the competition. Young had no qualms about confronting Neill over any issue. In training, he'd argue with Neill over absolutely anything, even if it didn't directly concern him, turning the air blue in the process. Alan Hudson recalls: 'A pint, a laugh and probably a bust-up over nothing, and Willie was happy.' In fact, he was no more likely to back down in an argument than he was to leave a pint of beer half-finished. Neill comments: 'He loved to argue, simple as that. He'd argue with his own shadow. Once or twice, I thought of asking him for a fight in the car park. It's lucky I never did, because he'd have kicked the crap out of me, no question.' Young reflects: 'Terry and me argued all the time, I've always argued back if I feel I'm in the right. Terry certainly wasn't in the right over everything. I'd never have punched him, mind. He wouldn't be around now to tell the tale if I had.'

Critics unfairly blamed Young's lack of mobility for Ipswich's shock win in the 1978 FA Cup final, as he failed to clear a ball that Roger Osborne gleefully rammed home. In reality, the whole team was under par but Willie felt guilty none the less. In the preamble to the following year's FA Cup final against Manchester United, BBC1's Tony Gubba intimated to Young that he could possibly have prevented Osborne's goal. Willie simply refused to answer the question and shot him a look which seemed likely to turn the interviewer to stone. Embarrassed, Gubba moved on to Graham Rix and asked him about the new female interest in his life. Again, with hindsight, this was probably not the most tactful question Gubba has ever asked. But that is a different story.

During that 1978–79 season, Young's fortunes had further improved. In the marathon FA Cup third-round encounter with Sheffield Wednesday, he powered in a late, late header to tie up the fourth match at 3–3, when the game had seemed to be up. He saved his best performance for the 1979 FA Cup final. Willie and Manchester United's Joe Jordan duelled relentlessly for 90 skull-crunching minutes in the Wembley sun, and United's toothless Scottish ogre hardly got a kick all afternoon. Many had Young down for man of the match; his performance was one of the key reasons for Arsenal's 3–2 success on that dramatic afternoon. Young recalls: 'It was an amazing occasion to be involved in. The greatest Cup final of all time, probably. Liam Brady proved what a class act he was and to get my winner's medal at the end of the game was the best experience of my career.' Equally as important was that Willie Young had now officially been accepted as an Arsenal man.

If anything, Young's performances reached an even higher pitch during the following season. This was to be a year stuffed with marathon cup clashes, nail-biting climaxes and sudden-death semi-finals. No player summed up Arsenal's fortress mentality that season better than Young. He played a starring role en route to the Cup-Winners' Cup final, scoring three vital goals under nervy conditions. The most memorable was a delicate chip against Gothenburg, which nearly brought the North Bank roof down. Young was even praised for his ball-playing skills by watching journalists. In *The Times*, Clive White spoke of Young's 'silky touches, almost unnatural for a big man'. The semi-final against Juventus cemented his reputation. In the first leg, he provided the assist for Arsenal's goal. A bulldozing tackle on Italian football's hard man Scirea at the Stadio Della Alpi in the return swung the tie in Arsenal's favour. As the Italians, who'd opted to defend a 1–1 away draw, grew more edgy in Turin it was only Scirea's midfield presence which had been holding Brady and Rix at bay. The Scot's jarring 80th-minute challenge removed Scirea from the equation and made the Italian question what day of the week it was. 'Those who live by the sword must die by the sword,' Young later commented. From that point, the Gunners were able to power forward and Paul Vaessen's late winner took Arsenal into the final.

Fourteen years later, Vaessen recalled: 'Willie and some of the others were speeding around the hotel grounds on motorbikes. A few of the lads were starkers.' Young thrived in such European combat zones: 'Away legs in Europe brought out the best in me and some of the other guys. We knew we'd got a hell of a task on our hands in the Juve game. They'd never lost at home in Europe. The atmosphere in the stadium was certainly noisy and colourful with all their smoke bombs going off, but I didn't think it was as intimidating as say, in Turkey. I remember once we played Fenerbahce and their fans were bloody mental, to be honest. They'd throw anything at you – bottles, cans, even smoke bombs, which would explode at your feet. Then some of the guys, if they took a throw-in, would get showered in spit. It was disgusting, but it also inspired us to win. Playing in those European games was fantastic. It was what being an Arsenal player is all about.'

Young also stamped – literally – his authority on the epic FA Cup semi-final encounters with the all-conquering Liverpool that season. Critics gave Arsenal little chance, unless, perhaps, midfield general Graeme Souness could be shackled. In the first goalless match at Hillsborough, Young noticed that fellow Scot Souness was beginning to take liberties with Brady and Rix. Young bided his time to exact revenge, but late in the second half he got it. Strictly speaking, his 'challenge' on Souness was within the laws of the game. Willie launched himself, with both sets of studs up, into a challenge and made slight contact with the ball. Souness, on the other hand, was sent flying onto the gravel track surrounding the pitch. After unsuccessfully trying to regain his dignity, Souness jumped to his feet, ready to square up to the perpetrator of the tackle. But there stood Willie, glowering and eyeballing him. As the Arsenal fans rapturously chanted 'Willie, Willie!' Souness slunk away and barely touched the ball again. Interestingly, Souness's contribution in the replays was described as 'subdued' by Liverpool boss Bob Paisley. Young simply smirked at the travelling hordes of Gunners and resumed his battle with Kenny Dalglish.

For all his heroics, Wembley infamy was only a few days away. With the Arsenal team shattered physically and mentally after a monumental fixture pile-up, West Ham's Second Division beard-faced blighters ran rings around the Gunners in the FA Cup final. Young commented: 'We'd all lost a couple of yards of pace, which was no good for me, as I didn't have any to begin with.' Trevor Brooking netted the Hammers' winner, but for many, the image of Willie hoiking down Paul Allen, just as the youngest player ever to play in a Cup final was about to kill the game, is the abiding memory of the final. Willie recalls: 'Paul was put through, about 20 yards outside the box. I had a split second to make up my mind. Either he would have most probably scored, or I had the chance to at least keep us in with a shout. So I thought "Son, you've gotta go." I was a defender and I defended. It wasn't a brutal foul – I just tapped his foot and he went down. Paul was very good about it and said "I'd have done the same, big man." I never lost any sleep over it.'

The critics immediately rounded on Young, despairing that he should have committed this most cynical of professional fouls. In effect, Young had destroyed a perfect fairytale ending: he'd prevented an innocent 17 year old from writing himself into the record books. The press got their 'DAVID SLAYS GOLIATH' story anyway, as West Ham won.

It was Young's reaction that infuriated neutrals. As the referee brandished a yellow card (today, he'd have Elleray or Durkin standing over him and waving him off the pitch), Young simply raised his hands, as if to admit: 'It's a fair cop.' To the nation at large, he was saying: 'It's all in a day's work, I do this all the time.' On that horrendous afternoon for Gunners fans, no one in the country seemed badder than big, bad Willie Young of the Arsenal.

He stayed at Arsenal for another full season, still bone-crunching anyone who chose to challenge him on the ground or in the air. Late in 1980, he famously booted Manchester City disaster Steve Daley all over Maine Road before marauding forward to grab the Arsenal equaliser. A few weeks later, he repeated the trick on Andy Gray, Wolves' £1 million striker, suggesting he bore a grudge against expensive footballers. Young also found the time to fall out with new teammate Peter Nicholas, with whom he'd had a running feud since the latter's days at Crystal Palace. He recalls: 'Peter Nicholas thought he was a hard man, but he wasn't very good at being hard. I think he began to play in Liam Brady's position after he left for Juventus, and Nicholas clearly wasn't Liam Brady. He'd tried to wind me up when he was at Crystal Palace and I hadn't forgotten. When he came to Arsenal, we played against Liverpool, and he went in high on Graeme Souness. It was a stupid thing to do. Nicholas was just trying to show off. I knew what would happen. Souness soon got his revenge: he put Nicholas out of football for a couple of months. As he was lying on the ground rolling around, I walked over to Souness. He expected trouble. "Oh, come on, big man, he deserved it," he said, preparing to defend himself. "I know – I'm just coming over to congratulate you," I replied. I'd never seen Souness lost for words before!'

For all the havoc he was wreaking, Young had to look to the future and at 30, after a career at the sharp end, he realised the clock was ticking. He'd already tried to earn some extra cash by going on Jimmy Hill's Rebel tour of South Africa in the late '70s, but the scheme collapsed at the last minute. Young knew that if he departed for a new club, he'd receive a £25,000 tax-free payment. This would be the equivalent of gold dust to him, as he'd never stayed long enough at his clubs to warrant a testimonial.

In typically brusque style, he informed his manager that he'd given excellent service, and would now be as awkward and difficult as possible, in order that Neill let him go. At first, Neill stubbornly refused, but as Young apparently became 'more and more of a pain in the arse' (according to Neill), he realised it was time to release the Scot.

Brian McDermott recalls Young's final days at Highbury: 'Willie was one of the funniest blokes I met in football. Even now, I look back to his arguments with Terry Neill and I just laugh. Once, in pre-season training, Terry decided to hire an aerobics instructor to help us with our "poise and movement". I think that's how Terry described it. So this woman gets on a box, stands up and starts doing all the movements to the music. One by one, most of us joined in, although we all felt like morons, to be honest. Anyway, Willie refused to do it. He just said: "Bollocks, I'm not doing it, boss." Terry said to him: "Yes you are, Willie, and if you don't, I'll fine you £50." This was actually quite a lot of money to a footballer back then. Still Willie refused. Anyway, Terry continued to up the fine, until it got to a full week's wages, if he wouldn't dance. At that point, Willie relented and said: "OK, OK, I'm fucking dancing. Yippee!!!" and he jumped up in the air and waved his arms and legs around. Even the aerobics instructor nearly killed herself laughing.'

The final row between Young and Neill erupted during

Arsenal's disastrous UEFA cup clash with Winterslag. The Belgian part-timers beat Arsenal over two legs and in Belgium, Neill was hit by a brick thrown from the terrace. 'It wasn't me who threw it before you ask,' Young tells me. In the second leg at Highbury, with Arsenal desperately requiring more aerial power, substitute Young begged his manager to bring him into the fray for one last hurrah. He recalls: 'Terry and I knew that Winterslag were shit scared of me. In Belgium, I'd put the ball in their net three times but each time it was struck off. At Highbury, we had to score again to get through and the crowd was chanting for me. But Terry refused to bring me on. I remember saying to him: "You and your stupid pride lost us the tie."' Unsurprisingly, when Neill received an acceptable offer for Young, he was allowed to leave. It was a sad end to the most colourful of Highbury careers.

There was only one concrete offer for Willie. It was faxed to Neill by Nottingham Forest boss Brian Clough in late 1981. At the top of the fax, which was newfangled technology at the time, Clough had written in unmistakable style: 'Welcome to the twentieth century, I want to sign Willie Young.' He offered Arsenal £170,000 for the player, which the board duly accepted. The move was doomed from the start. Neill comments: 'Can you honestly imagine Willie and Cloughie getting on? It's like pouring petrol onto a fire.' Young recalls: 'It was a terrible mistake. I knew the move was a mistake even before I got there.' Within a month of his arrival, Clough suffered a small heart attack. By chance, Arsenal played Forest shortly afterwards and Neill went to chat to Young in the Forest dressing-room. As soon as his ex-boss appeared and began to enquire about Cloughie's health, the Scot shouted: 'I know what you're thinking, but his heart attack was bugger all to do with me!'

His manager's heart palpitations increased when Young became Forest's PFA representative. Given his talent for arguing, it seemed an ideal job for the Scot, but Clough always despised barrack-room lawyers. The pair's first real flashpoint arrived over the matter of Young's removal allowance. This money was to be paid to the player some months after his arrival at Forest in order to fund his move to a new house. Young, instead, invested his (as yet unreceived) cash in an equestrian school in nearby Newark.

After hearing this news, Clough refused to pay Willie his money, on the grounds that the money should have been invested solely in a house. 'I never did see that money,' Young mutters.

Clough finally went 'nuclear' at Young after Forest had lost to Derby County in an FA Cup tie. Derby were under the control of Peter Taylor, Clough's former assistant and the two were now sworn enemies. Before the match, Clough said: 'Do a good job for me today, Willie. If you do, I'll never ask another thing of you.' But Forest lost the tie 2–0 and Clough accused Young of taking a bribe to throw the game. He told his centre-half to 'fuck off and talk to your mate Taylor'. Willie reacted in the only way he knew: 'Just to spite him, I did go and speak to Taylor. There was Clough, shouting "I can't believe you went to speak to him!" And I said: "But you told me to." "I didn't bloody mean it, though," was Clough's response. This was in front of several Forest fans. It was all a bit embarrassing.'

Miraculously, the Scot stayed at Forest for another season, before he was released in 1984. He had subsequent brief spells at Norwich, Brighton and Darlington. In one of his last-ever games at Darlington, he was involved in a mighty rumpus on the touchline with opposition players. When questioned about Young's actions afterwards, Darlington's boss spat: 'It's a man's game, not a sport for tarts.' Not so true today, perhaps.

Willie has retired happily and owns the Bramcote Manor pub on the outskirts of Nottingham. Remove the generous padding around the chin and the flecks of grey hair, and you can still visualise him terrorising '70s attackers. Nowadays, though, he is more interested in improving his golf handicap and carving Sunday roasts than scrapping with opposition strikers. He still finds the time to follow Arsenal's progress and particularly enjoys watching Dennis Bergkamp parade his skills. How would he have coped with facing the Dutchman in a game, I ask? 'God only knows,' he chuckles. 'I'd have used my "subtle" talents to put him off, I suppose.' Willie doesn't see too many of his old football chums, and, to date, neither Peter Nicholas nor Brian Clough – wisely – have popped in for a pint. Former manager Terry Neill still talks of Young's presence 'enriching' Arsenal. None of those Gunners fans who were party to Willie's unique persona during his stay at Highbury would disagree.

TEN

A Song and a Dance

People reckoned I spent all my time in Stringfellow's, but
I never went there that much. I preferred Tramp.
                              Charlie Nicholas, speaking in 1995

George Graham knew he was not assuming the command of a
happy ship when he arrived at Highbury in June 1986. The star
players Terry Neill and Don Howe had assembled at great cost
over the last three years had long since lost their sparkle. Despite
the glittery surface, the club was sinking fast, overburdened, as
George saw it, by a collection of prima donnas who were
unwilling to steer the ship in the right direction. The root cause
of the club's failure to win a trophy for seven years was, according
to observers, the demon drink. That, and the cancerous growth of
cliques at Highbury. The Arsenal drinking club was the most
notorious establishment in London, featuring giants such as
Woodcock, Sansom, Mariner and Nicholas. In journalistic circles,
the group was often referred to as the 'song and dance' brigade.
Whether or not all of these figures deserved their hell-raising
reputations is debatable, but to George, such minor details were
irrelevant. He had to change the spirit of the club, and fast.
Arsenal's other alleged problems, such as large debts, would be
eradicated by his prudent buying/selling policy. But destroying
the cliques would be the first real test of Graham's management
skills. The facts, however, were that these factions had become
engrained over the pevious three years and Arsenal's principal

'wide boy', Charlie Nicholas, just happened to be the crowd favourite.

The fanfare which had accompanied Nicholas's march south in August 1983 rivalled that which greeted the original Bonnie Prince Charlie some 300 years earlier. Here was the Messiah who would take Arsenal into the promised land, the dream player who would drive away the nightmares of Lee Chapman (laughably labelled 'Boy Wonder' when he arrived from Stoke a year earlier for £500,000) and Charlie's namesake, Peter. The vibe surrounding Charlie was sensational. Celtic manager, Billy McNeill, described him as 'the most exciting player I've ever seen', after Charlie plundered 52 goals in a season for the Glasgow club. Widely regarded as the best player to emerge from Scotland since Kenny Dalglish, Charlie had opted to sign, not for Liverpool, the dominant force in '80s football, nor moneybags Manchester United, but for the slumbering Arsenal. It was impossible to ignore the overwhelming feeling of optimism that surrounded his arrival. These, after all, were the regressive '80s and stories of pit closures, rocketing unemployment figures, and Thatcher's killer handbag remained at the forefront of press headlines. Football clubs were feeling the pinch, even the mighty Arsenal. Shortly before Charlie arrived it was announced that, due to 'severe financial constraints', free Christmas turkeys would not be distributed to players and staff that year. Charlie's brash entrance would reaffirm Arsenal as a major power; the 'Bank of England' club was open for business once again. In true '80s style, we could all stand up and shout 'Here We Go' at top volume. At least, that was the plan.

His reputation for 'larging it' around Glasgow was legion. Charlie knocked around with several teammates, dubbed the 'rat pack', and once commented: 'See four, five, six pints. That, to me, isn't a real drink.' Part of the Saturday night ritual was also indulging in a spot of horizontal training after leaving the nightclub in the early hours. Charlie admitted that by 21 he'd lost count of the number of women he'd slept with. Despite his heroics for Celtic, not everyone approved of his rabble-rousing. It was almost unheard of for footballers of that era to dance 'to the ear-splitting din of Kajagoogoo and the Thompson Twins,' wrote a Glaswegian journalist. On top of that, Nicholas had already been convicted for drink driving in early 1983. After knocking back a few cocktails, his ability to judge distances and drive in a straight line was somewhat diminished. Half of the Glasgow constabulary queued up behind him as his Vauxhall Chevette veered across the road, clipping the kerb on several occasions. Horror of horrors, Charlie also had an agent, a former bankrupt named Bev Walker. Walker reckoned that Charlie would be a millionaire within five years and, in order to maximise his commercial potential, encouraged him to develop links with music and fashion, and endorse anything and everything, it seemed. Here were the first palpable signs of his trailblazing tendencies, merging football with showbiz. Somewhat prophetically, Terry Neill commented at the time that in terms of commercial potential, Nicholas was ten years ahead of his time. He advertised fitted kitchens, sleeveless tank tops, leather trousers, Burton's gear . . . whatever. Once he'd dispensed with his New Wave wedge haircut, he decided to grow his fringe and his hair at the back, and modelled himself on U2's Bono. Listening to 'We Will Follow' became his pre-match gee-up. At last, a footballer had broken out of the Eagles, Dire Straits and ELO straitjacket.

For the tabloids, Charlie couldn't have timed his arrival in London better. He signed for Arsenal dressed in what can only be described as a leather catsuit, clutching an Italian custom-made handbag. Had Arsenal signed Emma Peel from *The Avengers* or Scottish football's hottest property? As he cruised into town, many secretly wished he'd fail. Nicholas recalls: 'To some people, especially journalists, I seemed a cocky so and so. You have to accept that some people wanted to cut you down to size. That's life. That's journalists!' The *Daily Mail* warned Charlie about the lure of the 'bright lights' and the perils that awaited him in the capital. 'Champagne Charlie', now on a staggering £2,000 per week (a mouth-watering sum for most of us even now), could enjoy the delights of upwardly mobile London, awash with new money, yuppies with mobile telephones the size of house bricks, and Arfur Daley types, ever ready to exploit footballers' marketing potential through personal appearances at Tramp and Stringfellow's. Although they were slapped down, the doubters were already comparing him with another young Scot whom Arsenal had signed in the late '60s – Peter Marinello.

Marinello had arrived from Hibernian in a blaze of glory for £100,000, and scored a great goal on his debut at Old Trafford in April 1969 – George Best's manor. It was probably the worst thing the young Scot could have done. It had been 16 years since Arsenal had won a trophy. This new kid was expected to be the man to deliver. Crushed by media expectation, 'London's George Best' went rapidly downhill and quickly drowned in a sea of bad modelling shots, dodgy newspaper columns and mediocre performances. Marinello was immediately devoured by hangers-on. Photographer Terry O'Neill later recalled 'feeling terribly sorry for the young man. He looked totally out of his depth'. Still, Marinello did at least get to appear with Pan's People on *Top of the Pops*. Like Nicholas, Marinello's musical tastes did not adhere to the stereotypes of that era. Citing Chicago and Spooky Tooth as his favourite bands, Marinello, in the 1971 *Fab 208* annual, commented that he liked 'hard swinging music, particularly in the underground style'. Tellingly, he also admitted to spending 'rather too much on clothes, but I believe that a footballer at the top level should dress well, as does a singer or an actor'. Indeed, he was linked with a cameo role in a low-budget horror flick. Like many things in Marinello's brief Arsenal career, it never came off.

Never able to establish himself in the first team, he drifted away from Highbury three years later. Bertie Mee referred darkly to the 'bad habits' he'd picked up in Scottish football (namely – 'a flashy temper on the pitch' and a 'tendency to let his head drop if things don't go well') and Marinello was embittered by the way in which 'friends' turned their backs on him when he faded from Arsenal's first team. 'I won't be making his mistakes. He was 19, I'm 21,' Charlie said defiantly when reminded of Marinello's disappointing spell at Highbury. Yet within a matter of weeks, he was penning his own naff *Sun* column and modelling all-white leather suits for the Top Man autumn collection, and was snapped up by Burton's for their new catalogue. 'It all got out of control,' Charlie recalls. 'I did too much, too soon, I suppose. The press saw to it that the ghost of Peter Marinello reappeared, but I didn't really help myself. Some of those leather suits I modelled make my toes curl when I see them now. I'm sure my family will never stop reminding me of them!' Groundhog Day was here and Charlie had not yet kicked a ball for the club, or had a chance to gel with his new teammates.

Though Charlie's arrival is often blamed for turning Highbury into a home for 'roaring boys', the club was headed in that direction anyway. In the 1982–83 season, Arsenal lost two cup semi-finals to Manchester United, and all observers agreed that a soft centre and an occasional lack of passion let the club down. Booze was perceived as being the main cause of the problem, something which Tony Woodcock later hinted at in his book *Inside Soccer*. Woodcock claimed that Peter Stringfellow, whose mullet was actually in fashion during that era, was only too keen to welcome Arsenal players to his club, on any night of the week. As was common with many '80s players, team-building activities included downing the odd pint or eight. The problem was that these 'bonding sessions' were occurring three times per week.

Of all the 'song and dance' brigade, it was Tony Woodcock who disappointed the most. One could be forgiven for believing, at times, that he came to London from FC Cologne in 1982 to wind down his career and party, after having won medals elsewhere. Woodcock never enjoyed a great relationship with fans, or some of his teammates. His displays could be horribly diffident as well as dazzling, and his barbed criticism of various Arsenal players' mates in his autobiography further undermined his position. It is believed that he led the faction that eventually persuaded Terry Neill to strip the captaincy from David O'Leary. Time would show that Woodcock often felt the need to speak out about team affairs. With his talent, he should have become a Highbury legend, but instead the number of alleged sightings of him in various London night spots would make even Charlie Nicholas appear like he had an extreme case of agoraphobia.

Rightly or wrongly, the public perception of Arsenal as Charlie arrived was of a team being torn apart by warring tribes. Stewart Robson, tellingly, refers to himself, Pat Jennings, David O'Leary and Brian Talbot as 'the professional lot'. Then there were the other 'young lads, like Paul Davis, Chris Whyte and Raph Meade, who tended to socialise together', and 'then there were the other guys'. The different factions got on up to a point, but in reality 'didn't gel very well'. At the Holiday Inn in Plymouth, Kenny Sansom and Alan Sunderland squared up to each other. Though the *News of the World* later suggested that Sansom had planted a couple of haymakers on Sunderland's jaw, the boozy argument did not get beyond the pushing and shoving phase. But the incident did demonstrate to Terry Neill the depth of the problem in the dressing-room, particularly when the paper also referred to Sunderland and Sansom as 'problem boys'. Neill realised immediately: 'I had to get rid of Sunderland.'

By 1983, the frizzy-haired Sunderland's career was heading off the rails. Although Arsenal fans remained forever in his debt, after his winner in the 1979 FA Cup final, his on-pitch displays, like Woodcock's, were worryingly inconsistent. Sunderland could raise himself for the big occasions, but games against the likes of Birmingham or Notts County appeared not to interest him. Neill was often concerned by the player's lacklustre approach to training and his growing bitterness as a player. Perhaps this was due to the fact that whilst Kevin Reeves and Brian Stein won England caps, the sublimely gifted Sunderland won none. The Holiday Inn incident with Sansom had been a long time coming. The sharpest of dressing-room wits, Sunderland was able to cut to the quick with a sarcastic aside. As a result, he ostracised himself from many of the other players. Terry Neill later commented: 'He was not a particularly popular player towards the end of his career with us.' Most infamously, Sunderland was dogged by tragedy off the pitch. In 1980, he'd been involved in a car accident that killed two people. Though he was found not guilty of driving without due care and attention, opposition fans frequently reminded him of the incident. Stewart Robson recalls his own debut against West Ham in 1981: 'There were 30,000 at

Upton Park. The thing I remember most from the game was that every time Alan Sunderland got the ball, their fans screamed "MURDERER" at him. I suppose he got used to that type of treatment, but underneath I wonder how he really felt.'

Left-back Kenny Sansom's immaculate displays meant he could never be accused of not pulling his weight. A £1 million signing from Crystal Palace, Sansom enjoyed his ale, but money problems beset him during his Highbury career. Upon his arrival, Terry Neill commented that Sansom had 'inflated expectations of what a million-pound footballer earns'. He was also concerned when Sansom, who lived just around the corner from Arsenal's London Colney training ground, bought himself a flashy Jag. 'He probably didn't even get it out of second gear. In his position he'd have been better off getting himself a push bike,' his manager later said. Gambling was Sansom's real vice. In a *Gooner* interview several years later he claimed his problems 'were exaggerated', but later contradicted himself in *Proud To Say That Name* by admitting that money worries occasionally took the edge off his game. It was all too much for Terry Neill, who was extremely uncomfortable with the large amounts of cash '80s stars earned. He said: 'These days we judge success by the size of someone's house, or car, or which parties they go to. That's fame, not success. Success is about self-worth, being professional and, in football terms, winning things.' He concluded by saying: 'Many people don't seem to realise there is a difference between those two things.' It was certainly a concept which the 'song and dance' brigade struggled to grasp.

Charlie Nicholas made his long-awaited Arsenal debut against Luton on 27 August 1983. The collective hysteria from Gunners fans that greeted his every move in that opening game would have given Duran Duran fans a run for their money. Ironically, on *Football Focus* earlier that day, an action sequence of him was backed by Duran Duran's 'The Reflex' with obligatory camera shutters clicking throughout. This was how life would be over the next four years. Charlie played quite well on his debut, Arsenal winning 2–1, and, three days later, scored twice at Wolves in another 2–1 win. Arsenal, for what it was worth, were top for the first time in a decade and the media frenzy grew apace.

Like Charlie George before him, the Scot was already becoming a creature of myth. The club decided that on his debut the Arsenal players should run on individually in an American football-type experiment, to herald the dawning of a bright new era. This was not the Arsenal way of doing things and the earth-shattering cheers which greeted Charlie when he emerged suggested that he was a bigger 'star' than his teammates. Several members of the crowd had a slight problem with that. This was Arsenal, not Spurs, where signing the occasional crowd-pleaser has been a method used to silence disgruntled, trophy-starved supporters. Though it was believed that Charlie lapped up the attention, he was acutely embarrassed. 'I just wanted to be part of the team,' he later told me. Another example of Charlie's uneasiness with some of the attention is shown when he recalls: 'Blokes of twice my age would come up to me and say: "Look, I've got my haircut just like yours." I found that a bit freaky, to be honest. Later, when people like Chris Waddle had the back perm done, I thought, "Christ, I've spent years trying to get out of all that!"'

It was all too easy to misrepresent Charlie during his four years in London, as had been the case at Celtic. The tabloids had mistakenly portrayed him as a rabid Catholic, due to his enjoyment of scoring hatfuls of goals against Rangers. Actually, Charlie hailed from a mixed religious background, socialised with Catholics and Protestants, and in questionnaires claimed to despise bigotry in all its forms. For a player who was often perceived as a big-headed poseur, his copious amounts of charity work with local schools and hospitals proved otherwise.

Yet for a man who claims, 'I was often lonely in London – most Saturday nights I'd stay in with a video and a bottle of wine,' Charlie had an unfortunate habit of being caught out at regular intervals by the ubiquitous paparazzi. Each time he boogied to A Flock Of Seagulls in his custom-made Italian shoes, a *Sun* snapper was there, it seemed. Charlie was even happy to whip off his top when asked. The fact that both of his nipples were still intact was a minor miracle, given the 'filing' affect of those tight nylon Umbro kits of his era. Charlie confesses, with a wicked chuckle, that a 'combination of elastoplast and Vaseline kept them alive'. A journalist claimed, in classic '80s mode, to have 'sipped Bucks Fizz with Charlie, who was dressed in a white leather suit, with Wham playing in the background'. Then, a photographer from the *News of the World* spotted him leaving Tramp at 2 a.m. with Suzanne Dando, the aesthetically pleasing gymnast-cum-TV presenter. Nothing wrong with that, but by now, Arsenal's form had slumped and Charlie's hectic social life was seen as the cause.

It was the Milk Cup that fully emphasised the 'song and dance' brigade's maddening inconsistencies. At Spurs, Charlie showed his penchant for the big occasion by netting the first in a monumental 2–1 win. Good news indeed, especially as Spurs, who'd won the FA Cup and inflicted Chas 'n' Dave records on the nation, had become top dogs in London over the last two years. Two weeks later, the team, in Terry Neill's words, performed like a 'bunch of pantomime horses' against Walsall at Highbury and crashed out of the competition. The Gunners, Nicholas and Woodcock especially, were awful, and a mass demonstration gathered outside the dressing-rooms to chant 'Neill out'. Nicholas had now scored just three goals in three months for Arsenal. Off the pitch, though, he continued to have few worries in the scoring stakes. He'd had a fling with Cadbury's Flake girl Janis Lee Burns. Charlie said of her: 'I just call her the Flake and if you'll pardon the pun, she's very tasty.' By now, Terry Neill was at the end of his tether with several other members of his team.

More tabloid exposés further undermined Neill's grip at the club. After a particularly inept 0–3 reverse at Leicester, Tony Woodcock publicly admonished David O'Leary for not 'taking responsibility in the team'. He reiterated that fact in his autobiography, published a few months later, in which he claimed O'Leary was a poor example to youngsters and that, far too often, Stewart Robson displayed 'a headless chicken' approach during games. It was not exactly conducive to a pleasant dressing-room atmosphere. A *Sunday Express* article then alleged that Arsenal's card-school sharks were gambling away their £1,500 per week wages on the team bus to away games. The author of the article, Anthony Holden, was later accused of making defamatory comments, as the maximum win/loss, apparently, was £10. Conventional wisdom held there was no smoke without fire. Just as a calm and rational approach was needed, the usually taciturn Peter Hill-Wood went public in the *Daily Mail* and accused 'the stars' of not trying. As the players continued to squabble and bicker among themselves, the public perception of Arsenal as a team stuffed with hedonistic prima donnas appeared to be confirmed. Unsurprisingly, in early December, poor Terry Neill was fired.

Nine months later, new manager Don Howe appeared to have healed the rift and turned Arsenal into renaissance artists. The boys ended the 1983–84 season in great style, losing just one game after Christmas. After an epic 3–2 win over Spurs, *The Times* described Arsenal as 'the home of fine arts'. At the start of 1984–85, Don Howe shifted Nicholas into a withdrawn role behind the front two and partnered Tony Woodcock with new signing Paul Mariner up front. To many, this was a clear admission that Charlie simply could not cut it in an orthodox striker's role. The arrival from Ipswich of the craggy Mariner, with Alan Sunderland making the reverse trip, meant that the Gunners had finally landed the target man they'd craved for so long.

Full-back Viv Anderson joined Arsenal in August from Nottingham Forest, increasing the number of full internationals at the club to ten. Many journalists believed that this would be Arsenal's year, and with devastating wins over Newcastle (2–0), Watford (4–3), Sunderland (3–2), Leicester (4–1) and Liverpool (3–1), Arsenal roared to the summit by the end of September. In front of an enormous 50,000 crowd, reigning champions Liverpool were played off the pitch. Charlie Nicholas's high-octane performances in those games suggested that, finally, he was justifying the hype. At last, he appeared to be getting his social and professional life in equilibrium.

Publicly, he remained much in demand, and it was rumoured that he'd asked punk heiress Clara Willan for a massive £4,000 just for the privilege of taking her out for dinner and to a nightclub. His new agent Frank Boyd denied that it was such an exorbitant fee, though he did comment that Charlie was 'in a high tax bracket'. Later, Boyd claimed the whole saga was down to tabloid rumour, but Charlie was informed that his agent would not be welcome at Highbury any more. Nicholas proved there was another side to him, becoming a sought-after interviewee for right-on music magazines like *New Musical Express*. He talked eloquently about the emergence of young Scottish groups like Orange Juice and the Cocteau Twins, and the rapid rise and fall of the punk phenomenon. With his back perm swaying in the breeze, designer stubble à la George Michael and 'serious music conversations' with The Alarm's Mike Peters, Charlie, in a distinctly '80s way, was the coolest footballer in Britain. Yet still, the 'Marinello millstone', as Nicholas puts it, was not lifted by tabloid editors. It is true to say that the pair's responses to questionnaires were uncannily similar. Nicholas's favourite food/drink combination had always been meat/lager. Marinello's, as told to the *Fab 208* annual, was 'massive steaks with all the trimmings. Perhaps a glass of beer.'

Arsenal's loftier ambitions and Charlie's excellent run of form couldn't last, of course. Nicholas blew his own cover, with a little help from his friends. He accepted an estimated £10,000 from the *News of the World* to sell a story entitled 'BIRDS, BOOZE AND ME'. Surprisingly, he said little about the former, but in regard to boozing, he claimed: 'The most I'll have is seven or eight pints of lager. To me, that isn't getting drunk.' Oddly, he claimed to have dumped Suzanne Dando because she enjoyed getting her photograph in the tabloids, not something to which Charlie himself was averse. A fortnight later, a frankly exhausted Therese Bazar (of Dollar fame), kissed and told in the same tabloid, confirming that Charlie and she had a fling when he'd first arrived at Highbury. The blonde bombshell, famous for singing 'O L'amour' with fellow Dollar co-star David Van Day, said: 'We talked about football but all he wanted to talk about was sex. I hear he's not been scoring many goals recently . . . But I can tell you he certainly scored a hat-trick with me that night.'

A catalogue of booze-fuelled stories then made the headlines, coinciding with Arsenal's slide from first to seventh place in the table. Nicholas, naturally, went further than anyone else. For the second time in four years, he'd been charged with drink driving. Charlie, who'd 'been enjoying a friend's hospitality' (according to his defence), drove home and, attempting to disguise the fact he was pissed, decided to drive at a steady 10 mph along a main road, zigzagging the car as he did so. For his pains, prosecutor Alistair McSporran (the gallery was in fits of laughter about his name) banned him for three years. Within a month, Graham Rix, Tony Woodcock and Viv Anderson were also up on drink-driving charges. After they too were banned, the joke went that Arsenal were now the most environmentally friendly club in football, as most of the players were forced to squeeze into a single taxi to get to training.

Don Howe's latest signing, Steve Williams, hardly improved the ambience. The abrasive Williams, who surely holds the record for shouting 'Fuck off!' most times during football matches, went public and criticised his new manager after he was only a substitute in his opening game against Spurs on New Year's Day. He says: 'I liked Don Howe as a bloke, I really did. But to me, it seemed like he often didn't have a clue. For that Spurs game, all my family were there and yet I didn't get onto the pitch until the 80th minute. I was really pissed off about that, and I told him so.' When I suggested to Williams that maybe he could have been rather more tactful with his new boss, he said: 'Well, I've always spoken my mind. And Arsenal had always been my club. But within five minutes of signing, I could see exactly why they hadn't won anything for bloody years. The morale was low and the attitude of many of the players all wrong. It was clear to me that Don Howe wasn't the man to turn the place around.' Though the rumours that he later had a punch-up with Charlie Nicholas aren't true, Williams' nadir and, for that matter, the 'song and dance' brigade's, had almost arrived.

The humiliating FA Cup defeat at York in February 1985, when Arsenal lost after a passionless display, was the club's '80s low point. It had been Williams who'd given away the penalty after pulling York's Houchen back, but Woodcock and Nicholas, in particular, didn't appear to fancy their luck against a bunch of Third Division roughnecks. As Stewart Robson later commented: 'We looked so dozy that day. The performance was a disgrace.

Some players just weren't interested.' Robson and Williams blame each other for the ills which blighted Arsenal during the latter half of that season. Robson comments: 'When Williams arrived, we had to shift the midfield around. He disrupted the balance of the side.' Williams counters by claiming: 'I told Don Howe and George Graham that the boy couldn't play. And he was supposed to be England's next big thing in midfield. What a joke!' Another ex-player, who wishes to remain anonymous, commented: 'At the time of the York defeat, there were high-profile players who rolled up to training smelling of booze. London Colney stank like a brewery at times. We all heard the stories going around at the time – wife swapping, cocaine abuse and a certain England striker kipping in his car after his missus threw him out. Most of these stories were totally untrue, but there was an element of truth in the car story! No wonder those giant-killings took place, with so many off-pitch distractions.'

From Charlie's point of view, the arrival of Don Howe's choice of first-team coach, the respected John Cartwright, put a massive black cloud over his head. Cartwright's no-nonsense, bull-in-a-china-shop philosophy signalled the beginning of the end for him and his cronies. Cartwright, renowned as a 'thinker', insisted on channelled passes and balls hit quickly into the penalty area. This game was totally alien to many of the stars, to whom JC took an instant dislike. 'Do you think this stands for Jesus Christ?' he asked Charlie Nicholas on the first day of pre-season training, pointing to the initials on his tracksuit. Cartwright and Howe introduced piecemeal changes, gradually phasing in the likes of David Rocastle, Martin Hayes and Niall Quinn over the winter of 1985. It became clear that many of Arsenal's yesterday men were getting a distinctly phased-out feeling.

They reacted in different ways to this slight. Steve Williams, who lost his place, on occasions, to Rocastle, admits to calling the coach 'a bastard – and much worse on several occasions'. Kenny Sansom, who was criticised by JC for not tackling hard enough, told him exactly what he thought of him 'after having one over the eight'. Tony Woodcock was certainly unhappy about losing his place to Niall Quinn and complained about his treatment by the club. Even the normally polite Charlie Nicholas claims to have learned 'bugger all' from Cartwright. One could argue that the stars got their revenge on Cartwright by repeatedly going to David Dein and criticising JC's training techniques. Paul Davis and Stewart Robson, both of whom continue to speak highly of Cartwright, confirm this was true. The stars received a sympathetic ear, particularly as Arsenal had endured yet another season treading water, finishing in seventh place. Dein and co. once again called for Terry Venables, but Tel apparently didn't like the way the club went behind Howe's back and declined the offer. After this piece of skulduggery by the board, Howe and Cartwright resigned. The 'song and dance' brigade appeared to have won the power struggle, but they'd already danced their last waltz.

They had achieved a pyrrhic victory. After failing to capture fellow cavalier Terry Venables, who would surely have put a sympathetic arm around Nicholas's shoulder, the board appointed his opposite as manager. George Graham, a Scottish Oliver Cromwell, was ready to sweep away Charlie and his pals. If Cartwright didn't quite have the clout to push through reforms, the new manager most certainly did. George marched into the club, looking every inch the zealous Puritan. With scalpel in hand, he was ready to cut away the twin cancers of sloth and complacency which were undermining the club. As well as getting rid of the smell of booze, he moved to try and fumigate the stench of decay as well. Within a week, Woodcock and Mariner, two of Arsenal's highest earners, were gone. Of the two, Woodcock hoped that George might award him a new contract. Graham didn't even bother to say hello to the player, let alone wish him bon voyage. In a vicious parting shot at Woodcock, who joined Cologne, Graham said: 'From now on, players will have to earn the right to play for Arsenal.'

George spent the rest of his early days at Highbury marking the surviving members' cards and dishing out verbal warnings. Few would have guessed that within 12 months, virtually all of the '80s crew would be expelled. One by one, the wide boys were hauled into the office and given the 'George' treatment. Kenny Sansom, a former teammate of Graham's at Crystal Palace, was informed that, from now on, he was to call Graham 'boss' rather than the more informal 'George'. Steve Williams was told to let his left foot do the talking, rather than his mouth and, naturally, Charlie Nicholas was given the biggest lecture of all. In the long term, he never stood much of a chance under Graham. Early publicity shots showed the fellow Scots grinning uneasily at the camera, with their arms around each other's shoulders. It was hardly a marriage made in heaven.

Charlie's discomfort was due to the fact that Graham knew all about his off-field excesses, because when he was Millwall manager he often joined the Arsenal players for a post-match pint. Nicholas remembers: 'One of our favourite watering holes was the Orange Tree at Totteridge. George often joined us for a drink. To be honest, he wasn't a great talker, there was a distance between us because he was a manager and we were players. But he listened carefully to what we said. He'd have heard about our social lives and what we thought of teammates. So he had, if you like, insider knowledge, before he got to be Arsenal boss. When he was appointed manager, I thought, "Oh Christ, I'm in trouble here", because he had this reputation of being tough on players who stepped out of line and he'd always told me that I'd made a big mistake joining Arsenal. It didn't fill me with confidence.'

During their first meeting, George accused him of wasting his precious talents through an over-demanding social life. On match days, George informed him, earrings were out and club blazers were in. Ominously for Nicholas, a mischievous barman had already posted a video to George, showing Charlie (caught on CCTV at 3 a.m.) cavorting in a nightclub with a 'busty, bubbly, blonde beauty', in the *Sun*'s words. Apparently, this took place just two days before the players were due to report back for George's first pre-season training session. Yet again, Charlie had demonstrated his knack for getting caught out at the wrong time. The incident led Graham to comment: 'London is a big place. It's easy for players to hide and not let us keep track of them.' That's unless you have a highly effective spy network in operation, of course. Nicholas also infuriated his new manager by becoming embroiled in a court case. Two years earlier, Charlie and friends had been holidaying in '80s-footballer's paradise, Ibiza's San Antonio. Nicholas had pinched a chip from student Lori

McElroy, at which point he was told to 'sod off' by the girl and her boyfriend. Charlie was then accused of having punched Lori and, along with his friends, attacking her boyfriend. Admittedly, this was out of character, as central defenders who'd nicknamed him 'Shirley' will testify, but judge Dennis McDonnell told him there were 'no excuses for his behaviour'. The judge argued that 'he had not been fully in control of himself' (about ten pints out of control, apparently) and that Christopher Brown of Brixton, who insisted it was he who had hit Lori McElroy, had told 'a pack of transparent lies'. Brown, who was unemployed, denied that he had been 'set up to take the rap for the footballers'. Nicholas was ordered to pay Ms McElroy £1,300 in damages.

George claimed that Charlie would get his chance in the first team, but he hardly fitted the image his new boss had for the club. At least his three-year drink-driving ban was lifted and, much to Graham's annoyance, Charlie arranged to pick up his custom-built Porsche on the very same day. His seething manager, desperate to destroy Arsenal's image as a club populated by Flash Harrys, spat: 'One day, this will be my Arsenal.' But axing the crowd favourite so early in his reign wouldn't be a good political move. He would have to bide his time.

Graham's first season was topped by winning the Littlewoods Cup final against Liverpool. It was the day when Charlie was finally crowned king, for 24 hours, at least. His two goals, both poacher's strikes, combined with his full repertoire of flicks and shimmies, lit up Wembley. But Graham wasn't taken in by the 'CHARLIE IS OUR DARLING' headlines. He'd seen what the team could do without Nicholas back in the autumn of 1986 when a leg injury had ruled him out for six weeks. Arsenal had roared to the top of the league. As Charlie commented: 'George knew, and I knew, that the team was moving in the right direction, with or without me in the side.' Even after the Wembley triumph, in which Sansom, Anderson and Williams played starring roles, things still didn't run smoothly for Nicholas. A tabloid headline appeared in *The Sun*, challenging Graham to 'SELL ME IF YOU DARE'. Charlie maintains: 'I wouldn't be stupid enough to say something like that,' but Graham never reacted too kindly to such boasts.

Over the next 12 months, the team was finally purged of the wide boys. The writing was on the wall for Kenny Sansom after the arrival of left-back Nigel Winterburn. During the 1987–88 season, Sansom publicly confessed to feeling 'betrayed', and later admitted to spending the season amidst the debris of 'empty bottles and shattered dreams'. Viv Anderson was allowed to 'fall out of contract' and joined Manchester United. Steve Williams was also disposed of by George. His foul-mouthed tirades, especially towards Ossie Ardiles, were still reassuringly regular, but George decided that the youthful exuberance of Mickey Thomas couldn't be held back any longer.

A three-match barren spell at the start of the 1987–88 season meant that Graham finally bit the bullet and axed Charlie Nicholas from the team for good. George later commented in his book *The Glory and The Grief* that Charlie had been 'a fool to himself' during his stay at Highbury. The symbolic axing of the Bonnie Prince made Arsenal fans realise it was time to revert to traditional Arsenal values of hard work, grit, professionalism and the eagerness of youth-team graduates. As if to further reinforce the point, George forced him to spend the final few months of his Highbury career in unhappy exile, banned from going anywhere near the first team. The smile had finally been wiped off happy-go-lucky Charlie's face. Coincidentally, the stock market's infamous crash on 'Black Thursday' in late 1987 ended the short-lived over-confidence and flashiness of yuppie London. The parallels between Nicholas's departure to Aberdeen and 'Black Thursday' certainly weren't lost on Arsenal fanzine writers at the time. Bust followed boom, as ever.

For all his faults, Charlie remains an all-time Highbury favourite, because his occasional sorcery on the pitch was a saving grace during Arsenal's fallow period in the mid-'80s. Many would claim, with justification, that along with several teammates, he never did himself justice. Tony Adams, in *Addicted*, claimed he'd 'lost respect' for Nicholas by the end because he wasn't giving his all for the cause. The player himself comments: 'I don't regret anything. I'm certainly not embarrassed to say that I enjoyed life in London. And I enjoyed my Arsenal career. In today's game, our lifestyle wouldn't be tolerated. It's a case of different time, different standards. The way most players looked after themselves was changing by the time I left Highbury. New diets, less booze. I was brought up with the previous generation of players, where drinking was part of club culture.'

So perhaps we shouldn't be too disapproving of the 'song and dance' brigade. After all, they were simply products of their era, having a ball in the boom-time London. In later life, the vast majority have settled down. Tony Woodcock is a respected football coach in Germany, Alan Sunderland in Cyprus, and Steve Williams owned a successful publishing business before selling it for a multi-million-pound sum. Kenny Sansom has maintained his reputation as something of a 'ducker and diver'. In 1998, he admitted he was bankrupt after piling up huge gambling debts. In order to offset his problems, he continued to play for different clubs into his 40s, winding up his career at Chertsey Town. There was light at the end of the tunnel, however. A big win on the National Lottery, and regular TV and radio work, means he's back on his feet. Charlie too has carved out a niche as a successful Sky TV pundit and businessman.

He's often asked for his opinions on radio football phone-ins. Recently, on Five Live, he commented wistfully: 'What I wouldn't give now to have played under Wenger for a season. I'm sure he'd have given me more belief in my ability than the manager I had at the end of my Arsenal career.' The former 'wild man' is happily married with two daughters and owns Café Cini in Glasgow. Times change – except for Nicholas's refreshing honesty and openness with this particular Arsenal fan. Overall, though, the club's policy of buying 'stars' was a disastrous '80s fad, like flecked jeans, Clive Sinclair's C5 and Stan Boardman's jokes. Charlie was a groundbreaker off the pitch at least, proving that football and showbiz could be combined. It is a marriage that seems set to last. After Nicholas had gone, George Graham promised that without the prima donnas, Arsenal would be making back-page headlines only. He certainly got that prediction spectacularly wrong.

ELEVEN

The Myth of King George

> I remember George, he was a bit of a poseur at first, a bit
> lazy ... Different now. He has poseurs for breakfast.
>
> Frank McLintock, speaking in 1992

> I would not like to play for him again. I have told him
> that, but I think he thinks I'm joking.
>
> Tony Adams, 1999

'He was many things to many people,' says Anders Limpar of
Arsenal's ex-manager George Graham. To Nick Hornby, George,
the immaculately dressed, dapper Scot, reminded him greatly of
his father. To many Arsenal fans, Graham was the saviour who
brought six trophies to Highbury during his eight-year tenure,
and for Limpar, and many of his teammates, he was a dictatorial
figure whom they nicknamed 'Gadaffi' – or worse, in Anders'
case. For the two disconsolate Sheffield Wednesday fans I
happened to get stuck behind in the queue for Arsenal Tube
station some ten years ago, he represented something else
altogether.

Their team had just lost 1–0 to Arsenal in a dreadful game.
Wednesday supporters spent much of the second half chanting:
'You'll never beat Des Walker.' In the 90th minute, Ian Wright
did just that, bagging Arsenal's last-minute winner. After
claiming that the Gunners were 'lucky' and 'boring' (it was hard
to disagree with them on that occasion), they went on to talk

about George. 'He's so bloody miserable,' one of them said. 'Yeah, he reminds me of Norman fucking Tebbit,' the other responded. Ironically, it wasn't the first time I'd heard George compared with the dour former Conservative party chairman. In the late '80s and early '90s, if one wished to be successful, it helped if you were ruthless, unsentimental and hard. George Graham was most certainly a man of his time. As John Lukic said: 'I wouldn't say he was ruthlessly professional, he was professionally ruthless.'

Analogies between George and Conservative Party members don't end there. When George became Arsenal boss in 1986, he sounded as pious as had Margaret Thatcher on the steps of Number Ten when she first became Prime Minister. Thatcher recited a poem by St Francis of Assisi, promising to 'bring hope where there has been despair'. George claimed, in holier-than-thou fashion: 'In society, standards are falling . . . I'm gonna try to make sure that's not one of Arsenal's problems.' By 1995, in the manner of disgraced Tory MPs like David Mellor and Neil Hamilton, George was also washed away on a tide of sleaze. Arsenal's white knight had been tainted, exposed as being less than honest. You half expected such stories to emerge about politicians, particularly as the media were always ready to expose scandal, but we didn't expect it from George, whom journalists had portrayed as pristine and perfect. Here was a man who was forever telling Ian Wright to 'watch your language', instructed players to wear the club tie and blazer to functions and before games, and deemed spiralling transfer fees as 'unethical and immoral'. We'd been fooled into believing that he was a paragon of virtue, but with hindsight, the evidence that he was hardly Saint George had been there for a long time.

On a boiling day at Wembley in 1971, George was involved in a 'sleight of foot' affair that made national headlines. Trailing 0–1 to Liverpool in the FA Cup final, Arsenal's John Radford hoisted a speculative overhead lob into the opposition area and Eddie Kelly nudged the ball gently towards Ray Clemence's goal. Graham ghosted in, swiped at the ball which crawled over the line and ran off, arm aloft, claiming the equaliser. Perhaps we'd always have believed that he'd scored that day, but for a reverse-angle TV replay which ITV broadcast on Sunday's *Big Match*. Presenter Jimmy Hill announced with glee that their rivals at the BBC were unaware of this particular 'case of mistaken identity'. TV was entering its high-tech phase and the replay proved conclusively that George made absolutely no contact with the ball. The goal was actually Eddie Kelly's.

In an interview several years later, shown on the *George Graham Story* video, he reiterated his belief that his 'shin had brushed the ball', before adding: 'Jimmy Hill has a lot to answer for.' For many years, he continued to stick rigidly to his story, despite all the evidence proving otherwise. On the day, it didn't hugely matter who scored Arsenal's equaliser and George deserved to win his man-of-the-match trophy anyway. But in 1995, when the 'Graham affair' was at its height, he once again stuck rigidly to his side of the story and denied he'd done anything wrong. Once again, George Graham was attempting to defend the indefensible. In a way, history had repeated itself, but on this occasion the fall-out shook Arsenal to its core.

His 1971 sleight of foot aside, George Graham the player had a reputation as a bit of a chancer: a 'geezer', in Talk Radio-speak. Like many players of his era, he'd always sought to supplement his wages through schemes outside football (a habit he obviously never lost). As a Chelsea player, he decided to expand his commercial potential by opening a tailoring business. Young George and his business partners, Terry Venables and Ron Harris, decided to name it 'Grateron', an unpleasant-sounding acronym formed through combining their names. The motley crew's business quickly folded. When your most famous client happens to be Norman Wisdom, you know there are problems. Graham's career at Chelsea reached the point of no return when George, together with Terry Venables and six others, broke manager Tommy Docherty's curfew and went boozing in Blackpool before an away match. One of the girls they met on their pub crawl was Pauline Monk, a Beatles-loving, bee-hived beauty, who confessed in the *Daily Mirror* to finding George 'charming'. To this day, Alan Hudson, a Chelsea apprentice at the time, remembers 'the exotic waft of expensive aftershave which the senior pros wore at the time. George was an immaculate dresser. He was the dressing-room style merchant. He looked like a cross between Cary Grant and Sean Connery.'

The Kings Road playboy ended up at Highbury in 1966. George's aristocratic, laid-back air meant he was given the nickname 'Stroller'. His neat dribbling technique and tendency to strut on the pitch also granted him the title of 'The Peacock' in some quarters. He was regarded as the vainest player of his generation. After he was kicked in the head during a game, he asked a teammate where the mark was. 'Above the hairline,' came the reply. 'Thank God for that, I'm going dancing tonight,' George is reported to have commented. His prodigious heading ability was a major asset, but he was regarded as one of Arsenal's slackest trainers and his unwillingness to track back in games was legendary. On one occasion, best pal Frank McLintock actually punched him because of George's apparent lack of effort. It is no exaggeration to say that George the player bore uncannily similar traits to Charlie Nicholas, even down to their Celtic heritage. Nicholas later commented: 'Ironic, but true. All the stranger when you consider how much George the manager disapproved of those kind of players. As a manager, he probably took the view, "Do as I say, not as I do." It's contradictory, I suppose, but that was George.' George, also aware of this contradiction, said simply: 'George Graham the manager would not pick George Graham the player in his team.'

Fifteen years or so after the 1971 Double triumph, the old stroller had miraculously transformed himself into a self-styled football dictator. The 'Ayatollah', as cowering Millwall and Arsenal players called their manager behind his back, was making his mark in football management. The laid-back product of the '60s quickly developed a clear understanding of the grim machinations of '80s football. He fitted in perfectly with the view that in order to succeed in football management during that era one had to be dour and Scottish. He'd begun to adopt his autocratic persona during a tough first managerial assignment at Millwall. In the mid-'80s, as Nena's '99 Red Balloons' topped the charts and filmmakers treated audiences to a spate of films about the nuclear holocaust, Millwall's rampaging fans did their utmost to turn several English grounds into an apocalyptic wasteland. Consequently, attendances at the Den nose-dived. On a shoestring budget, 'Iron George', who got this title due to his penchant for dishing out fines to misbehaving players, fostered a team spirit that was second to none. It was a trick he was to repeat in rather grander surroundings at Highbury. Old colleagues could hardly believe the extent of his metamorphosis. Don Howe later commented: 'If ever there was a player I felt definitely did not have what it took to be a coach, it was George Graham. Running a nightclub? Yes. A football club? Absolutely not.'

George swept through Arsenal football club in a manner similar to that of a swarm of locusts devouring a cornfield. With his sharp suits, business-like manner and crisply ironed shirts, he promised – Thatcher style – that anyone who did not concur with his vision for the new Arsenal would be destroyed. For want of a better phrase, he was a control freak. Just as Thatcher moved to crush the consensus-following wets, George steamrollered dissenters with ruthless efficiency. The Graham jackboot became as feared as Maggie's killer handbag in London N5. Charlie Nicholas recalls: 'Outside George's office, there was a row of chairs, and in his early days when he was manager, it always seemed to be full of anxious Arsenal stars who were concerned about their futures. When they were summoned by George, there was a few minutes calm, before the screaming and shouting started. It was always a sign that someone was out, or hadn't got the money they wanted. I remember that Paul Mariner's meeting lasted about ten seconds. Woodcock's was even shorter!'

Apart from getting stuck into the 'song and dance' brigade, he also got to work on two of Arsenal's brightest stars from the youth team: Martin Keown and Stewart Robson. Keown had broken into the team during the previous season and was regarded as the best central defensive prospect in the country. He crossed the Rubicon when he asked George for an extra £50 a week, in line with what other Under-21 starlets were earning at their clubs. George promptly sold Keown to Aston Villa for a pittance of

£100,000. His valuable services were lost to the club for six years, until George bought him back from Everton for £2.2 million. It was the first instance of George's ability to cut off his nose to spite his face. In his autobiography, he claimed it was essential that 'young Keown' was kept in line with the Highbury wage structure. Already the likes of Jimmy Greaves were able to crack jokes about 'tight-arsed' jocks. George had set a precedent that left him open to ridicule in the '90s.

Next to feel the full blast of George's wrath was Stewart Robson, already being touted as a future England captain. Graham confessed to finding Robbo 'deep' and 'intense', the kind of person with whom neither he nor his coaches could communicate. George also resented the influence of Robson's father, who believed that his son should remain in his favoured midfield berth rather than be moved around, which had happened under previous managers. He'd just been called into the England squad after five games for Graham's Arsenal, but already the injuries that would end his career were starting to affect him. Robson's version of events is as follows: 'I was in the England squad for the game in Sweden and there was a dinner for the players which I attended. In the end, I had to withdraw from the squad, as I'd done from every squad in the previous season. Then he began to question my loyalty to the club and my commitment. I said to him that was rubbish. I was a youth-team player who'd come up through the ranks. I loved the club and the fans knew I always gave of my best. And as for commitment, I said to him: "Well, you pissed off to Manchester United for more money when you were an Arsenal player." He didn't like that. He didn't like people who stood up to him. I got the feeling the end was near. He then accused me of putting country before club, something he often goes on about. When I had my hernia op and came out of hospital, he cold-shouldered me. You could tell I wasn't wanted any more. I didn't want to go to West Ham, but it was clear that George didn't want me at Arsenal.' In *The Glory And The Grief*, George pointed out, with some justification, that Robson's injuries would have made him a dead-weight within a few months. Yet once he'd bombed out Keown and Robson, the 'bully' tag never really left him.

Over the next two years, George's unpleasant habit of totally freezing out unwanted players was to be repeated with his treatment of Kenny Sansom and Charlie Nicholas, both of whom were classed as 'non-persons' by George, and obliging official club literature. In the Orwellian sense, they simply ceased to exist, stewing silently in the reserves before departing to Newcastle and Aberdeen respectively. Nicholas recalls: 'I was made to train with the reserves and the youth team. He made the decision to get rid of me, but I felt he was trying to humiliate me. He did the same to Kenny. Now we were tough minded, but we deserved better. He didn't need to be so unpleasant about the whole thing.' There was barely a murmur of protest from fans, because George's permafrost technique was a clear case of glorious ends justifying shitty means. After all, within a year of his appointment, Arsenal won a trophy and, two years later, the league title in 1989. Arsenal were rapidly on their way to regaining the 'most loathed team in the country' tag. The back four, led by Tony Adams and drilled to the point of overkill, perfected the art of springing the offside trap, and the likes of Thomas, Rocastle and Davis were forced to sacrifice flair and defend the back line with their lives. And there, on the touchline, stood dour George, mortal enemy of the beautiful game and master practitioner of percentage football, urging his troops to pinch a goal and lock out the opposition. At least, that was the popular perception.

To add fuel to the fire, George commented: 'I would rather win a game 1–0 than 5–2.' Even Arsenal fans would admit that watching the team wasn't always pretty, but the method was effective. The novelty of winning the title after an 18-year wait, and the sheer drama of Anfield 1989, silenced dissenting voices within the club, but not for much longer. After the 'treading water' season of 1989–90, when Arsenal finished a disappointing fourth in the league and crashed out of the cup in the early stages, George carried out another 'Night of the Long Knives' mini-purge of Highbury dissenters. Not all of them went quietly.

To confirm the often contradictory nature of the Graham regime, the first palpable signs of his losing the plot can be detected at the start of the 1990–91 season, just as Arsenal were about to cruise to the title. On the eve of the season, George seemed to be at the height of his autocratic powers. While the rest of the country sang 'Nessun Dorma' and basked in the afterglow of Italia '90, Graham, in the *Daily Mirror*, promised: 'I'll destroy anyone who steps out of line.' This obviously didn't apply to Paul Merson and Tony Adams, who'd been involved in recent booze-fuelled exploits. George was always far more concerned about barrack-room lawyers than bona fide bad boys. The first to be disposed of was winger and PFA activist Brian Marwood. One of the most popular Arsenal players of that vintage, Marwood, in George's opinion, had far too much to say for himself, and occasionally clashed with his boss in training sessions. More importantly, his PFA activities compromised his position within the club. After a rumpus with Norwich players back in late 1989, Marwood was asked by his PFA bosses to conduct an inquiry into the incident. George was not keen on this. To him, the inquiry should have been a strictly internal affair. After that episode, Graham became very distant, curiously accusing *The Sun* of contributing to their faltering relationship. The player realised that the root cause was Graham himself and disappeared to Middlesbrough.

A similar fate befell Kevin Richardson, a solid, workmanlike midfielder with a reputation for plain speaking. George sent him even further away, to Real Sociedad on a £1 million transfer. Record appearance holder David O'Leary dared to ask George for an extra week's rest before rejoining the squad for pre-season training, after his exertions for Eire in Italia '90. George's measured response was to let him stew in the reserves for the next three months. There was some grumbling in the fanzines, particularly regarding the treatment of O'Leary, the model professional. Kevin Richardson perceptively pointed out: 'Freedom of thought seems to be banned at Highbury . . . Who will Graham turn on next?' His concerns proved valid and Brian Marwood was also reported to have raised concerns about the 'human cost' of the Graham revolution.

George was simultaneously portrayed as a paranoid dictator and a bully, who trampled over feelings and reputations with scant regard for the angst it caused. A precedent was being set, but in the meantime, Marwood was replaced by new signing Anders Limpar and Richardson's place was taken by Paul Davis as Arsenal lost just one league game in that 1990–91 season. It is ironic that Limpar and Davis were next to feel the wrath of George. Make no mistake, these two were arguably the club's most creative players of that generation. Graham's persecution of them was totally self-destructive, reminiscent of Stalin's purges in the '30s, when he eventually realised he'd destroyed so many scientists and soldiers that he'd weakened the Soviet Union, not strengthened it. But even Stalin didn't import the likes of Jimmy Carter and Eddie McGoldrick to replace them.

Graham's treatment of David O'Leary should have provided ample warning to Anders Limpar not to cross swords with him over the club v. country debate. From the moment he arrived in north London, Limpar caused Graham as many headaches as he did opposition defences. As the Swede tersely points out: 'I was entitled to play for Sweden in friendlies, as my contract stated. But Graham would always say: "Anders, do you have to go? It's Arsenal who pays your wages."' In October 1990, just three months after his arrival, Limpar had already sown the seeds of his own destruction. On the eve of a Rumbelows Cup tie with Chester, apparently not fully fit, he jetted off to join the Swedish team, much to Graham's chagrin. Whilst away, Limpar evidently gossiped with some Swedish journalists. His comments appeared in the *Daily Mirror*: 'Mr Graham's always shouting at people' was one of them. He also claimed that George had stopped Michael Thomas from going to the toilet when he needed to. Limpar later denied he'd ever uttered those words. In signing Anders, Graham entered a new sphere. Here was a star player who hadn't learned his trade in Stoke's or Wimbledon's reserve team. He needed handling differently. This was a zone in which George didn't feel comfortable. As he has proved since, he is unable to handle star players, one of the key reasons why the 1991 side reached its zenith so soon.

From now on, Limpar was substituted with alarming regularity and endured public criticism from his manager for the next couple of years, something the boss claimed he'd never do to any of his players. The treatment of the Swede was a sign of a wider malaise regarding George's attitude to creative players. In the winter of 1991, Michael Thomas departed for Liverpool, grumbling in the tabloids about the Scot's growing insistence on long-ball tactics. For his troubles, Thomas was later fined for bringing the game into disrepute. More startling, and unforgivable, was Graham's treatment of Paul Davis, the only midfielder at the club capable of delivering defence-splitting passes. Davis endured an unhappy 18-month spell in the reserve team and suffered the ignominy of training with the youth team. He recalls: 'It was easily the worst spell of my career. During the European Cup match against Benfica, George claimed I went against his instructions and ventured too far forward. Put it this way – I didn't share that view! I thought an 18-month banishment from the first team was a bit over the top. The fact is that if you argued with George, you had to accept the consequences.'

By 1994, the all-conquering title side had mutated into a team stuffed with runners and battlers like Jensen and Hillier. The cup successes of that era couldn't disguise growing dissent from fans and that, in Alan Smith's words, 'Playing under George Graham just wasn't enjoyable any more. He'd said everything he could say to us. Everything was so stale.' When Arsenal embarked on a string of four consecutive 0–0 draws in late 1993, boos resonated around Highbury. This was supposed to be the new all-singing, all-dancing Premiership era and, watching from the newly built Brave New World North Bank stand, Arsenal fans realised it just wasn't good enough.

It didn't take a genius to work out that perhaps Arsenal's biggest problem was the manager himself. One of the requirements of bosses in the new era was that they possess a degree of media sophistication. Frankly, George was a public relations disaster. He'd never courted popularity, but in 1994, he began to consult a PR firm in order to rectify his dour image. The consultation process did not seem to work. It was a standing joke at Highbury that he wore a T-shirt with the logo, 'I'm trying to buy a midfielder', a response to those who criticised Arsenal's functional midfield. Yet, in public, the message he sent out to would-be signings was negative. Tellingly, he told Joe Lovejoy that Eric Cantona was 'a cry baby' and that he held no sway with 'pretty football'. He also confessed to 'mistrusting' star players. It was a barely disguised swipe at Anders Limpar, who was finally axed in March 1994. The Swede recalls: 'At the end it was impossible to talk to Graham. He kept avoiding me. I remember at the end, when he told me that he'd accepted an offer for me from Everton, he just walked out and left me there, after all those wonderful years at Highbury.'

His treatment of Limpar was later repeated with that of David Ginola at Spurs in the late '90s. George, in hindsight, rightly points out that both players achieved little after leaving his teams. The problem was that he didn't replace them with new blood. Without Limpar, Arsenal won the Cup-Winners' Cup, but as well as destroying the flair in the side, George was also destroying what little goodwill he had left in the crowd. Despite the silverware, something was desperately wrong in the court of King George, but at the time, no one realised precisely how rotten things were. If George had done his best to ignore Anders Limpar, he couldn't ignore the criticism he'd receive for failing to sign the country's hottest young stars in the mid-'90s, Roy Keane and Chris Sutton. The root of his problems was money related, inevitably. Resentment was building up in the first-team squad at the lack of bonuses and pay rises that came the players' way, despite the cup successes of 1993 and 1994. Yet none of the players were aware of the full truth: that behind the scenes, the boss was busy lining his own pockets.

The first clue arrived during a mundane training session late in the 1993–94 season. The usual gaggle of TV hacks hung about. As usual, George tried to ignore them, but a new face emerged from the crowd – Danish TV reporter Henrik Madsen – who waved a microphone in George's general direction. 'Mr Graham,' he shouted, 'do you know Rune Hauge? Have you ever taken money from him?' The camera continued to run, as George's face froze and went grey. He strode towards Madsen, snorted and said: 'Those are very serious allegations.' But he didn't deny them, and then he walked away. It's a wonder that Danish viewers didn't hear the pounding of George's heart going off the scale, but soon the sound of chickens coming home to roost drowned out almost everything else.

The Graham scandal officially broke in November. Ironically, it came just a week after Arsenal fans, throughout a match at the Dell, waved 'Bank of Grobland' notes at Southampton keeper Bruce Grobbelaar, who was under investigation for match-fixing allegations. The 1994–95 season proved to be Arsenal's *annus horribilus*, and the Graham affair became public knowledge just a week after Paul Merson confessed to drink and drugs-related addictions. Playing it cool, the *Sunday Mirror* announced that 'a top Highbury official' received a large sum of money from the John Jensen deal in 1992. In truth, the story seemed irrelevant to most fans. Admittedly, the thought that anyone should gain something from signing JJ, whose wayward shooting had troubled pilots beginning their descent into Heathrow, was strange, but the term 'Highbury official' conjured up the image of an office boy in a grey suit.

Those early stories were shrouded in rumour and counter-rumour, and littered with buzzwords like 'sweeteners', 'kickbacks', 'unsolicited gifts' and, of course, 'bungs', which further clouded the issue. When the mist began to lift, all routes led, staggeringly, to George. It was he, we were later told, that allegedly benefited from two 'kickbacks' from Norwegian agent Rune Hauge. The first was a payment of £140,500, allegedly his cut from the Lydersen deal; the second was £285,000, supposedly his take from the John Jensen signing. We later discovered that the board had known about the payments since August and that George had apparently told them only after he realised that Hauge's tax returns were being investigated. For some, that was enough to prove George's culpability, particularly when he admitted he liked to work alone on foreign deals. It all smelt suspicious. The man himself begged to differ.

In Graham's book, he notes that the board told him in October that they no longer trusted him and discussions over his likely resignation were already in progress. The press sniped at him for the next couple of months, although they did tone down their use of the word 'bung'. They spent the Christmas period frantically clarifying with their legal people the difference between the 'b' word and the term 'unsolicited gift'. George and the club, in the meantime, maintained a position of stoic silence, which simply added fuel to the fire. Come February, when the Premier League inquiry was set up and the press probed ever deeper into sleaze in football and politics, the term 'bung' would have as familiar a ring to it as 'back to basics' and 'cash for questions'.

During the uneasy peace, Gunners fans realised that the Graham dynasty really was coming to the grimmest of ends. Whether the money was a bung or a gift, George, the white knight who'd ridden to our rescue in June 1986, the immaculate, dapper boss under whom we had won so many trophies, was now forever tainted. For years, we'd questioned why, in the *Daily Telegraph*'s words, 'Graham, who should be shopping at Harrods, has had to make do instead with corner-shop players'. Just why were Arsenal regarded as one of the meanest payers in the Premiership? Had Jensen and Lydersen, never the most gifted or popular of players, really been bought simply in order for George to line his pockets? The puritanical Scot who'd sounded so virtuous nine years earlier had supposedly pocketed large amounts of cash, shoved them in an offshore bank account and hadn't declared it to the taxman.

An ex-player, who wished to remain anonymous, told me: 'I couldn't believe the stories. All those years when he'd been so tight over contracts, and then we find out he's been lining his own pockets. I could barely look him in the eye after that, to be honest. George's last signing was Glenn Helder. Now Glenn had a real mouth on him, and before long he started to blab about how much he was earning. That pissed off a lot of players, particularly those who had come up through the youth team and had done it all with George. Glenn never did anything for Arsenal. Helder was on two or three times what they were on. These lads, rightly in my opinion, felt betrayed by George. He'd reached the end.' Alan Smith recalls: 'I was amazed. For years, he'd always been the upholder of the badge. Then the story broke. Clearly things could never be the same again.'

It was the perfect, irony-laden story for the ravenous tabloids, who were convinced that football was awash with obscene amounts of cash and illicit payments. In an era of sleaze-related stories, the press remained convinced that malpractice was everywhere – in politics, the city, and football. John Major's disastrous 'back to basics' policy backfired and the press took delight in exposing men like Neil Hamilton and David Mellor as being less than honest. Unlike 'Honest John', of course. No jokes about late-night curries existed back then. In the city, the press had investigated insider dealing and exposed Nick Leeson's activities at Barings Bank. With so much cash sloshing around in football with Sky money, it was inevitable that they would start to investigate the football world, and George became the fall-guy. George was also boss of the Arsenal, everyone's favourite club to hate. He had had an uneasy relationship with the press since his divorce from his wife Marie, and you can bet that half of them rubbed their hands in glee when they learnt that he was at the centre of this scandal. Perhaps his business manager, John Hazell, was right when he admitted later that 'the press would never be happy until they had your head on a plate'. Still, the rapidly diminishing band of Graham worshippers reckoned that if results on the pitch could improve over Christmas and the New Year, the Scot may yet save his skin. They obviously didn't pray hard enough. Results did not improve and George was fired on Monday, 13 February 1995.

Although it was the FA hearing in March that banned him from football for a year, Graham had effectively been on trial since 19 September 1994, when he admitted to Peter Hill-Wood that he had pocketed the money. Essentially, the board and the subsequent FA enquiry asked four questions:

1. Did Graham engineer the Lydersen and Jensen deals so that he could make a profit from them?
2. Did he only 'declare' Hauge's 'gifts' because he realised that the Norwegian was under investigation, so the news would leak anyway?

3. Did the £425,000, which George pocketed, rightfully belong to the club?

4. Was Graham aware that the money he received from Hauge was in connection (i.e. his cut) from the two transfers?

Between them, the board and the FA enquiry believed the answer was yes to questions three and four, meaning that not only had George acted against the best interests of the club but he had also broken FA rules. Inevitably, there would always be a lingering suspicion that the answer to question two was also yes, though this can never be proved. He was found not guilty over what would have been the most heinous crime of all, that of engineering a bung, as stated in question one.

George has since hit back with some savage broadsides of his own, of course, although his agent informed me that he had 'no intention of contributing to your unofficial book'. Fortunately, Graham recorded his feelings about the whole affair in *The Glory And The Grief* and, most notably, the time he appeared on Clive Anderson's *Talk Back* show and stuck rigidly to his story. George has always insisted that the money was simply a thank-you present from Hauge for all the contacts that George opened up for him in England. Several Grahamites still claim that he was stabbed in the back. One staunch fan told me: 'There is no doubt that he had been foolish in accepting Hauge's money in the first place, which he admits. Stuffing wallets full of cash into a briefcase is, ahem, "dodgy" and you'd have thought that someone as smart as George would have had the sense at least to declare these gifts to the taxman. History shows that he eventually did this and the key thing is that George insists he never asked for the money. Such gifts are part and parcel of business life and there is no law in football which states "thou shalt not receive a gift". The handovers also took place in the lounge bar of the Park Lane Hotel. Now, if George really knew he was receiving a bung, would he have collected it in such a public place? In the City, it is a regular occurrence for expert brains to be picked (like George's was by Hauge) and rewarded with financial gifts. And, let's face it, if someone gave you a £425,000 gift, would you turn it down?

It is interesting to wonder if those who repeatedly criticise him would have flatly refused the gift. Ultimately, the board panicked. They believed that by sacking him, Arsenal would escape further punishment from the FA. They chose to believe a combination of hysterical newspaper allegations, three I.K. Start officials (Lydersen's former club) who couldn't get their story straight, and a three-man Premier Committee over their man who brought them seven trophies and countless millions of pounds in profits. David Dein's wealth is, in part, due to ownership of shares in Arsenal – the prices of which were sent rocketing by Graham's success. Maybe the vice-chairman and his associates should have remembered this before they acted so ruthlessly.

'George had a valid argument when he pointed out that the board had put up with the antics of Paul Merson and Tony Adams and forgiven them, while he was given no second chance. Then, having made the agreement that he would leave his job at the end of the season and receive compensation, the board decided to sack him without him receiving a penny of this. All this came after the evidence given by the laughable FA inquiry, from which there emerged so many leaks and rumours that it was impossible for him to receive a fair hearing. George rightly blasted it as a "kangaroo court". Surely the case would have been thrown out long ago by a proper court of law. So if George's actions were a little shabby, the manner of his sacking was positively grotesque.'

While there are several relevant points in the case for the defence, it would have been impossible for George to be given a mild 'slapped wrist' by the board. The FA had tied the board's hands, anyway, and not to take appropriate action would have left Arsenal open, as was rumoured, to relegation and a series of huge fines. According to George, being a manager was always a case of setting an example to his players. The board obviously believed that his was a very poor one.

Financial irregularities aside, George's time at Arsenal was up. Those final tragic shots of him after the team's meek surrender to AC Milan in the Super Cup showed a gaunt, strained man who'd reached the end. Being dumped out of the FA Cup third round in January by Millwall at Highbury was bitterly ironic. The club where George honed his managerial skills ended his Arsenal career, symbolically at least. The First Division club won 2–0, but it could have been far more embarrassing. Events at Highbury had now turned full circle under Graham. He recorded in his book that he felt he'd 'lost' certain players, a view concurred with by several of that team. The side now required as much internal surgery as it had when he took over nine years earlier.

George Graham provided many of us with our best Arsenal memories: Anfield 1989, Wembley 1993 and Copenhagen 1994. He also bought us Ian Wright and gave us a defence whose longevity defies belief. We're eternally grateful for that, but he believed that alone gave him the right to stay at the helm. Football management, though, is a ruthless and unforgiving business. George's protestations about 'what I did for that club' and the 'ungratefulness' of certain directors smack of pure sentimentality, an emotion he's always professed to hate. Charlie Nicholas, David Rocastle and Anders Limpar would all testify to that. Now, it was George's turn to be transformed into a 'non-person'. The Arsenal museum replaced his voice-over with that of Bob Wilson. The official programme, typically, simply made no mention of him, save for the briefest of comments by Peter Hill-Wood a couple of weeks after his sacking. It was as if George no longer existed. What went around finally came around, one might say.

In the aftermath of George's dismissal, *One Nil Down* ran the headline 'GRAHAM – THE BITTER END', but typically of the ever-resourceful George, it proved to be a new beginning for him. After serving his year-long world ban from football, he did some radio work, a little gardening and wrote his autobiography. Then, in October 1996, he was introduced as Leeds United's new manager. George did a decent job at Elland Road, but, interestingly, similar patterns emerged with those at Highbury. He was able to reap a rich harvest from Leeds' youth team, as he'd done at Arsenal in the late '80s. Yet, ultimately, he also stood accused of neglecting Leeds' youth team and grass-roots policies.

The same complaint had been levelled against him immediately after he left Highbury. Arsenal's reserve and youth sides of the mid-'90s were laden with Jensen and Hillier clones, none of whom possessed the talent to become first-team regulars. A top Highbury official muttered that the Scot had done 'serious damage' to Arsenal's grass roots. To date, Ashley Cole is the only British-born player to make the transition from youth to senior side since George's departure. He was also criticised by some elements of the Leeds crowd over his reluctance to 'splash the cash'. He preferred to ditch Tomas Brolin and Tony Yeboah, introducing instead a succession of canny purchases into the side, like Lee Bowyer and Jimmy Floyd Hasselbaink. Ostensibly, one of the reasons George quit Leeds in 1999 was due to his unhappiness that the Leeds directors were reluctant to fund more expensive purchases. Coincidentally, in *The Glory And The Grief*, he mutters that he would never have been given the money to spend on David Platt and Dennis Bergkamp. Yet the Arsenal board still claim that the necessary money had always been there for him. Ironically, Leeds chairman Peter Ridsdale, who gave David O'Leary around £60 million to spend on players, stated: 'This kind of money was always there for George to spend as well, before David took over. He chose not to spend it.'

The most bizarre twist in the Graham soap opera came when he was appointed manager of Spurs in late 1999. Arsenal fanzines portrayed him as a Darth Vader figure. Formerly an upstanding, whiter than white character, he'd been well and truly seduced by the dark side. 'Judas Graham' banners were unfurled for his return to Highbury for a north London derby, which ended in a typically tense 0–0 draw after George had been booed by most of the crowd for 90 minutes. Ironically, he'd always been given a standing ovation upon his return with Leeds. Managing Spurs, it seems, remains a greater crime than pocketing bungs. Arsenal fans felt George had committed treason by going to White Hart Lane and in Spurs fans' eyes he remained every inch an Arsenal villain. The *Daily Telegraph* revealed he was still making money from Arsenal's success. In 1992, he'd been issued with £8,300 worth of club shares. Their value had rocketed to £83,000 by the year 2000.

Though he was cleared of profiting from a 'conflict of interest', this, combined with his collection of Gunners memorabilia, proved that at heart he was an Arsenal man, albeit a tainted one. Spurs fans could never bring themselves to accept him. The hard core of their support could barely bring themselves to mention his name, chanting 'Man in a raincoat's white-and-blue army!' at several home games. They were intrinsically incapable of embracing the values for which he stood – good defending and trophy winning are not essential components of Spurs' *raison d'être*, after all. In the summer of 2000, he oversaw the sale of crowd favourite David Ginola to Aston Villa – echoes of the Limpar affair here – and faced a fan revolt. Finally, new owners ENIC decided that the more glamorous Glenn Hoddle was needed to appease the Spurs fans and they sacked him. George, as we now knew, belonged to a bygone era of harsh discipline, prudent spending and questionable accounting. ENIC officials were horrified to discover a biscuit tin stuffed full of tenners in George's office. 'It was for player fines,' he told them, but it hardly improved Graham's tarnished reputation.

For all George's faults, former Arsenal players retain a degree of respect for him. Paul Davis recalls: 'George always said "No matter what you think of me, you'll all look back with pride on all the medals you've won. We at Arsenal are all in the business of winning." I think there's a lot to be said for that view. History will probably judge him harshly because of what happened. But he was responsible for the rebirth of Arsenal. He made the club a force to be reckoned with again.' Arguably, his biggest crime was behaving like a dictator, destroying the side's flair and, as Arsenal's star fell, allowing Manchester United to dominate '90s football. 'With the team we had in 1991, Arsenal should have been the team of the '90s,' reckons Alan Smith. Six trophies in around eight years is an excellent record. It should have been an even more bountiful era.

The most obvious contradiction of his reign was that for all his early intentions, tabloid exposés on Arsenal's players and officials grew exponentially. Prior to the bung affair, even he was 'caught out' on several occasions. In 1993 George was snapped boogying,

Charlie Nicholas style, in a nightclub with 'bubbly blonde' Arianne Acristo. Then there had been his relationship with married mother of three Sue Schmidt, who owned a black Porsche with the number-plate '594 HOT'. Late in 1993, Arianne Acristo informed the tabloids that George paid her £30,000 'to get out of his life'. Tellingly, she also claimed: 'He has so much money he doesn't know what to do with it all, apart from save it for retirement.' Yet Graham confessed: 'It's the little brown envelopes which come through my letterbox each month that keep me going.' He'll be remembered for the two 'suitcases stuffed with cash' he was given by Rune Hauge, though. Whatever he had, George Graham always seemed to want more. As Arsenal fans are well aware, absolutely nothing was as it seemed in the Court of King George. This control freak was never quite as in control of his players as he liked to think. He was unable to prevent his two brightest stars from the youth team, Tony Adams and Paul Merson, from going completely off the rails. But that's another story.

TWELVE

Back From The Brink

I haven't pissed the bed for two and a half years.
                                    Tony Adams, speaking in 1999

My addictions are always there, waiting for me. They're
doing press-ups outside my door.
                                    Paul Merson, speaking in 1999

Founder of the Sporting Chance Charity, RAPT (Rehabilitation for Addicted Prisoners Trust) representative, UNESCO ambassador in Somalia, budding pianist, young manager on the steepest of learning curves at Wycombe Wanderers – these days there are no limits to Tony Adams' horizons, he tells us. But, as his regular and necessary visits to Alcoholics Anonymous prove, he mustn't ignore his troubled past. Not that he would be allowed to. In May 2002, during a visit to HM Swaleside Prison on the Isle of Sheppey (inmates are category B and have been jailed for acts of violent crime) he gave a talk on the perils of alcohol, both in and out of institutions. The talk, on behalf of RAPT, was extremely well received. As he left the site, he was subjected to some familiar taunts from inmates, who catcalled him from their cell windows. Not all the chants were good-natured. 'Adams, you donkey' and 'Eee-aaw' were fairly predictable. But the taunts about him crashing his car are more cutting, taking him immediately back to the events of over a decade ago.

It's much the same type of existence for fellow Sporting

Chance founder Paul Merson. Now a veteran with Walsall, I saw him almost singlehandedly demolish his future club whilst playing for Portsmouth at Fratton Park in late 2002. Quite simply, he was a couple of moves ahead of his teammates, let alone the hapless opposition. After the match, Merson obligingly signed autographs for Pompey's young supporters. A particularly repulsive-looking Walsall fan, bearing a strong resemblance to Gollum from *Lord of the Rings*, also hung around, quietly making snide comments in Merson's direction. 'I see he went up the line a lot today,' he repeated several times, as if we didn't get the gist. 'I bet he'd have scored if a pint of lager had been in the middle of the goal' came next. Believing that Merson hadn't heard him, Gollum slunk away. But the slightly flushed ex-Arsenal striker had heard every word. Merson told his companion: 'Years ago, that sort of idiot would probably have really got to me. But not any more. I've got to get to my Gamblers Anonymous meeting, anyway.' With that, he disappeared in his gleaming piece of German engineering.

Merson's comment tells us a lot about his transformation. Where once he was a fully fledged '80s roaring boy, he is now a sensitive new-age man, anxious to relate his problems to like-minded individuals. Once the very personification of *Men Behaving Badly*, his and Tony Adams' lives are now more akin to an episode of *Last Of The Summer Wine*, although Merson continues to battle his demons. Their lives have often been described as a journey back from the brink. Nowadays, they're reconstructed males. Role models, even. That seemed an unlikely prospect back in 1989, when the pair seemed hell-bent on self-destruction. In those far-off days last century, Thatcher clung desperately to power, the Berlin Wall still stood and Rick Astley was music's next big thing. Footballers were paid rather more modest salaries for playing a sport that still claimed to be 'the working man's game'. Fourteen years on and everything has changed.

That George Graham uttered the immortal words 'I want ambitious young men, allied with self-discipline, brought up in the Arsenal way' is now a cause for wry reflection all around. Not only because it makes him sound hugely pompous and hypocritical, but because the phrases 'young men' and the 'Arsenal way' took on an entirely different meaning throughout his tenure.

For a while, George's wish that stories about the club be confined to the back pages seemed to be coming true. Ironically, it was he who was first subjected to the 'red-top' treatment. A clutch of tabloids reported in late 1988 that his wife Marie had left him for her boss, dry-cleaning magnate Roger Bliss. Graham was granted a quickie divorce and *The Sun* reported her comment: 'He spends more time on football than with me.' Still, even the sad muppets who hounded George admitted there was a kind of perverse nobility here – he was effectively married to Arsenal Football Club. At the time, it seemed, only a crazed imagination could conceive of him getting involved in anything truly sordid or sensational.

With Adams or Merson, you didn't need to use your imagination; they kept Arsenal fans in drinking tales for months on end. It would have been easier for George if the duo had been merely average players, or past their sell-by dates, instead of the young legends they were becoming. From the summer of 1989 until their mid-'90s nadir, it was rare for a month to pass without feverish gossiping about them. They were portrayed as a couple of louts, as boorish and loud as Harry Enfield's 'Loadsamoney' character. Journalists, always keen to fan the flames of scandal, would suggest at regular intervals that George ban the pair from top-flight footie. To the vast majority of those inside Highbury, for whom Adams was a demi-god and Merson a prodigiously gifted starlet, this was an unthinkable prospect. As for George, when things did go pear-shaped for him in the mid-'90s, he knew that, along with Ian Wright, these two were the only ones capable of digging him out of the huge hole in which he found himself.

Tony Adams learned how to booze in the mid-'80s alongside Arsenal's infamous drinking crew. In those early days, his role models were Kenny Sansom and Graham Rix. For all his external brashness, young Tone actually felt quite overawed when he first walked into the Highbury dressing-room. Cheeky-chappie Sansom, with his string of Norman Wisdom, Max Bygraves and

Sergeant Columbo impressions, and his litany of pub jokes, was the life and soul of the dressing-room. Charlie Nicholas recalls: 'If it was a spot of communal singing you wanted, Kenny was your man to get it started. If you wanted dancing on the tables, he would be leading it. If you wanted terrible jokes about alligators or crocodiles walking into pubs, Kenny would tell them.' While Nicholas continued to cut up teammates' shirts and fill their shoes with talcum powder, Sansom perfected his impressions. On one occasion, Sansom, in his best Columbo voice, informed his uncomprehending England boss: 'Mr Robson, my wife thinks you're great.' Bobby Robson remained baffled, as his players fell about laughing around him. From Graham Rix, Adams sought advice on suitable beverages for a young footballer. 'Drink Guinness,' advised Rixy, on the grounds that it got you pissed quickly, but it wasn't long before Tone inevitably graduated onto lager. As he moved into the England set-up, he looked up to captain Terry Butcher, whose motto was: 'Win or lose, we will booze.' Adams lived by this adage for the next decade.

It was during a lengthy lay-off due to a broken leg in 1985 that Adams first discovered the mystical qualities of alcohol. To counter fears over his future, and boredom, he sought solace in ale, using it as a crutch to take his mind off things. Seeds were already being sown: Adams realised that alcohol was an effective anaesthetic to help him avoid dealing with strong emotions. Though there were no tabloid exposés on him during his early days, he was already on the Saturday night razzle each week and going on boozy holidays to Mediterranean hot-spots like Rhodes and Torremolinos with Martin Hayes and Coventry goalkeeper Perry Suckling. He later confessed to feeling embarrassed after slurring his way through an acceptance speech for his PFA Young Player of the Year award, which he received in 1987. Ironically, this came on the day when Arsenal beat Liverpool in the Littlewoods Cup final and Adams won his first medal as a Gunners player. It was to be the first of ten. But even in joyous victory, he found it hard to keep his emotions in check. 'Getting drunk was my way of dealing with the high points as well,' he later commented. In truth, few took any notice of Tony Adams' growing reliance on alcohol. Drunken escapades are woven into the very fabric of '80s football. If Terry Neill's and Don Howe's sides were labelled the best pub side in Britain, things didn't greatly change when George Graham became boss. Perry Groves recalls: 'Our big drinking sessions were in mid-week. Back then, English clubs were banned from playing European football, so apart from an occasional mid-week cup game we had a free day. Training ended early on Tuesday afternoon and then we could do what we wanted until Thursday morning, when we had to report back. It turned into a mammoth drinking session. It was usually an all-day bender. Most of the players went along – even the married ones would stay for most of the day. At that time, it was the done thing in the game. You'd go out, and you'd bump into lads from Charlton or QPR or Chelsea, whoever. It never struck me as being the wrong thing to do. We were young lads who worked hard in training. We had to. George made us. This was a way of letting off steam and bonding as mates. It worked for us at that time.' And George's attitude to the 'Tuesday club'? 'George turned a blind eye to it. The fact was that as long as you were doing it for him on the pitch, he didn't care. It only became a problem if you weren't doing it for him. And in Tony Adams' case, he was putting in great performances for the club every week.'

Within a year of Graham taking over, Adams was appointed Arsenal captain. Kenny Sansom was officially relieved of the role when he took his manager to task after he'd signed Nigel Winterburn. 'I'VE BEEN TREATED LIKE DIRT,' ran the *Mirror* headline. As Sansom later admitted, whingeing in the tabloids wasn't the smartest thing he'd ever done in his life. Tony Adams was a ruthlessly determined captain and he seemed to be an equally superb drinker. He was never over-reliant on his pace and, being naturally skinny, he didn't have to worry about marathon sessions weighing him down. Adams appeared to defy logic. The more he drank, the more he became the keystone to Arsenal's success. Skippering Arsenal to the title in 1989 required serious self-determination. In the European Championships during the previous year, he'd had the proverbial 'mare against Holland's Marco Van Basten. The Dutchman blasted a spectacular hat-trick, as Holland ran out 3–1 winners. Adams, whom the press had earlier labelled the 'new Bobby Moore', was blamed for two of the goals. He immediately began to glimpse the less charitable side of journalism.

The press began to gun for him. In April 1989, after Adams scored at both ends in a 1–1 draw with Manchester United at Old Trafford, the *Daily Mirror* pinned a pair of donkey's ears on his head on the Monday morning. 'EEE-AAW ADAMS,' ran the headline. It stung him deeply, as did the incident when Middlesbrough fans pelted him with carrots at Ayresome Park. Paul Davis recalls: 'The abuse which Tony had to put up with at the time was unbelievable. The ferocity of it was like nothing I'd ever heard. There was that game at Middlesbrough and as we prepared to kick off in the second half, their fans' chanting at him was so loud that you couldn't hear yourself think. I remember that Rocky and me just looked at each other and shook our heads. It was that bad. You have to remember that at one point, his parents stopped coming to games because he didn't want them to hear what fans were saying about him. Being such a young captain, and captain of Arsenal, left him open to criticism. As our skipper, he was second to none and the abuse didn't affect his game at all. He was the most inspiring player I knew at Highbury. In the true Arsenal style, he dug in and used it to motivate him. But, obviously, it hurt him inside.'

Adams responded in the only way he knew: keeping his feelings hidden whilst drinking to numb the pain, and leading Arsenal to victory at Anfield. In the days before the game, he recalled in *Addicted*, he'd embarked on a two-day bender, incorporating a day at Windsor races, with Niall Quinn, Steve Bould, and Paul Merson. It seemed that only superman could haul himself out of bed later that week, let alone think about taking on reigning champions Liverpool in Arsenal's biggest match for years. In his own book, Niall Quinn took issue over the dates of the 'Windsor bender'. This dispute even led to a brief falling out between the two.

Yet even after the Anfield victory, matters weren't straightforward for Adams. He confessed to feeling 'empty' the following day, after the adrenalin surge of the previous night. Only one thing could make him feel better, and during the team's victory parade through Islington on the Sunday, he gleefully swigged the cans of Heineken and Red Stripe the Arsenal fans threw up to the team. As he later commented, 'all contributions were greatly accepted'.

Once a terribly insecure and nervous apprentice, Paul Merson's life was already spiralling out of control by 1989. Brought up in a betting culture, his father had often disappeared for evenings to join his workmates in a card school. In unhappy echoes of his own adulthood, Merson's mother would often have to hide her husband's wages in order that the family would be able to eat during that week. A speech impediment and a feeling of failure at school left him an inarticulate and shy 20 year old. Yet he had few problems in expressing himself on the pitch. With his quicksilver bursts and spectacular goals, he was proving to be the perfect foil for Arsenal's main striker, Alan Smith, during the championship season. With his soul boy haircut and toothy grin, he struck up an instant affinity with Arsenal fans. In contrast with conservative family man 'Smudger', Merson began to perfect his 'Wild Man' image. Although notoriously inarticulate in interviews, he expressed his desire to run onto the Highbury pitch to The Troggs' 'Wild Thing' and, during the title-winning season, he mutated into the wild man of Borneo after refusing to cut his hair from January onwards, on the grounds that it was 'unlucky'.

There were always problems lurking just beneath the surface throughout his career. Even as an apprentice, he'd blow his wages down the bookies and now, as an established first-teamer, he gambled huge amounts on accumulator bets. Betting aside, his other passion was drinking lager tops. He could sink ten pints a session, no problem. Paul Vaessen described to me the temptations of a young player at a high-profile club: 'If you want it, you can get hold of everything and anything. There are so many sharks around, people who are ready to leech off you and introduce you to the "vices", like drinking, gambling and drugs.' I spoke to Vaessen before the Merson scandal broke in the mid-'90s and his words were prophetic: 'A lot of young players dabble in dope. For most, it ends there and is fairly harmless. A tiny minority, though, will got to the next "gateway" and get into harder drugs. The temptations are just too great.' Like Tony Adams, Paul Merson was busy during the week leading up to the 'Anfield experience'. An observant policeman noticed Merson's black Mercedes zigzagging across the road near his house in St Albans, Hertfordshire. As an unhappy taster of what was to come for both players in the '90s, a Breathalyser test revealed he was almost three times over the legal limit. He didn't believe it to be a problem. With his court date set for later that year, he showed all the signs of an alcoholic in development by simply laughing off the incident. Deprived of wheels for the foreseeable future, he moved to a new house that was less than a 50-yard walk from a pub.

Merson spent much of the close season flitting between his local pub and the betting shop. As it was for Adams, the summer was one non-stop Mardi Gras for him as he revelled in Arsenal's title success. Yet still, there seemed nothing sinister going on. He was just a young athlete in the prime of his life, having fun – right? But over the coming 12 months, Adams' and Merson's hedonistic lifestyle hit a new and dangerous pitch. Before then, dressing-room indiscipline had been confined to laddish pranks, along the lines of daring one another to put a condom on George's shoulder without him noticing, or throwing Perry Groves into the sea on pre-season tours and, on one occasion, watching him get washed up on Frank Sinatra's private beach in Marbella.

During the 1989–90 season, Arsenal would lapse into a post-Anfield doze, failing to defend their title by finishing a disappointing fourth. In the months leading up to Christmas, the tabloids laid siege to Highbury. Not only were journalists able to hone in on Arsenal's indiscretions against Norwich City, but Merson became star copy after a crazy October. He'd already received an 'unofficial' warning during the latter stages of the championship season. On transfer deadline day, George tried, unsuccessfully, to sign Celtic's Frank McAvennie in order to boost his striking options. A case for wry reflection all round, as the Scot's love of the Colombian white powder and Page Three models would have put even Merson's antics in the shade. Rapidly being portrayed as a Keith Moon-type lunatic, Merson's behaviour in local pubs became legendary. On one occasion, after Spurs fans heckled him during a pool game, he snapped his cue in half and became embroiled in a full-scale bar brawl. 'Bar stools and bottles were flying everywhere,' according to one eye-witness. The tabloids, unsurprisingly, played on this, with the *Daily Star* announcing 'MERSON IN LAST CHANCE SALOON'.

After a £350 fine and an 18-month driving ban, his final act during 'crazy October' was to be deducted two weeks' wages after misbehaving at an official club dinner. Comedian Norman Collier, famous for his chicken impressions and dodgy voices, could hardly make himself heard. 'YOUR LAST CHANCE MERSON,' boomed *The Sun*. 'ARSENAL TELL PROBLEM PLAYER TO STAY AWAY,' claimed the *Mirror*. In a sense, he was already in denial. In a *Sun* exclusive, he claimed: 'My bad-boy image is ruining my life . . . It's a burden around my shoulders, and at 21 years old I don't think that's fair.' Yet, in reality, he loved living up to his image, as he admitted in *Rock Bottom*. George, for all his promises to 'throw the book' at his starlet, continued to allow Merson to frequent 'last-chance saloon'. The question was, did 'the book' actually exist?

According to Perry Groves, it did. He recalls: 'At the beginning of each season, we would be given a list of rules and regulations from the club. Some of them were fairly obvious, like wearing an official club tie and blazer on match day. Then there was the one about you not being able to booze less than 48 hours before a match. Now, I'm not going to land any of my ex-teammates in it, but let's just say, the rule was open to interpretation. Ninety-nine per cent of the time, players stuck to the rule. But if you didn't, how George treated you depended on whether or not he had a soft spot for you. I leave it to you to decide which players he was more lenient with.'

Anders Limpar is slightly less coy. He comments: 'There was a time when either myself or Paul Merson would be dropped by

George. Now Paul was a great player and a good bloke, but I always got the impression that, at some point, Paul would get back into the side, whereas I might not. The comment George Graham made was that I tended to drift out of games. But so did Paul. And if he's talking about discipline, the only thing I ever did wrong was to get fined for jumping a red light. Being a bad lad – a naughty boy – wasn't a huge crime in Graham's eyes. From his point of view, it was worse if you argued with him like I did. At times, it was certainly a case of one rule for one and one for another.'

Adams and Merson were notoriously indiscreet drinkers. Arsenal fans in Essex and Hertfordshire claimed to have seen the deadly duo breaking numerous pre-match-day curfews. Adams was often spotted pub-crawling on a Saturday night along the Holloway Road and Niall Quinn took him to Irish bars stretching onto Camden Town. Gunners fans, delighted to be at such close proximity to their captain, would often conga with him, drink with him and occasionally even boogie with him. To the astonishment of fans, he'd buy monster rounds of drinks, stagger out pissed, but still play a blinder on a Saturday. He seemed to be a supremely well-oiled drinking machine, but the stress of being Arsenal captain was showing, making him guzzle even more booze.

Not only was he George's mouthpiece in the dressing-room, Adams was the conduit between players and the manager. In a recent *Football Stories* documentary, Lee Dixon claimed: 'George moulded us into a winning team by putting a lot of pressure on us.' He often used Adams to get his message across. Within the Tuesday drinking club, an air of discontent began to spread. Teammates, who'd just won Arsenal a first title in 18 years, nagged their captain to lobby the boss about a pay rise. Of course, George always claimed the board wouldn't budge, something that spread bitterness throughout the squad. Adams confessed to being 'scared of my boss', and became so angry with Graham's dogmatic approach that on occasions, he said, 'I wanted to hit him.' Perry Groves told me he was surprised that Adams felt under pressure from George, but teammates were also unaware of his feelings of guilt about letting his colleagues down through his failure to help secure them better pay deals.

Adams and Merson missed selection for England's squad for Italia '90, as did other Arsenal starlets like David Rocastle. Even worse, Gunners players were hardly enamoured to discover they had to go on an energy-sapping post-season tour to Singapore, with clear echoes of the Hudson and Macdonald affair a decade or so earlier. It was a tour from which Groves, Winterburn, Richardson and, inevitably, Paul Merson, were sent home after being caught drinking shandy on the eve of a match.

Tony Adams was extremely lucky to make the tour at all. Around lunchtime on the day of departure, Adams, scheduled to rendezvous with the other players at Highbury in the late afternoon, was stuck in Essex with friends. He decided to have 'one for the road' in Braintree, partly to deal with his anger at having to make the arduous trip at the end of a long season. Inevitably, one drink turned into several, and Adams and his buddy ended up at a barbecue in Rainham. Tone downed several bottles of lager and later played a game of drunken cricket in the garden, whilst the real fun took place upstairs. 'SEX ORGY AT ADAMS PARTY,' claimed *The Sun*. Host Mick Hynes boasted: 'It was one of the wildest I've hosted . . . There were couples bonking all over the house . . . but Adams got nowhere because he was completely plastered.' Blissfully unaware of events on the top floor, Adams continued to play wicket-keeper, before realising at 3 p.m. that he only had an hour to make the 60-mile dash to Heathrow.

What happened next has been written into the hall of infamy. Adams, barely able to stand up, sped off in his souped-up Sierra and, after rocketing over a dual carriageway at 80 mph, smashed headlong into a garden wall. The car concertinaed and the brick wall was completely demolished. It was a miracle that he survived, particularly since he did not tend to wear his seat belt at that time. After a breath test, he was found to be three times over the legal limit. The police allowed him to join the Arsenal squad at Heathrow after a friend drove him there. Upon arrival, he boarded the aeroplane, still with splinters from the windscreen in his hair and was cold-shouldered by his manager and club officials during the 13-hour flight to Singapore.

With his court date set for 19 December 1990, tabloids speculated frantically on what might happen to him. Although Liverpool's Jan Molby and Portsmouth's Mick Quinn had been jailed for motoring offences over the previous two years, many believed that, with respected figures like Bob Wilson speaking on Adams' behalf, he might be let off with a slapped wrist. They reckoned without the formidable anti-drink-driving lobby, keen to make an example of a celebrity in the run-up to Christmas, and the Essex courts, who had a reputation for Judge Jeffreys-type severity in such cases. Adams' feelings of persecution weren't helped by the week's events leading up to the trial. He'd been charged by the FA for flicking Vs at QPR fans during a clash at Loftus Road and, in his last Arsenal match for two months, he was sent off at Luton for a fairly innocuous challenge.

He was jailed for 57 days. The club rallied around and George, resorting to the mentality of the trench, vented his fury against the judge, claiming he'd victimised Adams. Yet, as the player later admitted: 'The reason I ended up in prison was my abuse of alcohol.' He brazened it out in prison, despite the *Daily Mirror*'s sensational claim that 'Adams is locked up alongside rapists and hardened criminals'. According to a cellmate, anxious to make some money out of the affair, Adams found it 'a joke in prison', but that wasn't true. He used the multi-gym daily and became a fitness instructor in order to get through his sentence. As a prisoner, he gained some respect inside for turning down the soft option of moving to Ford open prison and for having received a 'best wishes' letter from Reggie Kray.

Upon his release, Arsenal received criticism for continuing to pay him while he was in prison, and after a 7,000 Highbury crowd welcomed him back against Reading reserves, Simon Barnes wrote a cautionary article in *The Times*, headed 'HERO'S WELCOME CANNOT DISGUISE PERILS OF ALCOHOL'. Henry Winter referred to Adams' 'astonishing mental strength' in *The Independent*, but as events would show in the next few years, prison was not a form of exorcism for him. Not even the tragic tale of his former defensive partner at Arsenal, Tommy Caton, persuaded him to change his ways. Caton, only 31 and still a Charlton player, died from heart failure in late 1990 after years of alcohol abuse. He hadn't played a game for Charlton in 18 months, due to a succession of injuries. His ex-wife confirmed that Caton drank two bottles of gin a day because 'he didn't think he could do anything outside playing football'. The demon drink was now controlling Adams too. Having gone without a real 'session' for two months, he made up for lost time upon his release from prison.

As Graham's managerial reign entered its attritional period, punctuated with adrenalin-pumping cup runs and tepid league performances, Tony Adams' and Paul Merson's extremes were made startlingly public. With the advent of the Sky *Super Sunday*, Tone's drinking sessions lasted all day Sunday and into the early hours of Monday morning. 'I was turning up pissed to training on Monday morning,' Adams confessed. Tellingly, bed-wetting and blackouts were becoming more common, and now he began to mistime his drinking sprees the night before a game. On at least two occasions, against Everton and Sheffield United, he played while still under the influence, after a brandy helped to settle his dodgy stomach. He actually won the man-of-the-match award against the Blades. That may have said something about United's strikers rather than his ability, but even so . . .

As Paul Davis comments: 'Tony's displays during those cup runs under George were unbelievable. This was hardly the best Arsenal side ever, but with Tony leading, we always had a chance of winning a cup or two. I think we played about 20 cup matches the year we did the cup Double. It was pretty draining, and Tony scored the winner against Spurs in the semi-final. It was such a great win and gave us revenge for them beating us two years before. But I should think everyone remembers the FA Cup quarter-final against Ipswich, or rather the lead-up to it. That showed the kind of life Tony was living at the time. I just don't know how he did it.'

In February 1993, a week before the crucial Ipswich match,

Adams and some friends went to Towcester races on his day off. The opportunity was there for him to let off some steam and he did so. Having gulped down champagne in the enclosure, Adams adjourned to a favourite nightclub and got to work on the lager. After chatting to a friend at the top of a flight of concrete steps, he lost his bearings and crashed down to the bottom, requiring 29 stitches in his gushing head wound. Unbelievably, and still with the mother of all headaches, he recovered and played a blinder against Ipswich seven days later. He won the man-of-the-match award, the highlight being when his towering header smacked off the plaster, levelling the scores. Arsenal won 4–2. Yet even in the midst of triumph, 'public humiliations', as Arsène Wenger later called them, were never far away. It seemed that no matter how well he played, accidents always befell him. Just ask Steve Morrow, whom Adams dropped after the young Irishman had scored the winner in the Coca-Cola Cup final against Sheffield Wednesday, breaking his arm in two places. Diners at Pizza Hut in Hornchurch would probably also agree with Wenger's view. At three o'clock on an October afternoon in 1993, Adams and fellow Essex man Ray Parlour felt peckish and called into the restaurant for a bite to eat. Fed up with waiting for garlic bread and with the taunts of Spurs fans at nearby tables, Adams sprayed them with a fire extinguisher, giving a completely different spin on the phrase 'hit the hut'. George's response provided further evidence of his ad hoc attitude to discipline. Ray Parlour received the bollocking, while George simply shook his head at Adams. An aggrieved Parlour asked why he'd copped all the flak. 'Because he [Adams] does the business for me week in, week out. You don't,' came the reply.

Adams' final public disgrace came in the *News of the World* on 15 May 1994. On FA Cup final day, Adams and friends visited the Crown pub in Billericay, Essex. In a back room, stripper Alison Frost 'did a series of acrobatic somersaults to show off her physique'. According to onlookers, Adams stripped off (to cries of 'handball' from the audience) and the 'naked soccer ace' pressed against her. An onlooker commented: 'It was more fun than watching United beat Chelsea, I can tell you.'

Now almost a stone over his optimum playing weight, Paul Merson's physical condition was declining rapidly. With a growing paunch and an increasingly pallid complexion, his form flitted between the awful and the inspired. Playing while 'well drunk' in a league match against Luton was a symbol of his problems, but the Coca-Cola Cup final against Wednesday perfectly illustrated the 'Merse' phenomenon. He'd scored Arsenal's equaliser with a stupendous swerving drive. Yet, after the final whistle, his mimed gesture to fans of swigging cans of lager ('doing the Merson') made the real headlines. In August of that year, Merson crashed his £25,000 Land-Rover Discovery after losing control of it in Mill Hill. After he'd clipped the kerb, written off a Nissan Micra and smashed into a wall and a tree, he gave his name to the Micra's owner, Bhuendra Lakhaim. Lakhaim, who suffered whiplash injuries as a result of the crash, dialled 999 and informed Merson the police were on their way. Merson panicked, telling Lakhaim: 'You've not seen me, mate, all right?' before hopping over a wall and disappearing. Unsurprisingly, the police got hold of him and presented him with a large fine.

Little wonder that Merson and Adams became icons of the 'new lad' culture. *Loaded* awarded the pair a seemingly permanent residence in their Platinum Rogues list. Merson revelled in the attention, informing anyone who cared to listen about his astonishing drinking powers. Adams' party trick, smashing pint glasses over his head in front of astonished onlookers, became legendary in football circles. The pair were pulling the oldest tricks in the book to avoid detection. Merson would simply hold his stomach in to hide his gut and Adams wore a bin-liner under his shirt in training in order to 'sweat out the booze'. They would also resort to chewing gum or munching Trebor mints in order to disguise the smell of alcohol on their breath.

Arsène Wenger later admitted to finding it 'incredible that no one at the club noticed their problems', implying that George's antennae had failed once again. Graham has since countered by commenting: 'A manager cannot be responsible for his players 24 hours of the day.' True enough, but sometimes you wonder if he was ever as smart as we thought. Anyway, if the Gallagher brothers could roll up pissed to an Oasis gig and play a 'blinder', reasoned *Loaded*, then why not Adams and Merson, football's answer to Clunes and Morrissey? But even *Loaded* didn't know the half of it, particularly in Merson's case. *The Gooner* and *One Nil Down* suggested that Merson was cheating the fans. *One Nil Down* ran the headline: 'MERSON, SHOULD HE STAY OR SHOULD HE GO?' Seriously in debt, he was placing five-figure sums on sports as diverse as American football and bowls. A friend had also introduced him to cocaine and Merson, a shy bloke, enjoyed the buzz it gave him. He was regularly disappearing into pub toilets to hoover lines off the seats. As he later recalled, being a celebrity meant he often received it for free.

Ironically, as the 'new lad' era dawned, the culture of heavy boozing among Premiership footballers began to fade. As the first cohort of clean-living Continental imports arrived at Premiership clubs, they were baffled by their British colleagues' predisposition to guzzle booze like there was no tomorrow. The era of pasta, broccoli and water diets was here. Rather than go pubbing after training, your average foreign star would most likely 'warm down', have a massage on their aching limbs and go shopping in the West End. It was becoming harder to chuckle at Adams' and Merson's antics. Their behaviour had long since passed the tomfoolery stage. In George's latter days at Highbury, as the quality of matches declined and the players began to earn hefty salaries, far more was expected of the club's more senior professionals. Several members of the Highbury establishment believed the pair were a bad influence on their young teammates. Midfielder David Hillier made a frankly ridiculous sojourn into petty crime: he was accused of smoking cannabis at a party ('I thought it was a cigarette') and stealing two holdalls from Gatwick airport, unaware that a CCTV camera was recording his every move. Ray Parlour was also writing his name into the Highbury hall of infamy. In 1995, he was questioned by the police after becoming embroiled in a brawl at Bognor Regis Butlins, and a year later, was involved in the 'prawn-crackergate' incident.

Attempting to hail a cab in Hong Kong, Parlour lobbed a full packet of prawn crackers into Lai-Pak Yan's taxi. The cabbie screeched the taxi to a halt and chased Parlour with a wooden club. Parlour responded by punching him on the nose and the police were called. After a heavy night's drinking at the Hard Rock Café, 'witnesses' Tony Adams and Chris Kiwomya were unable to recall the incident. It simply reinforced the popular view that Arsenal was a club populated by boozers and brawlers. And it was well known that John Hartson, Arsenal's teenage signing from Luton, wasn't averse to a pint and a punch-up on a Saturday night.

The pressure on the pair to hide their addictions, keep their marriages together and retain their places in the Arsenal team became unbearable. Merson cracked first, hitting rock bottom after a particularly awful display against Brondby in a Cup-Winners' Cup clash in late 1994. He was substituted by George Graham after 60 minutes. Observant fans probably felt he'd reached his nadir in the opening game of that season, against Manchester City. After just five minutes, the bloated Merson (now a full stone and a half overweight), was doubled up with exhaustion, with sweat pouring down his face. On a typical night out, he was snorting between 10 and 20 lines of coke, and sinking 14 pints of lager tops.

He'd become totally amoral in his dealings with others. Merson became a nightmare to live with at home and was barely on speaking terms with wife Lorraine. He chose to unburden himself on 25 November 1994: 'I'M HOOKED ON COCAINE,' he admitted in the *Daily Mirror*. In the exclusive, he revealed how cocaine abuse helped him forget his other problems: 'I was doing line after line of cocaine throughout the night. It was the only way I felt I could cope with all the debts.'

Typically, amid a storm of protests, Arsenal stood resolutely by their man and paid Merson his £5,000 weekly wage while he underwent rehabilitation at the Priory Clinic over the next two months. It's always been Arsenal's way and while many claim that the club should have been tougher on its wayward stars, it provides further evidence of the 'Arsenal spirit', and the 'all for one' mentality. Trevor Brooking, for one, claimed a lengthy ban would have been in order, but Arsenal and the FA believed he'd already punished himself enough. It is a contradiction which runs through the club's history, that an institution which espouses high moral standards should have spawned numerous rogues and rebels and, stranger still, that in modern times, the club has tended to protect its bad boys.

George Graham surmised that, for all his problems, Merson remained a key player. After all, he was a rather more appealing prospect in the number 10 shirt than, say, Jimmy Carter or Eddie McGoldrick. Maybe George hoped that by showing faith in Merson, the board might be understanding towards his problems. He certainly got that wrong.

Tony Adams continued to drink for a further 18 months. As well as remaining club captain, he'd landed a new job, as a tester to ensure that Paul Merson's drinks were not spiked. As his marriage collapsed (his wife Jane was in rehabilitation for cocaine addition), Adams' recurrent knee injury meant that football, his first addiction, finally stopped 'working'. In the early months of 1996, during which time his use of crutches restricted his ability to go to the pub regularly, he came to realise the extent of his drinking problems. In the lead-up to Euro '96, after his knee operation succeeded, he fought his way back to full fitness, earned rave reviews for his displays in the tournament and stayed dry for two months.

Yet win or lose in Euro '96, Adams knew he'd make up for lost time afterwards. Gareth Southgate's missed penalty against the Germans sparked Adams' three-week bender. On a Friday afternoon in a dingy west London social club, he sank his last pint and went home. Cold sweats and delusions kept him awake all night. Adams decided, finally, to square up to his demons. After he'd confessed to his Arsenal teammates, he told the press. On 14 September 1996, the *Daily Express* printed the headline: 'ENGLAND CAPTAIN IS AN ALCOHOLIC'. It wasn't a surprise – it was probably the worst-kept secret in London.

But the reaction to Merson's and Adams' confessions among teammates, past and present, was one of bewilderment and confusion. They claimed to have had no inkling as to the extent of the problems. Paul Davis recalls: 'I don't honestly think that anyone was really aware. We all knew that Tony and Paul liked a drink, but in Tony's case, it never appeared to affect his performances.' Alan Smith recalls: 'I used to get changed next to Paul before every game. I got asked so many times about whether I guessed there were real problems, but, honestly, I didn't. Nowadays, there are much firmer tabs kept on players – but not so much back then.' Adams, once George's hard-drinking, tough-tackling lieutenant, became Arsène Wenger's thoughtful, ball-playing, tough-tackling lieutenant, skippering the Gunners to two Doubles. Teetotalism did little to diminish his powers of leadership. Merson, too, was rehabilitated and showed his true form under Bruch Rioch and Arsène Wenger, before leaving for Middlesbrough in 1997. Of the two, Merson's battle has been the most public. He left Middlesbrough due to the alleged 'betting culture' at the club and then fell temporarily off the wagon at his next club, Aston Villa. He did show a sense of black humour towards his addictions. In late 1996, a journalist asked him if he had any New Year's resolutions: 'No, mate, I've given everything up,' came the reply. Teammates were unsure of how to deal with the pair, often believing them to be self-absorbed 'recovery bores', a reflection of how hard it was for seasoned professionals to embrace the new thinking in modern football. Adams' teammates were bemused at their captain's new interest in playing the piano, writing poetry, studying Eastern philosophy and his on-off romance with supermodel Caprice in the late '90s.

A key Arsenal player from the mid-'90s comments: 'I think it was hard for Paul and Tony's teammates to really understand what was happening. Some of them really couldn't get their heads around it. David Platt, for instance, couldn't understand why Paul started to walk away from him when he opened up a copy of the *Sporting Life*. Some of the other lads were like: "Well, you can still drink alcopops or low alcohol beer, can't you?" It all got a bit edgy at times.'

Adams' reinvention has been the most startling. Once boorish in interviews, he has adopted an almost spiritual edge when he talks. He firmly believes that his Sporting Chance charity is his ultimate legacy to sport. Giving support to sportsmen and women from any walk of life who need it, it provides rehabilitation and counselling in various centres around the country. Now considered the positive face of football, Adams mentions that his UNESCO role 'is to show what a good force sport can be. It is a very powerful force.' Many in the game remain unsure of how to deal with the new Adams, believing him to be a pseudo-intellectual, a self-appointed 'evangelist' who only speaks for the tiny minority of footballers with addictive personalities. Wycombe Wanderers fans have a new perspective on Adams, having seen his cool veneer disappear on the touchline during the club's doomed fight for survival in the 2003-04 season.

Visiting Swaleside Prison in 2002 clearly brought back some painful memories for former prisoner number 669, but he commented: 'I feel so healed these days that the feeling didn't last. I have control in my life now.' A Five Live listener rang in to complain about Adams, claiming he sounded 'like Geri Haliwell. He's far too preachy, he thinks he's God.' A number of Premiership bosses were also unhappy with his stance on the gambling stories that circulated in early 2003. Adams reckons that gambling is rife in the modern game. Several Premiership managers begged to differ, accusing Adams of creating mountains out of molehills. Fact, or further evidence of the 'culture of denial' which Adams believes is undermining the modern game?

Twenty-first-century footballers are expected to be lithe, chiselled athletes. It is inconceivable that they could perform at the highest level and live the kind of life Paul Merson did a decade ago. Perry Groves comments: 'If modern Arsenal players sank as many beers as we did, they'd struggle to stay in the division. We were athletes, but these guys are pyrotechnic. They look different. The change is incredible.'

Clubs have stamped out heavy drinking among their stars, but in this era of telephone-number salaries, the temptation to gamble remains huge. As he winds down his career, Merson is becoming a potent force in warning players of these dangers. In January 2003, he claimed that 'lorry loads' of top footballers were blowing fortunes in the bookies and three months later admitted that although he'd resisted the temptations to drink and take drugs, gambling had 'spanked me all over the place'. In February 2004, he confessed to having 'blown £75,000 in a week on spread betting'. He remains a potent symbol of how difficult it is to kick the habits of a lifetime. As a leading light in the Divert Trust, the National Charity For The Prevention of Youth Crime, he claims investment in sport can 'rebuild young lives' and steer them away from breaking the law. Merson and his associates now offer free advice to clubs to warn players of the perils of addiction.

Paul Merson's and Tony Adams' careers encompassed the two opposite schools of thought in the English game. The sport is now trying to forget its boozy past and the Dennis Bergkamps of this world prefer to discuss their collection of vintage clarets, rather than how many pints they can sink in an hour. Neither Adams nor Merson has ever asked for sympathy, and that's just as well, because few addicts would have had such understanding employers, or access to expensive rehabilitation facilities like the Priory. But through their crucial roles in bringing success to modern Arsenal and their willingness to help others avoid the mistakes they made as young players, they deserve respect. Speaking a week after Paul Vaessen was found dead in his flat, Tony Adams said: 'It's very sad but that is the illness of addiction for you. I hope the kind of work I'm doing with my charity will mean that people like Paul Vaessen will know where to turn in the future.' He added: 'I have managed to put some money aside for my retirement, instead of throwing it down my neck. I understand that not all reformed alcoholics are so fortunate.' Financially, Adams and Merson can expect to enjoy a comfortable future, but even then they will still live a day-to-day existence. As Paul Merson says, they are only a single bet or drink away from plummeting to rock bottom once again.

THIRTEEN

Home Truths

I'm no longer part of Arsenal. To hell with the English
people.

Nicolas Anelka, speaking in 1999

Throughout the summer of 1999, civil wars raged in Kosovo and
Chechnya. In Britain, public debate rumbled over the exact cost
to the taxpayer of the Millennium Dome and, even more
importantly, if you were a *Sun* worshipper, precisely how much
'Beckingham Palace' would cost Posh 'n' Becks. Yet, judging by
my bulging cuttings file, these stories weren't the ones that
hogged tabloid headlines between June and August.
Astonishingly, the protracted transfer saga of a talented yet
moody French footballer who later commented 'I didn't realise it
would create a fuss' was considered a more newsworthy story.
Even *Mirror* editor Piers Morgan admitted that the whole saga
had received 'an unprecedented amount of coverage'. There has
never been a story quite like it. But then – as the player's brother
tells me – there's never been a footballer quite like Nicolas
Anelka. After 'Anelka-gate' had finally run its course, Arsenal,
and European football for that matter, had been rudely barged
into a new era. The sport, by and large, was controlled by the
whims of players and their advisers. The proverbial lunatics ran
the proverbial asylum. The serfs, whom George Eastham
liberated 40-odd years earlier, now claimed to be the masters.

The nearest thing Arsenal had experienced to 'Anelka-gate' in the past was Frank Stapleton's departure in the summer of 1981. The quiet Dubliner had been Arsenal's only regular goal-getter over the previous two years, but he became frustrated with Arsenal's lack of activity in the transfer market. Another issue for Frank was his relatively low wage: as a youth-team graduate, he'd never been one of Highbury's highest earners. He could double or treble his money elsewhere. A year earlier, Liam Brady joined Juventus for a ridiculously low fee of £600,000 (fixed by EC law) and that had been bad enough. But at least Brady was out of sight and, in some ways, out of mind. As the Gunners began their slide into mediocrity without the talismanic Brady, Frank also decided he wanted out. Liverpool were showing a strong interest in him and few would have failed to have seen the attraction for his going to Anfield. But Frank opted not to join Liverpool. Instead, he signed for Manchester United for £900,000. That hurt, because over the last few years Arsenal had always looked more likely to land silverware than the Mancs. Example: the 1979 FA Cup final. With Stapleton, it suddenly fitted into place. Frank was never given to much celebration after scoring, but there is one picture in which he looks truly elated. It was taken after the Cup final and there he is, in the Arsenal team group, beaming with joy. Yet the photograph is replete with irony, because, after having swapped shirts with an opponent, Frank is dressed in a United shirt. It was a foretaste of things to come.

They say there are no truths like home truths. As Liam Brady commented: 'At a time when Arsenal decided to tighten their belts, United and Liverpool loosened the purse-strings. It was a rough time to be an Arsenal fan.' According to Paul Vaessen, it wasn't much fun being an Arsenal player either. He recalled: 'Even though I probably stood to gain more than most from Frank's departure, the atmosphere at pre-season training was really depressing. With Frank and Liam gone, all the Arsenal players knew that basically, the club was on the way down.' Deep down, Arsenal fans realised their club was now regarded as a selling club, unable to fight off the circling vultures from the Continent, or up the M6. Over the next few years, Stapleton returned regularly to haunt his former club. While Gunners fans were forced to watch the likes of John Hawley and 'boy wonder' Lee Chapman, Frank got to play alongside million-pound players Bryan Robson and Ray Wilkins. The denouement arrived when United trounced Arsenal 4–2 in a Milk Cup tie at Highbury. Stapleton scored United's second and flicked his Vs at the North Bank in celebration, as a none-too-subtle riposte to the verbal abuse he'd received. It annoyed Arsenal fans that on Eire trips, Stapleton regularly called David O'Leary 'a mug' for staying at Highbury, bearing in mind the comparatively low wage he was on. There was a kind of justice, however, as O'Leary eventually won two title medals at Arsenal, whereas Stapleton got none with United. But no one would have predicted this outcome in the early '80s, and it doesn't erase the depressing memories of Arsenal's Dark Age.

Long ago it may be, but Stapleton has not been forgiven by many Arsenal fans. A couple of years back, he was making his way up St Thomas's Road towards Highbury's main entrance to do some radio work. He slipped through the throng largely unnoticed until he was spotted by a middle-aged man with his young son. The man blocked Stapleton's path and nudged his offspring. 'That man,' he informed the uncomprehending ten year old, 'is a fucking Judas.' Stapleton, used to dealing with the public, walked around him, but the man looked at him with genuine hatred in his eyes. 'He broke our hearts, didn't he?' he said. Then he too walked away, telling his son not to tell his mum that he'd used the F-word. But there were several vital differences between Stapleton's and Anelka's departures. Frank didn't spend months criticising Arsenal FC in public and, as he'd reached the end of his contract, he was technically free to leave Arsenal. Nicolas Anelka was not.

Back in 1997, Nico was Arsenal's international bright young thing. Clearly, Arsène Wenger had bought Anelka in order to groom him to succeed the ageing Ian Wright. In truth, Arsenal fans knew little about the raga-haired French teenager. He'd arrived under rather strange circumstances. Arsenal had, apparently, exploited a loophole in the French transfer system – full details only emerged years later – and signed him for a mere

£500,000 from Paris St Germain. In the brief glimpses fans saw of him at the tail end of the 1996–97 season, he looked a mouth-watering prospect, lightning-quick and alert. If this was the man to assume Wright's mantle, the future looked rosy. Anelka's signing was one of the first examples of Wenger preferring to purchase French produce, rather than relying on traditional British fare. Much as we appreciated Paul Shaw's honest endeavour, Phil Mitchell's dead ringer was several branches short of being top of the tree. So, Wenger decided, was John Hartson, who was sold to West Ham for £5 million. He decided that the Welshman spent too long injured or suspended. Hartson's propensity to pile the pounds around his midriff, largely thanks to his love of ale, had become another major headache for Wenger. Hartson was a throwback to a bygone age in English football. Wenger wanted teetotal athletes, not boozy, cumbersome target men. It was time for a dash of Gallic panache.

Wenger gave Anelka his first-team chance during the middle part of the following season. In November 1997, he whipped in his first Arsenal goal, a blistering 20-yard shot past Peter Schmeichel, in the Gunners' 3–2 win over Manchester United. As his manager later commented, there are worse circumstances in which to score your first Arsenal goal. In the second half of the 1997–98 season, Anelka's form was sensational. Under Wenger's guidance, and with advice from French colleagues Petit and Vieira, he quickly found his feet in the Premiership. Blinding speed and rapier thrusts took him through opposition defences at will, and he spearheaded the attack after Ian Wright faded from the first-team picture. Anelka's goals were befitting a team that had now thrown off the defensive manacles of the Graham era. There was the scorching brace of goals against Newcastle at Highbury, the quicksilver sprint and finish at Blackburn, and the crowning moment – his dash and pin-point finish against Newcastle in the FA Cup final, which secured the Double. At just 19, he was already making substitute appearances in the French national team. Life, it seemed, couldn't get much better for him. A golden future appeared to be mapped out.

There was just one slight problem. For a man who had the

world at his feet, he seemed to be carrying it on his shoulders. His body language suggested he possessed little self-confidence. In the Double-winning photographs, in marked contrast to the delirious Wrighty, the serene Tony Adams and the rabid Nigel Winterburn, Anelka seemed almost embarrassed to be a part of things. The one thing for which Anelka was criticised in that first full season was his frequently poor peripheral vision. With head and shoulders slumped, he was a stark contrast with the cocksure Ian Wright, who strutted around the pitch as if he owned it. And Nico didn't smile much either, not like Wrighty, who always knew how to flash his gold tooth at the right moment. In short, the Frenchman wasn't a new Ian Wright. He was the one and only Nicolas Anelka, a fact which, he believed, contributed to his problems. And there was one other thing. Rumour had it that Anelka's brothers, Claude and Didier, had rather too much to say about their brother's career.

In the summer of 1998, the air was full of it. Journalists who once slated Arsenal for being duller than a Sting record now queued up to pay homage to the Wenger vintage. 'ARSENAL WIN WORLD CUP,' claimed *The Sun*, as Vieira and Petit combined to construct France's third goal in the final against Brazil. Anelka didn't make it into Roger Lemerre's squad, but given his young age and Lemerre's baffling decision to play the hopeless Stefan Guivarch up front, it was understandable. *L'Equipe* magazine realised Anelka's vast potential, though, labelling him 'THE NEW STAR OF FRENCH FOOTBALL'. At Arsenal, his future seemed even more secure. With Ian Wright jettisoned in a cut-price transfer to West Ham, Anelka had the opportunity to take full advantage and really establish himself as a striking force.

The other main football story that summer concerned Nottingham Forest striker Pierre Van Hooijdonk's dispute with his club. The Dutchman refused to play for promoted Forest on the grounds that they had failed to adequately strengthen the squad in the close season. 'Dump him in the reserves and let him rot,' the club was urged. After two months, Van Hoijdonk did return to the starting line-up but it was a distinctly uneasy peace.

Teammates refused to celebrate goals with him, and manager Dave Bassett admitted that he'd wanted to 'shove the olive-branch where the sun doesn't shine'. Unsuspecting Arsenal fans didn't realise they would be reading similar headlines about another temperamental Continental striker by the end of the season.

Early season strikes against Manchester United, Everton and Southampton revealed Anelka's quality, but there were major problems with Arsenal's strike force. The Gunners decided against signing Patrick Kluivert, and with Dennis Bergkamp's troublesome hamstring injury and Chris Wreh still tripping over his feet with alarming regularity, the team was a striker or two light. Anelka did himself few favours and the slumping shoulders and downward gaze suggested all wasn't well. With Arsenal sliding into disastrous fifth place shortly before Christmas and falling at the first hurdle in the Champions League, sections of the Highbury crowd turned on the under-pressure Anelka. So too, on one memorable occasion at Blackburn, did Martin Keown. In full earshot of the Gunners' travelling fans, Keown, with blood-vessels in his head bulging, eyes popping and spittle flecking from his mouth, yelled: 'Look like you want to play for the Arsenal!' in the young Frenchman's face. As Arsenal laboured at home against a mediocre Middlesbrough side in December, cries of 'Ian Wright, Wright, Wright' were audible. No matter that Anelka saved his team with a last-minute equaliser; in the hearts and minds of many, he'd always remain in the shadow of the gold-toothed one.

As Arsenal got their championship challenge back on track in late December and the New Year, Anelka rediscovered his best form. Sparkling displays against West Ham, Chelsea and Leeds forced him into the French team, and he scored twice in France's 2–0 win against England at Wembley. It was at this point that he began to display the traits which have marred his career ever since. Later that week, the *Mirror* ran the headline: 'THE GLOOMY LONER IN COR BLIMEY LAND'. In an exclusive interview, Anelka confessed to being 'bored in London'. 'I don't know anybody here and I don't want to. I don't think I'll see my contract through,' he added graciously. What was it that

Dr Johnson once said about people who were switched off by the capital – that they were 'tired of life itself'? Inevitably, the Arsenal publicity department quickly denied that Anelka had ever made such comments, but he was obviously troubled. In an off-the-record comment to a journalist, he said: 'For a week I had been waking up in the middle of the night, running with sweat. I don't know why. I had the impression of playing against ghosts. I don't know whether they are dreams or nightmares.' So, just what, or who, was eating at him? Strangely enough, he seemed to believe that it was teammate Marc Overmars.

The Dutch winger had been the catalyst behind Arsenal's 1997–98 Double success. It's been the story of Arsenal's modern-day league triumphs: an in-form wide man has equalled title success. For a while, Overmars appeared as if he was destined to become better than any of the Armstrong/Marwood/Limpar legacy. Scorching pace, direct running and a guaranteed ten goals a season – Overmars had it all. But after that first season, he started to display some rather annoying habits. As the usually diplomatic Alan Smith commented: 'He began to evade challenges as if he had a pole vault up his backside.' This, combined with a tendency to 'go it alone' in the opposition penalty area, clearly got to Anelka. 'It's true that Overmars only plays for his own mug and will never give me a ball that I can score from,' he commented. He also bemoaned Overmars' and Bergkamp's tendency to speak Dutch to one another on the pitch. He felt shut out by the pair.

Arsène Wenger faced a potential crisis. Already, press hacks were lamenting his reliance upon foreign cavaliers rather than English roundheads, and a protracted international dispute between Holland and France would prove that petulant Continentals were undermining the true spirit of Arsenal. Surely George Graham would have metaphorically banged their heads together, labelled them prima donnas and shoved them in the reserves for a couple of months. Wenger advocated a more cunning approach. He knew that Overmars didn't speak French and that Anelka barely spoke any English. So in his mother tongue, Wenger got Anelka to confirm that he felt Overmars was selfish with the ball. Then in English he asked Overmars for his view. The Dutchman argued that he 'looked out' for Anelka whenever he had the ball. Although nothing had yet been sorted out, both players seemed more relieved now that they'd aired their grievances. Wenger, realising that non-communication could be a virtue in such circumstances, made two individual statements to the pair. He told Overmars, in English, that Anelka 'doesn't have any kind of a problem with you', and Anelka, in French, that 'Marc promises to pass to you more often'. Both players, satisfied with the outcome, shook hands and walked out. Wenger's outrageous gamble paid off. But he was only papering over the cracks.

When Wenger's foreign stars first arrived at Highbury, they found it amusing that established English professionals referred to the manager as 'the boss' or 'the gaffer'. In Holland, dressing-room bust-ups are de rigueur. Dennis Bergkamp, with painful clarity, recalls how the Dutch team self-destructed on the eve of two successive World Cups. It is accepted that teams in the Dutch league are riddled by cliques and that the manager's decisions are questioned on a regular basis. It is a different story at Highbury, where, in Lee Dixon's words: 'Team spirit is everything – we fight and die for each other.' Anelka walked into a culture riddled with war analogies at Highbury. Captain Adams had instilled a trench-like mentality amongst his troops. There was little room for dissenters, or those who felt themselves to be above the law. Anelka can be spiky, outspoken and moody, in the manner of most French rebel icons. Here is the man who insists: 'I live my life how I want to, even though it makes things complicated. The future will show who is right.' No wonder Arsenal's old guard feared and mistrusted Anelka's stroppy tendencies. As Adams sent his troops into 'battle', with talk of 'death and glory', there could be no room for a loose cannon who didn't feel part of the collective. Already Anelka was portrayed as a disturber of the peace, a troublemaker. But he wasn't acting alone. With agent Marc Roger, and brothers Didier and Claude, the Anelka side-show was destined to become the most infamous and gossiped about in football by the end of the year.

It emerged that, despite Nico's considerable wealth, the three brothers remained holed up in a drab, rented Edgware flat. This hardly suggested that Anelka planned to stay around for long. As his advisers and guardians, Claude and Didier allowed him to score some fairly spectacular public own goals. There was the embarrassing episode when Nicolas simply refused to turn up to collect his PFA Young Player of the Year award, preferring to spend the evening clubbing instead. ('Nicolas didn't realise the fuss this would cause,' Claude later told me.) The award subsequently took pride of place on the mantelpiece in the brothers' flat, befitting Nico's often-contradictory nature. Then there was the chilling warning issued by Anelka in February 1999, when he commented: 'They talk about loyalty and love of the shirt. All that is dead. Only the national team is important.' ('Nicolas was only telling the truth. Why fob off the media and the fans with complete lies? That's how things really are,' Claude comments.) Nico's ruthless brand of honesty hardly endeared him to an increasingly twitchy Arsenal faithful.

This, after all, was the period when he scored a sensational first-half hat-trick against Leicester, after combining superbly with Dennis Bergkamp, but then proceeded to look completely miserable in the process. The 'Incredible Sulk' nickname had its origins in this match. What did Claude Anelka make of this infamous episode? 'Nico never said he was Ian Wright,' he says, rather tetchily and tellingly. Maybe not, but surely an occasional smile and shirt kiss wouldn't have gone amiss?

Teammates never understood him. At times, he was every inch the nerdy teenager, who sat with his eyes fixed rigidly on his laptop watching DVD movies on the coach back from away games. He could also play the stroppy adolescent role, having to be cajoled onto the team coach by Wenger after an argument with Marc Overmars at Coventry. Then there was the teenage prodigy who drilled in two beauties during Arsenal's stunning 6–1 win away at Middlesbrough in April 1999. The truth is that he was all three rolled into one. So what makes him tick? Gaining access to Anelka – he has always claimed that he wishes to be 'left alone' – is nigh on impossible. However, in a brief telephone conversation four years ago, I discovered that Claude is slightly more forthcoming. To understand his brother, Claude tells me, you have to consider his background.

The Anelka family originally hail from the Caribbean island of Martinique. During 'Anelka-gate' in the summer of 1999, the *Mirror* interviewed Nico's grandmother, Horta, who still lives on the island. Practically illiterate and living in abject poverty, her only valuable item is a signed photograph of her famous grandson. It says simply 'Yours, Nico'. The implication was that the Anelka boys would have faced a similarly grim existence if their parents had not emigrated to Trappes, a poor ('but not that poor', my French friend informs me) Parisian suburb. Anelka's parents found menial work in local government and Nico showed footballing talent from a young age. The brothers were frequently stopped and questioned by the police, as racial tension in the area grew higher. It was the beginning of Nico's tendency to feel picked on and partly explains his dislike of authority figures. Claude and brother Didier have acted as Nico's advisers for several years. Is Nico's role, I asked Claude, to act as the Anelka family's main breadwinner? Claude wanted me to clarify my meaning. 'Do Nico's earnings now support the whole family?' I asked. 'You mean, is he the golden goose?' he responded. I told Claude that this showed an excellent grasp of the English language, considering he didn't understand my previous question. He laughed, saying: 'I've heard it before. You're suggesting that unless we keep him moving around, we kill the golden goose. But it's purely down to him what he does with his money.'

I'd asked the question because, in a recent interview, Jimmy Floyd Hasselbaink, who comes from a similar background to the Anelkas, admitted that his wages supported the extended Hasselbaink family. I put it to Claude that it was in the family's interests to keep Nico moving, as the resultant 10 per cent signing-on fees would feed and clothe the family – including Claude and Didier – for a while longer. Claude told me: 'I'm not answering that question.' But he didn't deny the allegation, either. A rather different view of Nico and his brothers emerges during the player's interviews with French journalist Dominique Fourniol, the only hack on the planet, it seems, with access to him. Anelka, invariably charming and polite company, with plenty of time to sign autographs for the kids, refuses to allow hangers-on near him. He embraces Islam and the three siblings have used their cash to good effect in Trappes, where they have funded the local football team for several years and are leading lights in regenerating the whole area. But that was of little comfort to Arsenal supporters as the 1998–99 season reached its climax.

A listless display in the FA Cup semi-final against Manchester United led to him being booed by some Arsenal fans. He redeemed himself somewhat in the replay by rounding on Peter Schmeichel and slamming in what appeared to be Arsenal's equaliser. Nico, this time with a touch of the Ian Wrights, went ballistic and virtually jumped into the contingent of Arsenal fans at Villa Park. If only the linesman hadn't raised his flag for offside seconds earlier. After further gossiping in the press and a dreadful display against Aston Villa in what proved to be his last match in an Arsenal shirt, a journalist wrote: 'Nicolas Anelka is the unpleasable in pursuit of the unobtainable.' Wenger, seven days later, reported Olympique Marseilles for 'tapping Anelka up'. His brothers were effectively offering him around Europe to the highest bidder. The crazy world of Nicolas Anelka was rapidly spiralling out of control.

Arsenal fans were resigned to the fact that he would leave, despite having two years remaining on his contract. The bizarre way in which Anelka contradicted himself in public led Wenger to claim: 'He has had his head turned.' It wasn't hard to fathom that Wenger believed his brothers were weaving a dark spell around Nico, destroying his ability to think clearly. A day after the Villa game, Anelka claimed: 'Of course I'll see through my contract.' Then, three days later, an allegedly 'homesick' Anelka announced – through brother Claude – 'the club of my heart is Real Madrid'. Three weeks later, he had his heart set on a move to the Eternal City of Rome, describing Lazio as 'a dream team'. By now, even the Pope had got to hear of Anelka's obstreperousness. Through the *Vatican Daily*, he described the player's proposed £18 million move to Rome as 'an offence to poor people'. A week later: 'The club of my heart is Juventus.' The British press, aware that Jimmy Floyd Hasselbaink was treating Leeds in a similarly truculent way, believed this to be the thin end of a destructive wedge. The Anelka brothers were portrayed as mafiosi, intent on destroying the last vestiges of loyalty and decency in the modern game. Arsenal were urged to let Anelka stew. In public, at least, the club followed this advice. In early June, he was informed: 'You are going nowhere.'

The popular view of the Anelka clan as pantomime villains has been exhaustively written about in the media. Their perceptions of Arsenal and English football are usually ignored. But Claude Anelka, despite his prickly approach to our conversation, does deliver some rather uncomfortable home truths. I asked him directly whether or not his blatant disregard for contracts was likely to kill the game. His response was unexpected: 'I've been asked that question so many times. But I always take another view. Say, for instance, that Nicolas had lost his form, or failed to recover it after a bad injury. Don't you think that Arsenal would have shipped him out, in mid-contract, to the highest bidder? Players may be high earners, but basically clubs treat them like pieces of meat for sale. It's a business, pure and simple. You talk to me of loyalty. The days of players like Tony Adams are over. You fans find that difficult to understand. But in reality, there is no loyalty from clubs to players. There never has been. Once a player is of no use to a club, they're finished. Most players don't finish their contracts any more, and that's often due to the club's say-so. I put it to you that you're annoyed he left because he's a good player, not due to your principles. If an obscure reserve wanted to leave mid-contract, would you create the same fuss? I doubt it. People talk about lots of things, but what is important is Nicolas's career. People say he's selfish and disloyal. But clubs have been suiting themselves for years. Let's be honest – it suited Arsenal very nicely to sign him from Paris St Germain in the way they did. But all Arsenal will say on that issue is "that's another story".'

Claude Anelka's final comment is one that still rankles with Arsenal officials. Under French law, a player is obliged to sign his first contract at the club that developed him as a youth. In Anelka's case, this was Paris St Germain. However, the law cannot be applied internationally. 'So Nicolas could have signed for Arsenal but not Marseilles or Bordeaux,' Claude said. Wenger's Arsenal, in signing Anelka for a mere £500,000, cunningly exploited a legal loophole. A leading French manager described Arsenal's actions back in 1997 as 'technically legal, but hardly upstanding'. Doubtless, the club would also rather not be reminded of the manner in which record signing Sylvain Wiltord arrived at Highbury back in August 2000. The Frenchman, who'd just been voted player of the year back in his native country and had helped France win Euro 2000, informed his club, Bordeaux, that unless they agreed to release him immediately from his contract and let him join Arsenal, he would have no qualms in launching a one-man strike. Echoes of the Anelka affair just 12 months earlier? Most certainly. On this occasion, the Gunners were the beneficiaries of player power, and it was no surprise that in the press, Claude Anelka accused Arsenal of applying double standards. Gunners officials calmed troubled waters in unmistakable style, claiming: 'You can't really compare the respective cases of Nicolas Anelka and Sylvain Wiltord.' No further explanation was given.

My final question to Claude, before he slammed the telephone down without so much as an *au revoir*, was whether Nicolas's career hadn't benefited hugely from Arsenal's 'exploitation' of the loophole. 'Of course it suited Nicolas that Wenger gave him his first-team chance, especially as Paris St Germain are not a club which tend to give youth graduates a chance. But then Arsenal got my brother for a tiny sum. They gained even more,' he told me. Claude neglected to mention that the Anelkas, through their family lawyer, Marguerite Fauconette, planned to exploit a legal loophole of their own. In what would have been a court case as sensational as the Bosman saga, Fauconette planned to invoke an obscure European employment law, whereby Anelka, in paying Arsenal three months' wages (around £200,000) in compensation, would be legally exonerated from fulfilling the rest of his contract. Doubtless this law will be invoked by the end of the decade.

By late July, the Anelka brothers, attempting to escape Europe's ravenous paparazzi, holed themselves up in an economy class Martinique hotel. There were no telephones in the rooms, so Didier and Claude called the shots, contacting officials at various European clubs via their mobiles. On 27 July, the family doctor deemed Nicolas unable to return to pre-season training at Highbury. He was said to be 'suffering from stress'. A week later, the teenager, who'd cost Arsenal just half a million pounds two years earlier, moved for 46 times that amount, finally joining Real Madrid for £23 million. Reports speculated that he would be earning in excess of £60,000 a week. The player has always denied that he moved simply in order to line his pockets. 'I moved because Real Madrid are the biggest club in Europe,' he later commented. Clearly, he didn't listen to Wenger's warning that Real were: 'a big club run by little men'. Typically, Anelka refused to go quietly. David Dein was accused of 'dragging out the dispute for two months', and being interested in 'money, money and only money'. English journalists were lambasted for being 'all rubbish. They are frustrated players who never made it as professionals.'

Yet for all his bluster, Anelka's brief stay in Spain revealed an incredibly naive side to his nature. As new Real Madrid teammate Steve McManaman warned: 'English journalists are pussycats compared with Spain's.' For a man who claimed to dislike media attention, Madrid was the worst possible destination. Raúl and Morientes had already discovered just how fickle the Spanish media could be. Within weeks, Anelka missed training after an alleged bust-up with Vincente del Bosque over his role in the team. Nicolas claimed his manager refused to speak to him, but del Bosque saw it another way. He commented: 'I think he is just confused, that he lives in a world of his own and he will just have to get out of it.' The player, in typically obstreperous style, claimed: 'I know perfectly well what I did. I expressed my feelings, because as no one wanted to listen to me, I had to do something. I am a little bit crazy but I know the consequences of what I did.' His stay in Madrid was little short of disastrous. He now claims:

'I didn't fit into the style of play,' but there was more to it than that. The final ignominy for him came in the 2000 Champions League final, when del Bosque replaced Anelka, who'd played well, with loyal club servant Manuel Sanchis, who, in Tony Adams style, had served Real faithfully for two decades. The Madrid fans gave Sanchis a rapturous reception, but booed the outward-bound Anelka off the pitch. A journalist later put it to Nico that for all his wealth, he was destined to find nothing but unhappiness and fans' contempt if he displayed such a gung-ho attitude to contracts. Anelka declined to comment.

In the summer of 2000, he decided it was time to go home and rejoined Paris St Germain for £20 million. The team, sponsored by Canal Plus, was expected to coast to the title. As it was, PSG finished a poor seventh in the league. Anelka failed to hit it off with new coach Luis Fernandes, whom he accused of being 'impossible to talk to'. When disgruntled PSG fans unfurled the banner 'www.shit.com' at a home match, they had the sullen Nico in mind more than most. Toe and hamstring injuries contributed to his poor form, but he also found that so-called old friends in Trappes were not so keen to see the prodigal son return. Anelka reckoned they were 'envious' of his wealth.

Over the last two years, he has resumed his career on these shores, even though he originally claimed he'd never return. After a poor start to season 2001–02, he informed PSG coach Fernandes – 'an unintelligent man' – that he wished to leave the French capital. Fernandes, who'd watched the 'Anelka-gate' affair carefully two years earlier, admitted: 'I cannot keep a player against his will.' First, he was offered on loan to Chelsea or Fulham, before departing for Gérard Houllier's Liverpool. Four teams in just over two years? You can almost hear the old Tommy Docherty gag about him having had 'more clubs than Jack Nicklaus'. Houllier opted not to sign him on a permanent deal and he ended up at Manchester City for £13 million. His stock had fallen since his Arsenal days; he didn't make it into France's 2002 World Cup Squad. Roger Lemerre said of him: 'God helps those who help themselves.' Yet Anelka continues to display a bizarre combination of charm, arrogance and a total unawareness of accepted codes of conduct.

Anelka has adapted well to life in Manchester and, along with Shaun Wright-Phillips, was the only success story in City's disappointing 2003–04 season. Yet City fans shouldn't bank on Anelka sticking around for long. Shortly after his arrival, he claimed he'd like to rejoin Real Madrid at some stage and he hasn't ruled out the possibility of playing in Italy either. Rome appears to be especially attractive to him. Yet you cannot help but feel that he's angling for a return to Highbury in the near future. It is no secret that Wenger – whom Anelka describes as 'the best coach I've ever worked with' – wanted to link him up with Thierry Henry during the 2001–02 season. Anelka is still not overly keen on David Dein, but naturally he chooses to take an unconventional view on his Arsenal departure. With the £23 million received for him, the Gunners, he claims, were able to sign Double winners Robert Pires – who Anelka encouraged to join Arsenal rather than Real Madrid – and Thierry Henry. There's still that distinct whiff of cockiness about Anelka, mixed with a tinge of regret that he left Wenger's Arsenal so quickly. It wouldn't be a huge surprise if he did return. Anelka's key critics within the Arsenal dressing-room – the 'old-guard' defence – have largely disappeared and Nico remains good friends with the French contingent.

Yet Wenger appears reluctant to buy established stars, especially at a time of tightening purse strings at Highbury. In signing the likes of José Antonio Reyes, he is buying players who will hopefully appreciate in value, just like Nico did when he was at the club. He would also have to win over his critics in the crowd. Anelka insists that he bears Arsenal fans no malice, but many Gunners fans bear *him* a grudge – witness the crescendo of boos every time he has touched the ball on his return to Highbury with Liverpool and Manchester City. Aside from his 'messing Arsenal around', his departure delivered another set of painful home truths. Anelka dared to mention that Real Madrid were 'a bigger club than Arsenal'. Like Brady and Stapleton in the early '80s, he made us feel unhappy about ourselves. With Overmars' and Petit's departures to Barcelona a year later, the Gunners regained the unwanted title of being a 'selling club'. On the grand European stage, Arsenal were at the mercy of the wealthier La Liga clubs. Hindsight has since proved that the Gunners' ability and team spirit remained undiminished, but that was no thanks to Anelka. Yet even his detractors would be silenced once the goals began to flow. Just like players and managers, we're also guilty of applying appalling double standards at times.

For all his claims of wishing to settle down in his career, controversy dogs him. Anelka has always let it be known that he values playing regular club football above representing the national side. When asked about playing for his country, he refuses to be even remotely subtle. Was he disappointed to have missed out on France's World Cup venture to Japan and South Korea? 'No – it was a good thing, as it turned out. I had a nice holiday in Miami, instead,' came the bullshit-free reply. Then, in late 2002, he refused to join training with the national squad after a late call-up. In the manner of Alan Hudson and Charlie George, he felt insulted about not being selected the first time around. Unsurprisingly, Anelka is already being compared with the unpredictable German midfielder, Berndt Schuster, who went into self-imposed exile in the '80s. Recently, Anelka extended the olive branch to the French national manager. 'I'm not a movie star – I don't want all this fuss,' Anelka is often reported to say. But if you walk out on three of Europe's biggest clubs in three years and opt not to play for your country at 23 years of age, you deserve the nickname 'Trouble Man'.

With three Premiership runners-up spots and two defeats in cup finals between 1999 and 2001, Arsenal were becoming the perennial bridesmaids and supporters grew twitchy. Wenger was stalling over signing his new contract, the Ashburton Grove stadium plans were on hold and £40 million of talent had gone abroad. The club, it seemed, was being pulled in a downward spiral. The only consolation was that Manchester United hadn't got their hands on any of Highbury's foreign stars. In the summer of 2001, Arsenal fans' worst nightmare almost came true. Patrick Vieira's frustration at the club's failure to build on the 1998

Double success was visible right throughout the 2000–01 season. After the defeat against Valencia in the Champions League quarter-final, he expressed huge fear that without significant additions to the squad, Arsenal's stock in Europe would fall. The FA Cup final defeat against Liverpool, when Arsenal snatched defeat from the jaws of victory, seemed the final straw. On 27 June, after weeks of speculation, the *Mirror* ran the worst possible headline for Arsenal fans: 'VIEIRA – I'M OFF'. Via the ubiquitous 'close friend', he expressed his disappointment with the way in which Arsenal's season ended. Before Sol Campbell's arrival from Spurs, Vieira had been none too impressed with the club's summer signings. Giovanni Van Bronckhorst, he reasoned, was an 'untested' Premiership player and Francis Jeffers 'just a boy'. With hindsight, Vieira's doubts over the pair were justified, but that's another story.

In the manner of Nicolas Anelka two years before, Vieira also allegedly threatened to strike if Arsenal refused to release him immediately. Real Madrid appeared the likeliest destination, with Manchester United rumoured to be lining up a mega-bucks deal to link him up with Roy Keane in United's midfield. In a dramatic show-down with David Dein and Arsène Wenger, he warned that he would go 'where and when it suits me'. What actually occurred behind the scenes remains a mystery. The full truth is unlikely ever to emerge – Arsenal's spin-doctors have seen to that – but Dein and Wenger somehow convinced him to stay for another year.

In an exclusive *News of the World* interview in August 2001, Vieira attempted to adopt a 'clear the air' stance. He didn't make a very good job of it. His barbed comments about the club and the new signings earlier that summer were attributed to a treacherous former acquaintance of his. Then he finally revealed the worst-kept secret in football: Manchester United 'tapped him up' during the summer, which only went to worsen relations between the two clubs. Yet Vieira hardly seemed offended by United's advances. He admitted: 'I considered joining United,' adding: 'If I see at any time that Arsenal's ambitions don't match mine, I'll leave.' The club persuaded Vieira to dump his agent, Marc Roger, and become the latest addition to the Jerome Anderson stable, like so many of his teammates. It was Arsenal's attempt to exercise a degree of control over the Frenchman.

Vieira had made several thinly veiled threats against the club, and admitted that, for him, contracts were there to be broken. Yet at the first game of the 2001–02 season, away at Middlesbrough, Arsenal fans gave him the usual rapturous reception, the author included. But to be honest, I didn't really mean it, and I wondered if Vieira, who pointed to the cannon on his shirt and gave fans the 'thumbs up' sign, really felt comfortable either. Maybe his outburst that summer was simply down to the frustration he felt, but there was an uneasy peace afterwards. As Tony Adams prepared to retire at the end of the season, Vieira seemed poised to assume the mantle of Arsenal captain, if he chose to stay. Soon, he would be required to embody the spirit and determination of Arsenal, but his actions in the summer suggested he wasn't exactly a 'new Tony'.

I asked the guy next to me, who applauded Vieira for far longer than me, if he didn't feel uneasy pandering to a player who'd been ready to walk away, mid-contract, only a few weeks earlier. The man seemed to ignore the question, but a couple of minutes later he tapped me on the arm and said: 'You're right – it is wrong to pander to these players. But I bet you'd still rather have him at Arsenal than at Madrid. It's basically a business for them. It's a love thing for us. He will leave us sooner or later. Enjoy watching him while you can.' In 2003–04, Spanish clubs continued to make eyes at Arsenal's French contingent. Barcelona and Real Madrid sounded out the Gunners over taking Thierry Henry to Spain for a £40 million fee. Chelsea now have the financial might to consistently unsettle Arsenal's leading stars, and made a formal £50 million bid for Henry in January 2004. The Vieira rumours have never died away. Recently, an 'un-named' Arsenal player was reported to have commented: 'If Arsène Wenger leaves Arsenal to manage elsewhere, there will be an immediate exodus of French players from Highbury. No question.' And that's the truth.

FOURTEEN

Handbags and Verbals

We give people what they like to see – pace, commitment, attacking football – and sometimes if we go overboard, I am sorry.

Arsène Wenger, 2002

As Arsenal players and fans know, dust-ups and brawls during games can be both a blessing and a curse for the team. On the one hand, they result in large fines and lengthy suspensions for the protagonists, and a spate of unwelcome headlines, along the lines of: 'ARSENAL'S DAY OF SHAME'. The flip side is one that the FA and the club gloss over, but probably realise deep down is true. Many of Arsenal's most infamous run-ins with other clubs have cemented team spirit and created a common enemy upon whom players and fans can focus. It is a fact that during every successful Arsenal season in recent times there have been a clutch of high-profile incidents, large numbers of sendings-off or a headline-grabbing brawl – sometimes all three. In other words, scrapping Gunners may officially bring the club into disrepute, but in practice they indirectly strengthen it.

It was George Graham who, whilst insisting on 'high standards', oversaw the most newsworthy of the bust-ups. He would then collect the relevant newspaper clippings, detrimental to the club and individual players, and use them as a gee-up in order to get the team to respond. 'George used what I call "negative energy" to great effect,' recalls Alan Smith. 'He'd say, "Look what they've said about you. How are you going to respond?" And he knew we'd go and win our next game.' Yet before George arrived on the scene, Bertie Mee had not been averse to using such kidology and, latterly, Wenger has also used negative sound bites about the team to motivate his stars and identify a common cause – to better Alex Ferguson's Manchester United.

The late David Rocastle once commented: 'If you see your teammates in trouble, you go in to help . . . it was our teammate, our blood brother, in trouble.' Rocky was talking about Nigel Winterburn being pummelled during the 'battle of Old Trafford' in 1990, but he could have been referring to a host of incidents during the last 15 years or so. Even by the early '70s, Arsenal had a reputation as a club that occasionally overstepped the mark and a team that, in Frank McLintock's words, would 'fight and die for each other'. Ex-Leeds striker Duncan McKenzie once said: 'Arsenal remind me of the army a little bit – a group of highly trained professionals who can so easily step over the line into illegality. They are simply too close to the edge.'

In truth, heated encounters on the pitch have been the norm since the '40s, but with the advent of TV and Sky's penchant for highlighting every incident, it has become much easier to home in on trouble. Arsenal's first high-profile spot of bother occurred in the 1968 League Cup final against Leeds. 'It was not a pleasant game in which to play,' recalls Ian Ure. 'You wouldn't believe the amount of shirt pulling, sly kicks and time wasting which Jack Charlton, Johnny Giles and Norman Hunter were using.' Striker Bobby Gould, who also played in that game, remembered his treatment at the hands of Leeds defenders: 'Jack Charlton used to volley you up in the air, and then the scythe – the left foot of Norman Hunter – used to thwack you on the way down. And boy, could they dig.' Arsenal lost the game to a Terry Cooper volley, while Jim Furnell was impeded by Jack Charlton on the goal-line. In the second half, the Gunners also lost their rag. A 'handbags at dawn' encounter involving all 22 players kicked off in the Arsenal penalty area, after Furnell was impeded once again by Charlton. 'Something inside us snapped and we just decided that we weren't going to take it any more,' recalls Ure. Along with Storey's running battle with Johnny Giles, Arsenal had, at last, proved their point. 'That wouldn't have happened under Billy Wright,' laughs Bobby Gould. Though the Gunners lost the match, they'd demonstrated their ability to mix it with the bully boys. During the attritional '70s, this was to become a prerequisite for success.

Two years later, Arsenal players became involved in another confrontation, far away from the gaze of TV cameras and the British press corps. Lazio had been 'entertaining' Arsenal in Rome for a Fairs Cup match, and the 'ultras' – the right-wing faction of their support – gave the Arsenal players their usual friendly greeting of fireworks, smoke-bombs and verbal abuse. Lazio's players had a noteworthy reputation for riotous indiscipline and there was the omnipotent presence of referees who, it was later proved, fixed games in the Italians' favour. John Radford put Arsenal 2–0 up, but Lazio fought back and, with the dodgiest of last-minute penalties, levelled the tie at 2–2. With tempers still simmering, players from both sides attended a banquet in a plush Roman restaurant. Denis Hill-Wood, Arsenal's chairman, thanked Lazio for their 'warm hospitality' (cue sniggers from the Gunners players) and, as a token of their 'goodwill', Lazio officials presented Arsenal players with a set of distinctly girly handbags. Such fashion accessories were trendy among Latin males, but not burly Anglo-Saxon footballers.

Ray Kennedy recalled that at the end of the meal, some of the bags were thrown around like frisbees by the Arsenal players. It seemed fairly good-natured, and even the Lazio players laughed at their antics, but when the teams left the restaurant, it was a different story. Immediately, Kennedy was set upon by a couple of Italian players and the fight spilled out onto the street, turning into a full-scale brawl. George Armstrong was slammed against the side of the bus, and several of his teammates were punched to the floor. In the thick of the action was John Roberts, not the greatest central defender in the world but proving himself to be a decent heavyweight boxer. He defended his colleagues with his life, as did manager Bertie Mee, who according to eye-witnesses 'had a neat right-hook on him'.

It was then that the Italian *gendarmerie*, with sirens wailing, roared up in their Fiats. It sounds like a scene from *The Italian Job*, but it was set to become more serious than that. Wading in, complete with truncheons and guns, they randomly picked on Eddie Kelly and held him at gunpoint. Bertie Mee, clearly fearing for their safety, ushered his players onto the coach. As Frank McLintock later commented, this was one of the turning points of the 1970–71 Double season – teammates had shown 'their willingness to lay down their lives for each other'. FIFA investigated the incident and Lazio were fined heavily. In a fit of pique, they threatened to withdraw from the second leg at Highbury. They did turn up and, for all their bluster and talk of revenge, were easily defeated by the hyped-up Arsenal. George Graham, who played in both matches, learned a thing or two about the importance of team spirit during that episode.

George's sides always had a reputation for being tough, occasionally menacing, and for haranguing referees and baiting authority when they felt they had been wronged. In recent years, Graham has been referred to, mistakenly, as the inventor of Arsenal's offside trap. George actually modified the system, instructing his defenders to operate as a single defensive unit. The 'unit' became the most stubborn and impenetrable in European football. In George's early years, his full-backs, Viv Anderson and Kenny Sansom, were instructed to 'work' on the linesmen. Anderson recalls: 'George reckoned they lost concentration – that they dozed off. He told Kenny and me to give them "gentle" reminders. That meant shouting at them on a fairly regular basis. Kenny was a lot better at doing this than me.' Anderson is being modest. Those fans close enough to the action often heard the pair screaming 'OI, FLAG' at the startled linesman and, Inspector Gadget style, the obliging official raised it. Tony Adams was even less subtle, simply raising his arm and looking pleadingly at the referee, another reason why purists didn't take to him. They chuckled when he misjudged the situation by a fraction of a second, and the frozen Arsenal defence allowed opposition attackers to pour through the gaps.

If all else failed, Steve Williams led the swarm of protests around the referee and proceeded to turn the air blue, using the f-word as many times as possible in a ten-second onslaught. Even Joe Pesci, in Scorsese's *Casino*, would have had trouble beating Williams in a swearing competition. Williams later told me: 'I was a big Arsenal fan and I just hated to see the team lose. I suppose I'm best known for my battles with Ossie Ardiles in north London derbies. Now, he was a great player, but very, very sly. He was a bit like Johnny Giles. He'd look innocent enough, but he'd leave his studs in. Then, as all hell was let loose, he'd try and walk off and pretend he didn't know what the ref was saying. That annoyed me even more. He spoke perfect English. Ardiles is a very intelligent man. So I would phrase my verbal protests to him in language anyone could understand. Four letters long – it's simple enough. People would accuse me of being a "nutter" and a "psycho", but I wasn't going to let anyone take liberties with the Arsenal midfield when I was around.' Unsurprisingly, Graham's Arsenal gained a reputation as a team that was difficult to referee, a fact raised at the Referees' Forum in 1988. The biggest change in behaviour was that Arsenal players now hunted in packs. Groups of four or five circled hapless officials and argued about every decision, or so it seemed. It was team spirit gone 'over the edge', as Duncan McKenzie had put it. Yet the Arsenal players were clearly manipulating the system, doing just enough to avoid being booked.

To the unwitting observer, the only hard evidence that Arsenal's tempers could collectively boil over came in early 1987, during a filthy match with Manchester United at Old Trafford. Norman Whiteside had been booting lumps out of Rocastle and David O'Leary all afternoon. Rocky responded by aiming a well-placed kick at Whiteside's stomach and, to the amusement of new United boss Alex Ferguson, was red-carded. Although the Rocastle dismissal was widely condemned, it proved to several critics that Arsenal's experienced professionals were training up their young protégés to 'carry on moaning'. Viv Anderson could actively be seen encouraging David Rocastle to vent his spleen and Kenny Sansom was doing his best to coach Nigel

Winterburn, the new left-back, signed from Wimbledon. During a blistering FA Cup clash with Manchester United in early 1988, Winterburn and Brian McClair niggled each other through the game. With the score standing at 2–1 to Arsenal in the 90th minute, McClair blasted over a penalty which would have forced a replay. As fans on the North Bank jumped around in celebration, and the United player trudged disconsolately back to the halfway line, Winterburn walked alongside him and launched into a torrent of verbal abuse. Lip readers were outraged by what they saw on ITV's *The Big Match*. It wasn't the last time the pair locked horns, and it was only the beginning of an ongoing feud with Ferguson's United.

These remained isolated incidents, but in early 1989 Pandora's box swung open. An investigative team at ITV decided to make a football documentary on referees, in order to gauge their opinions on the modern game and, more titillatingly, discover just what was said on the pitch in the heat of the moment. The *World In Action* special was officially titled 'Offside'. For the first time, a referee, the young David Elleray, was to be miked up for the full 90 minutes. Both sets of players were blissfully unaware of this. The match chosen just happened to be Millwall v. Arsenal. The pre-programme blurb deemed it a run-of-the-mill league match. It was anything but. This was a London derby, taking place one year after Millwall fans had smashed up the pubs around Highbury before an FA Cup clash. George Graham was returning to his old club, with his new team's title challenge wavering. And, of course, his Arsenal team contained a cohort of black players, who were about to run out in front of Millwall's notoriously combustible crowd. Southampton v. Coventry it wasn't. It hardly took a genius to work out that the programme makers expected, and wanted, trouble.

They weren't disappointed. Arsenal players, especially David Rocastle, Kevin Richardson and David O'Leary, questioned the referee after each decision was awarded against them. The Millwall team, featuring luminaries such as Terry Hurlock and Keith 'Psycho' Stevens, also hassled Elleray at every opportunity, but these excerpts ended up on the cutting-room floor. The monkey noises aimed at Davis, Rocastle and Thomas were also conveniently filtered out. In the second half, the moment arrived which everyone seemed to be waiting for. From a Brian Marwood free kick, Millwall goalie Brian Horne fumbled the ball and Tony Adams narrowly squeezed his shot over the line. Elleray disallowed the goal, on the grounds that the ball had not gone in. The Arsenal players went bollock-nuclear. First, Kevin Richardson and Paul Merson surrounded Elleray: 'WHAT'S WRONG WITH THAT, EH? WHAT'S WRONG WITH THAT?' Richardson shouted, with Merson screaming obscenities in the background. Then, Adams stormed over and, within a yard of Elleray's face, shouted at a thousand decibels: 'THAT WAS OVER THE LINE. THAT'S OVER THE LINE. THAT IS OUR GOAL.' Elleray was still having none of it, at which point Adams ran off yelling 'Fucking cheat!' at the referee. Elleray, adopting his Harrow tutor persona, called Adams back, told him to 'stand up straight' – amusingly, Adams did so without hesitation – and booked the Arsenal captain.

The programme, shown at 9.00 p.m. on ITV, was deemed to be so explosive that it has never been repeated. To this day, a football referee has not been miked up again. Quite why it has been withheld is a mystery: *A Clockwork Orange* it isn't. Arsenal's reputation as being an intimidating crew was confirmed, but George Graham's reaction, given his 'iron-fist' attitude to other disciplinary matters, was unexpected. 'I want my teams to compete,' he said. 'I don't think our behaviour was that bad. This, after all, was a heated London derby.'

David Rocastle commented at the time that it was 'something out of nothing'. Looking back on those events from 15 years ago, Perry Groves comments: 'That was probably the first occasion I can remember where the media poked around into indiscipline on the pitch. It had to be us, didn't it? Some of the lads were a bit embarrassed about what came out, but footballers swear all the time. Nowadays, with Sky's cameras everywhere, you can lip read everything, but this documentary did close-ups and the voices. I suppose it was ground-breaking reality television, and it was the first time the club was really in the spotlight. The label seems to have stuck.'

Yet it wasn't simply mortal combat with their London cousins that caused Arsenal players to blow their tops. Tempers were to explode in more unlikely circumstances before the year was out.

When Arsenal played Norwich City on 4 November 1989, it was originally supposed to be a day of celebration. David O'Leary, making his 608th appearance for the Gunners, stood poised to overtake George Armstrong and become Arsenal's record appearance holder. Everyone seemed delighted that the genial Irishman, one of the nicest guys in the game, should have reached such a milestone. What better opposition could there have been on such a day than those chirpy 'canaries' who, even in their pre-Delia Smith days, were the friendliest and most inventive team in the old First Division? After 90 tempestuous minutes, the pomp and ceremony surrounding O'Leary was forgotten as both sides got stuck into one another, in every sense of the word.

The game, refereed by George Tyson, was the proverbial cracker. With Norwich 3–2 up, O'Leary, amazingly, equalised with a clever header. The crowd was stunned – general elections came around more frequently than a goal by the Irishman. Most observers reckoned he was lucky to still be on the pitch, though, after repeatedly clashing with Malcolm Allen for most of the match. In the last minute, Norwich's Andy Linighan was harshly adjudged to have handled the ball, and from the spot kick, Lee Dixon firstly missed, then, from the rebound, bundled the ball home to give Arsenal an unbelievable 4–3 win. Norwich players were furious and piled in on those Gunners players celebrating in front of the North Bank. Alan Smith, who'd run to collect the ball from the net, was elbowed in the face for his trouble and Dale Gordon, nicknamed the 'disco king' on account of his wet perm, tried to throttle Nigel Winterburn. Adams and 'history man' O'Leary also ran forward to join the fray. For the first time in several years, the police were called in to restore order, allowing the remaining minute to be played. Even then it wasn't quite finished, as O'Leary once more tried to exact revenge on Malcolm Allen after the final whistle. Alan Smith recalls it as being 'something out of nothing. Things got a bit heated, but I think both sets of players went for a drink in the bar afterwards. It was all forgotten quite quickly.'

Interestingly, George Tyson was perceptive enough to realise that another 'handbags' encounter had occurred and recorded in his referee's report: 'No serious individual incidents occurred.' Matters were quickly taken out of his hands by the media, who sensed some juicy headlines from the affair, and the FA, keen to restore the game's tarnished image after the Hillsborough disaster. 'YOU'VE SHAMED OUR GAME,' boomed *The Sun*, before adding that a possible loss of three points and severe censure could occur. As soon as other Sunday tabloids hyped up events, the FA's chief executive, Graham Kelly, decided to get tough. He reported that the match had been 'shown throughout Europe and the rest of the world' and that both teams 'had a collective responsibility' to 'behave properly'. Kelly also claimed that the managers bore the largest burden of responsibility. Officially, George Graham concurred with this opinion, but he always took the view that players should be mature enough to be in control of their own actions.

Talk to any of his former charges and few remember a collective bollocking after the Norwich game of any more seriousness than, 'Watch your behaviour, lads'. The likes of Paul Davis and Alan Smith do remember Graham using the incident for his own gain. 'Look at this article. Look what they've said about us. We'll show them, won't we?' was the bog-standard response to this 'crisis'. And, just to concur with Graham's view, the effects did not seem to be especially serious, for all the tabloid bluster. Arsenal were handed a £20,000 fine and warned about future conduct. No top-flight team had been deducted points on the grounds of players' bad behaviour for over a century, and it seemed highly improbable that this would happen. But the next 'explosion' occurred against a more famous foe than Norwich, and the fall-out would be more serious.

The match at Old Trafford on 20 October 1990 was a tempestuous encounter. On a grey, misty day, 47,000 watched as Manchester United, without a league title in 22 years, took on

George Graham's unbeaten Arsenal. Anders Limpar had already pick-pocketed a goal for the Gunners, after his whipped-in shot caught Les Sealey napping and crept over the line. Several of the United players believed they'd been cheated, but TV replays proved otherwise and the game got more niggly as the infuriated Mancs fought back. A mistimed tackle, it seemed, could cause mayhem.

Midway through the second half, the ball pinged around between Irwin, Limpar, McClair and Winterburn, fairly combative and combustible individuals all. Limpar left his foot in on Irwin, at which point Winterburn charged in from the other side to 'sandwich' the United defender. The next 18 seconds saw 'mayhem' (or so it was reported). Players from both sides pushed, shoved and wrestled each other, the only punches being thrown by Paul Ince and Brian McClair. The tabloids were not going to miss out on this one. 'THE BATTLE OF OLD TRAFFORD,' reported *The Sun*. Despite Arsenal protestations that 'most of the players were trying to stop it' and George's claim of 'We have had only one suspension in the last three years', the prospects of a slapped wrist didn't look good, particularly as less than a year had passed since the rumpus with Norwich players.

The consequences were even more serious than could first have been imagined. Heavy fines were handed to George Graham (as manager he took ultimate responsibility), Rocastle, Winterburn, Davis, Limpar and Thomas. The club was fined £50,000, but, most seriously, Arsenal were deducted two points, putting them a whopping eight points behind leaders Liverpool. Hindsight is a luxury and most of the players involved accept they went too far. But at the time, Arsenal players felt totally victimised by the decision. David O'Leary said: 'They've just handed the title to Liverpool on a plate.' Anders Limpar recalls how George Graham turned the situation around in the club's favour: 'Graham handled it really well. He went on about the injustice of it all, how we'd been cheated, how the only way to respond was to approach each game with renewed energy. Victory, he reckoned, would taste all the sweeter if we could come back from this. And he was right – we won the league. I think it's what you Arsenal fans call the fortress mentality.' Alan Smith is even more succinct. He recalls: 'From that point on, Arsenal fans sang: "You can stick your two points up your arse." We agreed with that. It became our philosophy too. And it worked.'

Amateur psychologists attempted to explain why the team became involved in such incidents. They didn't do a great job. A few pro-Arsenal hacks claimed it was purely a case of the Gunners being made scapegoats. For instance, while the 'Battle of Old Trafford' raged, body punches were actually thrown in a game between Derby County and Manchester City. No disciplinary action was taken against those players involved. Others claimed the Gunners were simply a bunch of thugs. The only way to get into the psyche of those involved is to ask them what being an Arsenal player is really all about. Paul Davis, who graduated from the youth team, says: 'I played for the Arsenal youth, reserve and first team. Right from day one, as a schoolboy, you're told, "Arsenal is different." This club is geared to win things – finishing second is not on the agenda. Playing for Arsenal is about fighting for each other, team spirit and an "all for one" mentality.' This becomes hard-wired in your head after a while. In 1990–91, with so many youth-team graduates in the first team, the natural progression was to a "them and us" situation. As you saw, it gave us an intense, unbelievable team spirit. If one player in the team is in trouble, you're duty bound to defend him.' History was to be repeated at the same location some 13 years later.

Ian Wright didn't graduate from the Arsenal youth academy. Nor was he a 'blue-collar' player who'd worked his way up from Stoke or Wimbledon, à la Dixon and Winterburn. Technically, he didn't owe George Graham a debt of gratitude for giving him his chance at the big time. After all, he was already an England international with Crystal Palace. Yet in his unmistakable style, he was seen to epitomise the spirit of Arsenal, at least in his first few years at Highbury. He was the exception to almost every rule. Until the comparatively late age of 22, he'd played semi-pro football while digging tunnels for Greenwich Borough Council during the day. In his youth, he'd mixed with the wrong crowd and spent seven days in Chelmsford prison for non-payment of car fines. He knew that when he signed for Arsenal from Crystal Palace in 1992, time was very much of the essence. Simply speaking, the 28-year-old Wright was a whirlwind, ready to wreak havoc on opposition defences. Although his epic goal feats made him a hero for most Arsenal fans, his explosive temper and abrasive nature meant he was perceived as a villain by almost everyone else. Example: when he received an MBE for 'services to football' in 2001, at the same time as England's 1966 heroes Alan Ball, George Cohen, Nobby Stiles and Roger Hunt, *Express* writer James Lawton claimed that Wright's achievements lacked any 'dignity' and his award proved that the game's values had 'gone to hell'. All this vitriol, incidentally, was poured out under the headline: 'WRIGHT'S HONOUR AN INSULT TO REAL HEROES'. Writing for the *Telegraph*, Michael Parkinson was also a fiery critic, and the *Sun*'s Mike Langley was quick to diminish Wright's achievement after he broke Cliff Bastin's scoring record.

Whenever a discussion on Wright's character and persona arises, the debate tends to revolve around his skin colour. He is quick to point out that he has suffered and been galvanised because of it. He argues that he's been regarded as a role model and a spokesman for his community. Throughout his career, he always professed to admire Martin Luther King, as shown in Mercury's One-2-One TV ads. In his early career, he was forced to endure a 'hard time' from Palace's senior pros, George Wood and Jim Cannon. However, Wright also voiced respect for Malcolm X, leading many to claim that his politics were confused. Wright often took Malcolm X's philosophy, 'Actions speak louder than words', out onto the field. Whenever he was the target for racist comments or actions, he hit back immediately.

A key reason for his move from Palace to Arsenal was the comments of (then) chairman Ron Noades. Black players, he'd claimed, were good for 'fancy flicks' but useless on 'frosty pitches in winter'. Wright reported Noades to the Commission for Racial Equality and expressed a desire to leave Selhurst Park immediately. Early in his Arsenal career at Oldham, he was spat at and racially abused by home fans. When he scored the equaliser, he flicked his Vs and spat back. He was fined £1,500 and ordered to apologise. There were no apologies from Oldham Athletic to Wright. Then there was the raging injustice he felt over his feud with Millwall. During Wright's England debut, for the B team, he was racially abused by sections of the crowd at the Den. The grudge he bore against the club never left him. Prior to an FA Cup clash with Millwall in early 1995, he commented: 'They try and intimidate you. It makes you want to stuff it up them.' The club's chairman, Reg Burr, was infuriated, but during the game Wright suffered verbal abuse throughout, including being fouled by a Millwall player after the final whistle. No wonder Wright was one of the prime movers and shakers in the 'Let's Kick Racism Out Of Football' movement. No wonder he made many football writers uncomfortable. With the anger-management classes he attended and his vigilante attitude, Wright, who'd always rebelled against authority, was hardly likely to follow their bog-standard advice to 'turn the other cheek'.

Back in the 1992–93 season he was to endure a tricky second year at Highbury. He compared this time in his life with 'living in a goldfish bowl', but many of his problems were self-induced. If Gary Lineker, who'd just departed to Japan, had been English football's Luke Skywalker, Ian Wright was about to become Darth Vader. He was the most marketable black sportsman in the country, ahead of Linford Christie and Lennox Lewis. He'd been snapped up by Nike a year earlier and made a series of advertisements with them that did more harm than good to his image. At a time when Lineker was renegotiating his transfer to Grampus Eight, Wright was portrayed as an anti-hero, sneering out of posters, saying 'Gary Who?' and 'Sayonora, Lineker-san'. Receiving much closer attention from defenders, he occasionally lashed out, clomping Wimbledon's John Fashanu (and breaking two of his own fingers into the bargain) and Tottenham's David Howells during a tetchy north London derby.

Sky TV's cameras became an omnipotent presence at football grounds – and they tracked Wright's every move. Lip readers could tell just what he said to the likes of Southampton's Ken Monkou during games. The abuse he gave opponents gained him notoriety and caused embarrassment among his teammates. Anders Limpar recalls: 'Off the pitch, Ian was a lovely man, but on it he could be an animal. At times, his language was terrible. I mean, we all swear on the pitch during games, but his language was industrial, to say the least. I've never met a player who came close to matching his persona. So much anger and hunger – he was like a man possessed in pursuit of goals. George Graham used to speak to him about his language but, basically, I think he realised he couldn't change Ian. Take away his sharp edge and you'd only have half the player. And being honest, Ian carried that team for a couple of years, so I think Graham realised that Ian's aggression did Arsenal more good than harm. But with players like Ian, they would inevitably get themselves into trouble because of it. That's the deal.'

It was Wright's ongoing feud with Manchester United goalkeeper Peter Schmeichel that made national headlines during the 1996–97 season. By the time Arsène Wenger became manager, it was clear that Wright was reaching the twilight of his career. Questions had long been asked about his all-consuming desire to receive the ball and whether, overall, this was having a detrimental effect on the team. Some believed he'd destroyed the Highbury careers of John Hartson, Glenn Helder and Kevin Campbell through his constant haranguing, and he'd shown a more spiteful edge to his nature off the pitch. The FA censured him for two verbal outbursts that season. He'd called David Pleat 'a pervert', and insisted that a disabled linesman 'get your flag up'. His mood was worsening as 'the end' drew nearer.

Something that clearly annoyed him was his inability to score for Arsenal against United in a competitive match. He'd done so in the 1993 Charity Shield, unleashing a spectacular volley past Schmeichel, but that hardly counted. Only Liverpool and Chelsea, as we know, appear to treat the Shield as a truly desirable piece of silverware. In the Premiership, he'd played against the red-nosed Dane on no less than ten occasions and failed to hit the back of the net each time. Like Wright, Schmeichel is a force of nature. Towering, intimidating and prone to screaming obscenities at his central defenders, he was the key factor behind

United's successes in the '90s. He was also capable of getting into spats with opposition strikers, Alan Shearer and Ian Wright especially.

During the game at Old Trafford in late 1996, Wright had three one-on-ones with the Danish goalkeeper. Each time, Schmeichel blocked him. On one occasion, when it was clear Wright could only blast the ball at the Dane, as the route to goal was blocked, the gold-toothed one unleashed a venomous shot at Schmeichel's gonads. It narrowly missed, cannoning off his thigh, but the United player glared at Wright, knowing full well what he'd intended. With Arsenal desperately chasing an equaliser after Nigel Winterburn's own goal, Wright once more stormed through and challenged for a 50-50 ball. He slid in on Schmeichel and the Dane promptly went mad, protesting so vociferously that the referee booked him, at Old Trafford too. In the midst of his fury, he made a racist comment to Ian Wright. Wright clearly heard it and viewers of *Match Of The Day* also knew exactly what Schmeichel said. Yet after Wright made a formal complaint to the FA, inquiry chief Steve Double said: 'It's very difficult to prove exactly what was said by viewing TV evidence.' Wright was incensed. After all, trial by TV had been used against him in the past, but even with a seemingly watertight case, it didn't work in his favour when he most needed it.

With the war of words between Wenger and Ferguson in its infancy (Fergie had already suggested that Wenger didn't have the 'relevant experience' to comment on English football's cluttered fixture list), the return match at Highbury was another grudge match. Arsenal lost 2–1, ending their title chances, but the Wright v. Schmeichel duel raged. After just ten minutes, a clash between the pair resulted in the ball being punctured – the atmosphere was truly explosive. With 20 minutes remaining, Vieira's pass put Wright through again, but the referee had already blown for offside. Fully three seconds later, Wright, who'd carried on running, made a two-footed lunge on Schmeichel. He touched the ball first, but Schmeichel spun around, crying out in agony. In slow motion, it looked nothing less than a spectacular attempt by the Arsenal striker to break the Dane's leg. He failed to complete his task, but was immediately surrounded by a pack of angry Mancs, including Roy Keane, who was informed by Wright that he was an 'Irish c**t'. The next morning Five Live seized on the incident, with some claiming that Wright's comment to Keane was as despicable as the abuse he'd received from Schmeichel two months before. The debate, which effectively revolved around the question: 'Is it worse to abuse a person's skin colour or call someone an Irish c**t?' was inconclusive. It brought Wright's contrary persona into the limelight once more. Again, he'd hardly done himself any favours, and it reflected the increasingly high stakes of Arsenal v. United clashes. On this occasion, Schmeichel and United had proved their point. The Dane seemed intent on having the last word on the matter. In 1999, he publicly stated that he'd always considered Wright 'something of an idiot'.

Arsène Wenger's managerial reign has not been marked by the brawls that typified the Graham era. But the fact that over eighty players have been red-carded in seven years and that there have been so many FA misconduct charges lodged against Gunners players means Arsenal's disciplinary problems regularly make the news. Wenger may not be an 'Arsenal man' in the strictest sense, but he still understands precisely what the 'Arsenal way' entails. An ex-Arsenal star who also played under George Graham told me: 'For all his revolutionary ways and new ideas, Wenger is still a great believer in the *esprit de corps*. He knows all about Arsenal's tradition and history. You could tell from his first-team talks that he realised what the Arsenal spirit was all about.' Clearly, the personnel were starting to change, as Wenger merged his 'cavaliers' with Graham's 'old guard'. The nature of the scraps has also changed. Isolated incidents on the park and verbal sparring matches conducted through the media are now the order of the day. But the main enemy, Manchester United, remain, and due to Wenger's insistence on backing his team to the hilt, Arsenal's fortress mentality remains as potent as it was at the end of the Graham era.

If Wenger is the archetypal twenty-first-century manager,

Patrick Vieira is certainly the prototype of the modern midfielder. Towering, athletic and with lungs the size of balloons, he is the perfect fusion of swashbuckling Gallic skill and Anglo-Saxon grit and aggression. No wonder he took the Premiership by storm; he has been the driving force behind Arsenal's recent successes. But his short fuse has also revealed the essential contradiction lying at the heart of most successful Arsenal teams. Wenger once commented: 'I'd never try to change him. It would take away the edge to his game.' This is the same 'edge' which George Graham realised he couldn't take away from Ian Wright, and Bertie Mee from Charlie George, without reducing their effectiveness as players. An ex-Arsenal star puts it to me bluntly: 'Do you want Arsenal to finish top of the Fair Play league, or the Premiership? You can have one or the other, but I honestly don't think you can have both. Take Patrick, for instance. He's expected to be a combative midfielder and help out the defence. He's niggled throughout most games by rivals intent on winding him up. I believe he's the most fouled player in the Premiership. With the rule changes about two-footed tackles, it's inevitable that he will, and others will, get into trouble with refs from time to time. Football is a contact sport and sometimes people get angry and get stuck in. To be honest, I'd be worried if Arsenal players weren't in trouble from time to time. It would suggest they weren't being combative enough.'

Wenger's public defence of his players has sparked controversy ever since his arrival at Highbury in late 1996. He was immediately called to task after John Hartson's ridiculous sending-off against Middlesbrough in December of that year. His response stunned the gaggle of press hacks: 'I cannot condemn the behaviour of my team because the three red cards we got before we didn't deserve.' It isn't difficult to see why Wenger has his detractors. His stock phrase, 'I didn't see the incident', is as repetitive and tedious as a Status Quo riff. His insistence on backing his charges to the hilt symbolises to many that he is refusing to acknowledge Arsenal's disciplinary problems. Interestingly, the only time he bucked the trend came when Francis Jeffers was sent off in the Community Shield match with

Manchester United. Jeffers' actions were labelled as 'stupid' by the Frenchman, and three days later he was farmed out on loan to Everton for the rest of the season. As we saw during Bruce Rioch's brief tenure, dressing-room morale collapses when the boss publicly puts the boot into his stars. Rioch now knows, it just isn't the Arsenal way. Over the years, Wenger never criticised – in public at least – Gilles Grimandi's string of dismissals (for stamping on hands and bouncing a ball on another player's head), or Dennis Bergkamp's stroppiness when mere mortals laid a hand on him. Jokingly, Wenger once commented: 'We tend to play better with ten men anyway.' His teams have had plenty of practice at this, and the 'them and us' attitude that George Graham cultivated continues to flourish under the Frenchman.

At the start of the 2000–01 season, Vieira was given his marching orders for elbowing Sunderland's Darren Williams in the face during Arsenal's 0–1 defeat and again for a two-footed lunge at Liverpool's Hamann, three days later. Wenger, fearing that Vieira was about to quit English football, made some typically provocative comments. He claimed Vieira had been 'victimised by referees' and that 'some people are on the field just to upset him'. Between them, Sunderland's Williams and Kilbane had been trying to rip Vieira's shirt off all afternoon and even Liverpool's Gary McAllister (also sent off in the Arsenal v. Liverpool game) reckoned that Vieira's dismissal 'hardly even merited a yellow card. Footballers have to be allowed to tackle. It is a contact sport.' As a general summing up, Wenger concluded: 'Referees have an instinct to give us red cards.' The reaction from the media proved that few agreed. Michael Parkinson remarked: 'Wenger never lost an opportunity to defend his players, particularly Vieira, whom he would have us believe is the victim of a sinister plot.'

Unsurprisingly, Alex Ferguson also felt compelled to give his opinion, pointing out the differences between United's and Arsenal's disciplinary record. The mutual apathy between the two managers went back to the start of Wenger's Highbury tenure. Within weeks of his appointment, he fired an opening shot across Fergie's bows. The Frenchman claimed that the fixture list could be manipulated if Ferguson wished and that opposition teams would be 'fortunate to ever win a penalty at Old Trafford'. Ferguson was not happy with such claims, commenting: 'He's come from backwaters in France and Japan. He's never managed in Italy, Spain or England. He should spend more time controlling Ian Wright's behaviour than criticising this club.' During Arsenal's Double-winning season of 1997–98, Ferguson indulged in mind games. With Arsenal in the middle of a ten-match run of straight victories, he claimed: 'Arsenal, sooner or later, will feel the heat. They too will drop points at a crucial stage.' Arsenal didn't. Presumably, the Scot believed that Wenger, doubtless a highly strung, combustible Frenchman, would explode under pressure. Fergie hadn't done his homework rigorously enough. Wenger, born in Alsace, a region that borders Germany, often displays Teutonic-type coolness under pressure. The 'backwater' of Japan had also taught Wenger a lesson or two in the art of self-control. 'There, people will laugh at you if you're not in control,' he commented.

Quite simply, Ferguson, used to bullying players, United shareholders, fellow managers and journalists, had met his match. In early 1999, the Scot launched his most scathing attack yet on Wenger's Arsenal. He announced: 'When they're not doing well in a game, they turn it into a battle to try to make the opposition lose concentration. The number of fights involving Arsenal is more than Wimbledon had in their heyday.' When told of Fergie's comments, Wenger laughed and the Scot was forced to offer a grovelling apology, claiming he'd been 'stitched up'. Joe Lovejoy of the *Sunday Times* witnessed Fergie's comments and said this wasn't true. The United boss also claimed to have sent a written apology to Wenger, who reckoned it must have been sent 'by horse and cart, because I didn't receive it'.

Ferguson's verbal attacks raged on throughout Wenger's second Double-winning season of 2001–02. Fergie claimed that despite Arsenal winning their final 13 games and Liverpool pinching second spot, his side had been the better in the New Year. 'And everyone knows he's got the prettiest wife at home,' was Wenger's cutting, yet enigmatic response. Wenger further fed Ferguson's paranoia during the close season with talk of 'shifting power bases' and Arsenal's proposed new stadium, which would massively increase Arsenal's revenue. The climax to the 2002–03 season proved that both comments were distinctly premature. Nonetheless, the United manager was rattled. Cheeks purpling, Fergie reckoned: 'Every Arsenal player would like to play for Manchester United.' Wenger gave arguably his most effective response yet. He didn't bother to comment.

The Frenchman also locked horns with (then) Chelsea chairman Ken Bates, who firmly believed that his club were London's premier attraction. Bates, for many years, has nicknamed him 'Arsène Whinger', partly in a bid to wind up his former rival on the FA management committee, David Dein. In early 2000, Wenger gave a press conference, when he commented that certain Premiership clubs, Chelsea included, were stealing a march on their rivals by overspending on transfer fees and player wages. Listening journalists chewed over the sound bites and the *Mirror* came up with the headline: 'WENGER ACCUSES CHELSEA OF CHEATING'. Bates, true to form, threatened to sue Wenger for his comments. The Frenchman responded: 'If Ken Bates is thinking of suing me, he must be a very sensitive boy. But I am not worried about what he says.' Needless to say, the writ did not arrive.

Roman Abramovich's arrival at Stamford Bridge means Chelsea are likely to become a major threat to Arsenal in the next few years. Yet Wenger had a clear respect for manager Claudio Ranieri, describing him as 'one of the most decent men in the game'. Such sentiments are unlikely to be reserved for Alex Ferguson. The latest instalment in the feud between the two clubs bore uncanny similarities to the original Battle of Old Trafford in 1990.

Tension had been growing since Sol Campbell's sending-off against United in the previous April. Wenger, who 'felt cheated' by the decision, reckoned Arsenal would go on 'to win the title for Sol'. Arsenal didn't, which proves that Wenger's mind games do not always work. The club protested to the FA about Campbell's four-match ban, a reaction deemed 'nauseating and absurd' by Alex Ferguson. Wenger then suggested that rather than Manchester United winning the title, 'We threw it away'. Four months later, Campbell was fined £20,000 for retaliating against Eric Djemba-Djemba's late tackle on him in the Community Shield clash with United. This, combined with Jeffers' sending-off in the same game, and the controversy surrounding Robert Pires's blatant penalty-winning dive against Portsmouth, meant the side's behaviour would be under the microscope during the 21 September clash with United.

In a sense, this game – as in 1990 – marked the end of an era, temporarily at least. Unbeaten Arsenal's disciplinary record markedly improved afterwards. Patrick Vieira firmly believes it was 'the turning point of our season', a view shared by several of those who played in the 1990 game. When the Arsenal captain was sent off in the second half after kicking out at Ruud van Nistelrooy, the tension grew. The jostling of United players at the final whistle, after the Dutchman's penalty had crashed against Arsenal's crossbar, inevitably made the headlines for weeks afterwards. The scenes were reminiscent of what happened 13 years before, except that United's players did not respond. An Arsenal player, who wishes to remain anonymous, told me: 'I wouldn't say we were proud of what happened that day, but that's how it is against United. Some of our players were furious about what van Nistelrooy did, and they believe that he was sneaky and got Patrick sent off. The two of them had a real barney after the match in the tunnel.'

Allegedly, the Dutchman told Vieira: 'You have no class.' Vieira responded: 'If you come near me, I'll put you down properly.' My source confirms: 'Some of the older lads who used to play under George Graham came to the training ground the following week and said it would be the springboard to a great season, and that it was the slice of luck we needed. After all, if Ruud had scored that penalty, the season could easily have gone the other way. Don't forget we'd stopped United at Old Trafford. That was a big achievement.'

The events in Manchester placed one member of that 1990 team in a rather difficult situation. Now a *Daily Telegraph* journalist, Alan Smith openly criticised Arsenal's poor disciplinary record. As an ex-player who knows only too well how Arsenal often turn a crisis into a triumph, he commented: 'Some of the Arsenal players weren't too happy with me saying that the disciplinary situation had to change. They felt that as an Arsenal "old boy", I should be more loyal to the cause. But I felt that I had to say it as I saw it. I thought the team's indiscretions reflected badly on the club and could damage them in the long term. And in fairness, the team's disciplinary record after that was excellent.' Wenger, who'd originally wanted his players to plead not guilty to the misconduct charges, was overruled by Arsenal's board. They clearly felt that such a response could lead to an angry FA extending the bans which were likely to be handed out to Lauren, Vieira, Cole, Keown, Parlour and Lehmann. There were also dark mutterings in the weeks leading up to the hearings of points deductions.

During that period, Arsenal's manager reverted to type. Wenger created the fortress mentality which George Graham once expounded. He commented: 'If you want to see Martin Keown as a devil and Ruud van Nistelrooy as an angel, then you have a big problem because van Nistelrooy is quite provocative.' He added: 'Of course we will fight for our players . . . football is a sport not a ballet dance.' Wenger went on to claim the whole episode, was in any case, a 'trial by Sky TV'. Here was another example, the Frenchman claimed, of 'Arsenal against the world.'

In November, when the bans were finally handed out to the six Arsenal players, Alex Ferguson was furious. 'We have to win the league without any help,' he said, suggesting that Arsenal had 'cut a deal with the FA' to reduce the sanctions taken against the players. Wenger was still smouldering over the perceived media vendetta waged against his team. He claimed: 'Some people want my players hanged from a tree in Hyde Park in front of the whole city.'

My source claims: 'We were told, in no uncertain terms, to "cool it" and focus on what we do best – winning football matches. None of us really know whether the manager was told off by the board, and instructed to "sort us out". But we got the message from a number of figures at the club. I think our disciplinary record speaks for itself, and only Ashley Cole and Martin Keown were sent off in the remaining games. Yet history will show that the Old Trafford game served its purpose and created the injection of anger which successful Arsenal teams need.'

On 18 April 2004, ITV's *On The Ball* ran an end-of-season review, and reporter Gabriel Clarke asked Arsène Wenger to describe 'Which of the season's games will live longest in your memory?' Wenger paused. After all, he had a treasure trove of memories to recall. Any number of stellar Henry goals, marauding Robert Pires runs, or pyrotechnic moves would seem the most likely choice. Yet Wenger was certain in his choice: 'Manchester United away. We got a point against the champions with a lot of trouble around. It was a turning point.' The image of a snarling, vein-popping Martin Keown, it appears, will burn longer in the memory than any moments provided by the French foreign legion.

Gabriel Clarke seemed nonplussed: 'So, of all the beatings you handed out, you go for a nil–nil with all the aggro?' Wenger replied: 'Absolutely, what else do you expect me to say?' Some things, it seems, never change at Arsenal.

FIFTEEN

Bound

A man with fingers in every footballing pie you can think of.

     Sam Hammam, talking about David Dein in 2001

One has to tread extremely carefully before suggesting that David Dein is anything other than the visionary who has taken Arsenal into the promised land. Even though he's safely ensconced in his position as the club's prime mover and shaker, as well as being a key figure on the FA Committee and on the UEFA executive, he is notoriously touchy when he receives criticism of any kind. Dein was furious with the *Mail On Sunday* after journalist Lawrence Lever made various allegations about the financial health of his business ventures back in January 1995. After numerous publications threatened to print details of the article, they were warned off by talk of libel writs. Even Alex Fynn, who's slaughtered a few sacred cows over the last 13 years in his two books, always stopped short of actually criticising Dein. This is despite Fynn's clear disapproval of the Arsenal board's behaviour during the process of turning Highbury all-seater. And there lies the unavoidable point: that Arsenal Football Club as we know it is an almost unavoidable consequence of actions inspired by Dein.

Of course, now he is widely accepted and largely forgiven for any past misdemeanours after his direct intervention brought Ian Wright, Dennis Bergkamp and Arsène Wenger to Highbury. But considering he's a lifelong Arsenal fan, his attitude to the club's supporters has been contradictory. On the one hand, he has argued that the all-seater process was necessary to protect fans in the wake of the Taylor Report. He even listened carefully to the views of an action group claiming to speak for Arsenal fans back in 1984. But the flip side is his and the board's continued reluctance to communicate effectively with supporters during the past 20 years over issues that really matter. In 2003, as you sit in your comfy North Bank seat, thrill to Thierry Henry's 'va va voom' and watch the replays on the Jumbotrons, Dein is regarded as the most influential power-broker in English football. But there was a time when many regarded his presence at Arsenal as a disaster waiting to happen.

Of course, it's hugely symbolic that Dein bought his way onto Arsenal's board in 1983, as revealing, say, as Charlie Nicholas's arrival during the close season. If the signing of Charlie ushered in a glitzier era in Arsenal's recent history, Dein's entry showed that not even football could escape the insidious influence of Thatcherite new-right economics. Dein appeared to represent the new kind of working-class hero championed by the Conservative Government. He'd inherited no shares, hadn't relied on old-boy networks and hadn't gone to a top public school. On top of this he'd made his fortune without exploiting his workforce, unlike many tycoons of that era. David Dein seemed to be the more acceptable face of the new enterprise culture.

If several members of the Arsenal board he was about to join had been born with silver cutlery in their mouths, Dein started on his way in life with no more riches than a good upbringing. There was to be no effortlessly smooth transition to the top for him. He came through with sheer willpower, hard work and a willingness to gamble. Dein's ancestors were poor Jewish émigrés who arrived in east London at the turn of the twentieth century. His father became a successful tobacconist and, from a young age, Dein and his brother were expected to help out in the family grocery shop. At 15 years old he was out 'selling dented tins of Christmas pudding . . . beans or soup or something and they had no labels,' recalls Alfie Fletcher, who still owns a stall opposite what was once 'Dein's Food Stores'. Presumably, if Dein had yelled out 'Rodney, you plonker!' it wouldn't exactly have been a surprise. The opportunity for him to get seriously rich arose through the foresight of his mother, Sybil. Along with her eldest son, Arnie, she would fly out to Jamaica and Barbados, jot down a list of popular recipes, and arrange to import yams, avocados and mangoes, aware that London's burgeoning Caribbean population were missing authentic home cooking. By 1970, the business's annual turnover was £2 million. Dein quickly climbed onboard and his fortune grew to such an extent that, by the early '70s, he made an audacious attempt to marry his American fiancée on the Aga Khan's yacht. Though Dein's request was turned down, it was his first attempt to ingratiate himself with the truly rich and famous.

In the manner of other '80s tycoons, you'd imagine that Dein would be happy to discuss his humble origins and espouse the virtues of hard work and endeavour. But you'd be wrong. Dein never discusses his past and remained a mystery man back in 1983. One reason for his reticence could be that in mingling with leading hoteliers, lawyers and merchant bankers, he felt insecure about his background. Or it could be that, despite the hype, Dein's business record was hardly unblemished. In the early '70s, a haulage company he'd co-owned with his brother collapsed, two years after it was sold by the pair. And, at the time Dein joined the Arsenal board, few realised his import/export company, London and Overseas Sugar Limited, was falling into serious financial trouble. Dein's business deals were not discussed at the time, but the fact that he'd invested his money in a football club was proof to many that he'd lost his touch anyway.

Old business acquaintances were shocked by Dein's absurd venture. Here was a character who'd always been regarded as a 'lucky gambler'. Some years earlier, Dein and friends decided to go dog racing at a track near Brent Cross. Dein placed a £20 bet on a 6–1 rank outsider. It won, and Dein was left with £120. Despite encouragement from his mates, who suggested he bet again, Dein went home, clutching his winnings. He was known as a canny wheeler-dealer with a clear eye for a bargain. Yet the

£330,000 outlay that gave him a 14 per cent stake in Arsenal was described as 'dead money' by Peter Hill-Wood. Terry Neill told me: 'We all thought his investment was about as wise as buying shares in a Sahara irrigation business. A pointless venture.' As for Dein himself, conventional wisdom held that he was just a good-time guy and friend of the stars. Tony Woodcock and Kenny Sansom, amongst others, were his buddies and as a lifelong fan, Dein relished going to nightclubs like Annabels and Tramp with them even before he became a club director. Dein, it was reckoned, would be happy as long as he could entertain his associates at the game and get his name in the gossip columns. It was the first sign that leading figures in football misread him. As any financial adviser will testify, he'd invested at precisely the right time – when a depressed market had reached rock bottom. Behind the bonhomie lurked a sharp, ambitious operator, intent on making his presence felt within the club. Others' underestimation of him and the value of his shares played directly into his hands, and in time this tilted the club into Dein's grateful embrace.

He needed no reminding that he was to be part of the most traditional and upright board of directors in the country. The Hill-Wood dynasty had been at the club for the previous 60 years. In 1927, Eton-educated Conservative MP Samuel Hill-Wood ventured south from the mill town of Glossop. At that time Glossop Town Football Club were a struggling Division Two outfit and, with the cotton industry in decline, Hill-Wood, leading mill owner and club chairman, sold up and moved to the capital. In the wake of the Norris scandal, Hill-Wood was elected chairman of Arsenal. Shortly afterwards, Glossop failed to gain re-election to the Football League and disappeared without trace. Hill-Wood was accused of turning his back on his Yorkshire homeland, like Chapman had when he left Huddersfield.

Neither Samuel Hill-Wood nor his son Denis regarded the ownership of shares as anything less than a waste of time and money. Grandson Peter felt the same way: 'One sort of stepped into grandfather's shoes and father's shoes – one did not buy one's way in having suddenly made a great fortune . . . I have never looked at a football club as a financial asset. In the old days, when any shares came up for sale, we used to draw lots for them at board meetings. We used to buy them at 30 bob each, and if you got them, you were inclined to think of them as a waste of money. One didn't view it in a commercial way.' Hill-Wood agrees that Dein was to be aided by the chairman's lack of foresight on how English football could develop. Unlike Hill-Wood, whose family prided itself on a non-interference policy, Arsenal's new whizz-kid executive chose to be strictly hands on. Not for the last time, football interests and business ideas would clash. Terry Neill was to be the first to feel the blast of the Dein revolution.

It is no exaggeration to say that Dein annoyed Neill intensely. The tales are numerous: Dein allegedly telling Neill, a professional of 25 years, that he was 'satisfied' with training routines; Dein often visiting the dressing-room shortly before kick-off, and continuing to party with Rix, Sansom and Woodcock on a regular basis. Neill clearly thought Dein was encroaching on his territory, leading to an uncomfortable relationship between the two. The Irishman recalls: 'When Dein told Don Howe and myself that he was "satisfied" with training, I thought it was an absolutely ridiculous thing for him to say. It was patronising and downright rude. I didn't think he had any business interfering on the playing side. None of the directors had ever done that before. Then, when he started to visit the dressing-room just before kick-off on match day, I got really annoyed and threw him out on one occasion.' Initially, Dein found it difficult to come to terms with the vagaries of Arsenal's fortunes. Neill recalls him shaking his head and muttering: 'This isn't like my business,' after another Arsenal collapse in the latter part of 1983. It didn't help that Neill had for some time felt as if an insider was undermining his position as manager.

A newspaper article in April 1983, prior to an FA Cup semi-final against Manchester United, had predicted Neill's sacking and the Irishman still believes an insider leaked the story to the newspapers. Dein wasn't at the club then, but with his arrival Neill was even more convinced that his position was being threatened. One can assume that when Arsenal's league form slumped in late 1983, it became a question of when Neill would be sacked, not if, and Dein had clearly seen enough by then. At this point, Dein became embroiled in one of the seamier episodes in modern Arsenal's history. He began to liaise with the Arsenal Action Group – initially with Neill's blessing, it should be said.

Action groups are strange beasts. They certainly gained publicity during the '90s, particularly in the case of the 'No to Murdoch' campaign at Manchester United. Action groups of the 1980s are less well known, simply because football wasn't as high profile back then. The public face of the Arsenal Action Group was Alan Esparza, himself a controversial and (in some corners) unpopular figure. He told me: 'Basically, we set up the group because we were dissatisfied with Terry Neill's management. Since we'd done the Double in 1971, we'd won one FA Cup and we were mediocre, to say the least, in the league. This was Arsenal and it wasn't good enough. It was time for a change. I remember I waited outside the Rotherham ground after they'd beaten us in the late '70s and I slaughtered Neill. He said: "I haven't seen my family for two weeks and we're trying to sign the Van Der Kerkhoff brothers." I wasn't interested – he got paid to deal with that, it wasn't my fucking problem. In 1983, some of us in a café on Gillespie Road formed the group and we stood with clipboards outside pubs and stations and the ground getting names on a petition against the management. There was a lot of ill feeling and I tell you what, there were 20,000 to 25,000 names at the end of it. So we were definitely representative. We also met David Dein on more than one occasion. He listened, he sat and listened to what we had to say. I got the impression he agreed with many of our comments.

'I waited for Dein, Friar and Hill-Wood after the Walsall game where we lost at home. It was embarrassing. I said to them: "Are we no better than this?" They said: "What do you think we've been talking about up there? We haven't been playing cards." Obviously, Neill got sacked soon after this. I think you can say we brought some pressure to bear and brought it to the forefront of the press. I can't deny that the person we had most to do with, and. who listened to us most intently, was David Dein.'

It is recorded in Neill's book that Dein later took members of the group 'for a burger' and it is public knowledge that Dein attended a public meeting after Neill had gone. Esparza claims that the meeting had been arranged before Neill was axed. Significantly, Neill tells me he believes that 'some of my bosses were paying too much attention to the views of the Arsenal Action Group'. Dein has never commented on this strange episode in Arsenal's history and later claimed that the team's long losing streak cost Neill his job, rather than the Irishman's personality clash with Arsenal's new executive, or his own dealings with Esparza and company. Either way, Neill has never fully forgiven him for the way his sacking was handled and traditionalists never quite lost their suspicion of Dein after this.

When, two years later, Don Howe unexpectedly resigned, Dein was again cited as a prime reason for his departure. With several members of the first-team squad taking an instant dislike to John Cartwright, Howe's new coach, they exacted revenge by complaining to Highbury's top brass about training techniques and team morale. Stewart Robson takes up the story: 'The likes of Woodcock and Williams had their noses put out of joint by John Cartwright. He'd begun to phase in younger players like Hayes and Rocastle. They believed that if they could get Cartwright out of the way, they could safeguard their futures. Several of them whined to the board and it was no secret that David Dein was good friends with some of the players. That's when it all got nasty. The board, I was told, went after Terry Venables without informing Don Howe first. But they got egg, and a lot more, on their faces, when Venables found out that they were going behind Howe's back and refused to come. Then Don Howe resigned anyway when he got wind of what was happening. The board looked like idiots. A few of us believed it served them right. For a club who has a reputation for doing things in the correct manner, they didn't exactly cover themselves in glory here. And nor have they since, with Rioch's and Graham's sackings.'

As it turned out, second choice George Graham arrived and the board got lucky anyway. No one disputed the fact that Arsenal needed a change of direction, and George provided it. The problem remained the manner in which Howe disappeared. It was hardly ethical. In the press, Terry Neill muttered darkly once more about business activities trampling all over good manners. Dein simply commented once more that he was 'just a fan'. How ironic that within six years, he forced many Arsenal supporters to question what being a fan actually meant.

By 1989, Dein was British football's most prominent executive figure. As Arsenal vice-chairman, he now controlled 41 per cent of club shares and was carnivorous in his approach to gaining more. On one occasion, Terry Neill claims that Dein completed an 800-mile round trip to acquire just two shares from an elderly Scottish lady. He was also responsible for the slow modernisation of Highbury. Dein, who followed American sports closely, was in the process of expanding Arsenal's commercial outlets, which he likened to a 'Manchester bus shelter' when he first arrived at the club. The Superstore next to Finsbury Park station appeared, and the number of 'Make Money With Arsenal' girls at games increased exponentially. But this was merely the thin end of the wedge. Dein was moving the club in precisely the direction he wanted, much to the chagrin of swathes of fans, who'd finally found a voice through the burgeoning fanzine movement.

In late 1987, the proposed £6.4 million development of executive boxes at the Clock End was announced. Ultimately, this was the first concrete evidence that football clubs were keen to attract a new corporate class of fan, and that the game was on the path to domination by media tycoons and the money men eager for their pound of flesh. David Dein described the Clock End development as 'the very best in executive and catering facilities, an exciting prospect as we head towards the twenty-first century'. Fanzines, such as the *Arsenal Echo Echo*, took a different stance, realising that a fundamental shift in the relationship between fans and the club was taking place. Supporters had been kept in the dark over the details of the redevelopment. Surely it made sense to consult the fans, to reassure them that they weren't being priced out, or that at least now they could stand in the dry on the previously uncovered Clock End. The fact that fans first read about the proposed changes in the *Daily Mirror* spoke volumes about the arrogant attitude clubs had towards their fans by the late '80s.

The club continually fudged the issue, claiming that 'some' Clock Enders would now be under cover (only some?). There were no guarantees that areas of terracing wouldn't disappear. Even then, a new construction consisting of only 48 executive boxes seemed incredibly short-sighted. Most fans agreed that a stand similar to Aston Villa's away end would have been preferable. After all, an extra 5,000 seats as well as the boxes really would have helped the club make the stadium more comfortable and modern for all fans (their proposed aim), not just executive fat cats drinking champagne.

As well as redesigning Highbury, Dein and his cronies were busy sculpting the football model of the future. Chairmen had just negotiated a £44 million deal with ITV whilst at the same time addressing the knotty issue of a Super League. Though the First Division was never cut to ten or twelve clubs as Dein proposed, the Premiership, which kicked off some three and a half years later, had its origins in these negotiations. The *Echo Echo*'s complaint that 'Arsenal's league match with Tottenham in January will kick off at 5 p.m. to prevent a rescheduling of *Coronation Street*' now seems quaint. After all, in these days of an embryonic European Super League, an hour's delay to a north London derby would barely register. The fans' game was in the process of being hijacked by the likes of Maxwell and Murdoch, who cared little if supporters were put out at all by rescheduled kick-offs. Dein's role as one of the main speakers for the so-called 'Big Five' and his campaign for the breakaway Super League reflected the widely held view that he was primarily interested in profit and balance sheets.

At this juncture, the view of Dein as a visionary was hardly justified. It has since come to light that his 'vision' of a Super League was actually gleaned from a meeting at the offices of marketing consultants Saatchi and Saatchi in London. Like his mother back in the '60s, Dein was canny enough to recognise a good business idea when he saw it. But the concept of a breakaway league certainly wasn't his. As punishment for his Super League discussions, Dein was labelled 'unforgivably arrogant' by the *Echo Echo*. When a pigeon shat on his shoulder as he left the Saatchi briefing, Arsenal's vice-chairman seemed to have received an unequivocal message from above.

Fans' growing paranoia was fed by the proposed ID card membership scheme devised by Margaret Thatcher and her sports minister, Colin Moynihan. Born from the problems caused by hooliganism in the '80s, it was a hot political potato. Liberals pointed out that having to pay an extra £10 simply to attend only one team's games was an infringement of civil liberties. Conspiracy theorists also claimed that it was a pilot scheme for a national ID card venture. Arsenal fanzines were at the forefront of the 'say no to ID card' schemes, amidst claims that if floating supporters were killed off, attendances would be halved and many Third and Fourth Division clubs would go to the wall.

Ultimately, fanzine lobbying, together with a very rare government admission that the scheme would be unworkable, meant that the threat never materialised. It was a rare victory for the fan in a world where many felt that they were mere pawns for politicians, financial tycoons, television magnates and football executives. It was hardly Dein's fault that he liaised with Colin Moynihan – possibly the most loathed politician from the later Thatcher years – but fans criticised him for doing so nonetheless. Within two years, Arsenal fans' feelings of paranoia would increase hugely.

In May 1991, a storm was brewing in London N5, the like of which hadn't been seen since Sir Henry Norris relocated the club to Highbury. Norris had used his contacts in the local press to silence the protesters who complained about the 'vulgar project' in their midst. Eighty years on, it was impossible to gag the protesters. As this book has shown, it was nothing new for drunken stars or scrapping players to attract controversy. This was a crisis with a difference: a raging battle between Gunners supporters and the board of directors. After this messy episode, some Arsenal fans chose never to return to Highbury. For them, the link between themselves and the club had been permanently broken.

The club pretends the whole saga never happened. For example, Phil Soar and Martin Tyler devote one sentence to the furore surrounding the scheme in their official history of the club. In the very best traditions of club propaganda, the incident has been forgotten. Several of the fans who opposed the scheme now admit that Arsenal had no option but to pursue it, but they can't forget that it signalled the death knell for football as the working-man's game, or the appallingly high-handed manner in which the club went about it. Dein was at the centre of the cyclone.

In a souvenir Coventry City programme, compiled after Arsenal secured the 1991 league title, it was announced that the club had decided to finance the £22.5 million cost of making Highbury all-seater through a bond or debenture scheme. The club hoped to sell £16.5 million worth of bonds to fans, while the rest would come from within the club's not unsubstantial coffers. Rangers redeveloped Ibrox through such a scheme, as had several clubs in America. For an outlay of either £1,200 or £1,500, buying a bond would entitle a fan to 'exclusive rights' to a season ticket for up to 150 years, and a bond certificate signed by Peter Hill-Wood and George Graham

The battle to save terracing had long since been lost. Hillsborough had changed everything. In the wake of 95 Liverpool fans dying in April 1989, clubs were informed that if they refused to comply with the findings of the Taylor Report, their safety licences (i.e. right to stage matches) would be revoked. It was a *coup de grâce* – over a century of tradition was all but over. What rankled most of all was the way in which Arsenal proceeded with the all-seater process. Rumours about the Bond Scheme were leaked in the *Evening Standard*. The consultation process with fans that the Taylor Report advocated consisted of a few vague public meetings and a half-baked questionnaire in an Arsenal v. Leeds programme. The questions were hardly designed to gauge public opinion on the all-seater debate. In truth, the most important information the club received through the survey was contained in the box after the word 'Address'. Those who responded, an estimated 15,000, were sent a glossy brochure on the merits of the scheme. As for the findings of the questionnaire, they were never made public.

Immediately, it became clear that, if pursued, the Bond Scheme would have a major impact upon the social make-up of the Highbury crowd, due to the necessary outlay in instalments (around £100 a month for a year or more) or as a lump sum of £1,000. This was on top of the price of a season ticket. One band of Arsenal fans spent the summer of 1991 establishing the Independent Arsenal Supporters Association (IASA). In the words of one of its founders, Ian McPherson: 'We were incensed that the club thought they could push through these proposals at the last minute, unchallenged, and hope that everyone would forget it over the summer. It was unforgivably arrogant on the board's part.' Arsenal directors stood accused by the club's own fans of two heinous crimes: social engineering and an inability to communicate effectively with supporters. The IASA achieved a notable early success. In June, a *Time Out* article publicised the movement, which prompted David Dein to threaten legal action against the group. Dein had obviously calmed down a few days later, because the movement's leader, Dyll Davies, and *One Nil Down*'s editor Tony Willis were invited into the inner sanctum to meet with Dein and Ken Friar to discuss their differences.

The meeting was heated but fairly good-natured. A transcript from it was reproduced in *One Nil Down* some weeks later. One part of the conversation summed up the gulf between fans and the board. When asked the question: 'What provisions are being made for loyal fans who cannot afford a bond?' (namely the majority of teenagers, students, OAPs and the core of the North Bank), Friar and Dein apologised but said that 'the club is not run as a charitable institution'. A fair point, but in a nutshell, they'd admitted that no provision was being made for lower-income fans. Dein's and Friar's responses at the meeting were terse and sharp. The reason for this was that bond sales were slow. Out of 16,000 bonds, only an estimated 5,000 (£5 million worth) were sold by Christmas 1991. The IASA's campaigning was proving to be a serious pain for the club.

Ian McPherson wrote several articles for *One Nil Down* and helped put together the IASA newsletter. He recalls the prevailing attitude amongst many fans at the time: 'I don't think that the club ever really understood what our grievance was. The North Bank had always been the traditional stronghold of our support. In general, it was populated by the lower-income sections of fans. It was, therefore, of real symbolic importance. The Bond Scheme was an exclusive, elitist scheme which asked those people to shell out a large sum of money. It was money that many did not have. In effect, the club was telling people on the North Bank that money was more important than loyalty. They were constructing a new kind of football audience: a well-heeled, middle-class audience who would then be able to spend a fair proportion of their cash on club merchandise. In effect, it was a form of social engineering. Someone told me that the directors, including Dein, allegedly, used to call us the "intelligentsia" – which kind of hints that they found the IASA intimidating. That's actually quite amusing, but it just goes to show that for all their claims of being a "progressive club", it was being led by an archaic elite with no PR skills at all.

'We saw it as our responsibility to come up with an alternative plan for financing the conversion of Highbury into an all-seater stadium. We proposed that, firstly, a debenture scheme should guarantee season tickets at a reduced rate, which meant that fans would get a real return on their investment. We suggested issuing a maximum 6,000 of these. Secondly, we suggested setting up a membership scheme which, for £20 a season, would enable fans to obtain an option on buying a ticket for every home match. Thirdly, we put forward the idea of a limited share issue raising between £2 million and £4.5 million. Added together, this would have brought in between £12 million and £14 million. The membership card scheme mysteriously appeared the following year – the club's idea, of course!'

Dein's version of utopia at Highbury seemed to be a nightmare in the making for North Bank regulars. It filtered through that over the next two years, when the capacity was to be slashed to around 28,000, the club hoped to sell all 16,000 bonds. They also hoped to make 'up to' 12,000 tickets available to fans on match days. By the time the away side had received their share and the touts had got their grubby hands on some of them, closer to 6,000 tickets would be available to non-bond holders for each game. It would, in effect, have turned Highbury into Fort Knox, with enough cash to buy a bond seemingly the prerequisite for regular entry to the ground. Once fans comprehended this news, letters of support and cash donations flooded into IASA headquarters. Ian McPherson allowed me to see the wodges of letters they received. They all express similar emotions, namely a sense of betrayal at the club's willingness to liquidate them and a fear that Saturday pilgrimages to Highbury would soon become a thing of the past. One of the letters stated:

> I enclose a cheque for £5 to help you in your campaign. Due to financial constraints, I am finding it increasingly difficult to turn up at home games. The team's recent performances are not a cause of this, but David Dein's attitude towards fans. Not just the ridiculous price rises on the admission and programmes, but the whole contemptuousness he has displayed . . . I am not going to buy a bond, Dein can shove that up his arse!

Finally, it seemed, Dein had gone too far. Tabloids, anxious to report another Arsenal crisis, reacted with gusto. 'FANS STAGE BOND DEMO' ran the *Daily Mirror* headline, whilst *The Sun* reported: 'FANS BLAST TO HIGHBURY TOP BRASS', before adding: 'Arsenal guru David Dein was last night accused of ripping the club apart.' The *Daily Star*'s Bob Driscoll reckoned Dein's ideal would be 'a world which turns the terraces into poseurs' parlours'. When, in late 1992, Islington Council blocked the club's original plan for the North Bank stand, commenting that 'David Dein will have to reduce the size of his ego', it appeared Dein was becoming a liability. Just like Sir Henry Norris 80 years earlier, he was accused of gambling away the club's soul. But football's ultimate politician wasn't finished. He had one crucial factor on his side – pure luck.

With the Premiership era dawning, the Big Five, with Dein acting as a key spokesman, backed ITV to continue screening games on *The Big Match*. As Ken Bates later commented: 'If that decision had stood, Sky TV may have folded there and then. Who knows how different the future for English football would have been?' Sky TV, with Alan Sugar keeping Rupert Murdoch abreast of developments during the meeting with ITV bosses, proceeded to blow the rival bid out of the water. Primarily through Murdoch's millions, football became cool. If Dein had got his way, Premiership clubs would have taken the Betamax option rather than the VHS route. He believed he'd lost a key battle, but as it turned out, he'd inadvertently won the war. Within a few years, his 13,000 shares in Arsenal were worth a staggering £35 million. As gambles went, his decision to invest in Arsenal back in 1983 now seemed inspired.

Gradually, as rival clubs' grounds resembled building sites during those formative Premiership years, the criticism aimed towards Dein subsided. As one fan told him shortly before the new North Bank stand was officially opened for the game against Coventry in August 1993, 'If I have to sit at football matches, then this stand is the dog's bollocks.' Other hardened terrace dwellers admitted that forsaking the delights of standing at games wasn't such a chore after all. Unlike other clubs, who'd invested all available funds into rebuilding their antiquated stands, George Graham was still able to break the club transfer record to sign Ian Wright for £2.2 million in 1992, partly due to Dein's personal intervention. Under George, Arsenal won the Cup-Winners' Cup in 1994, at which point Dein was appointed to the UEFA committee. And there lies the (still) unpalatable truth for some, that Dein did well for Arsenal in the '90s, but that the club did even better for him. Members of the IASA, which inevitably faded away, alleged that Dein's primary motivation was self-enrichment. It was in his interests for Arsenal to turn over a good profit, because it boosted the price of his shares and raised his profile. The more well-heeled clientele which flocked to Highbury was also good news for Dein, as they could spend more money on official merchandise than working-class North Bankers could ever have done. Those who bought bonds realised a return on their investment and a decade or so on were able to buy a season ticket at a discounted rate.

After the board chose to sack George Graham in 1995, Dein successfully turned the crisis into a personal triumph. Once George, who'd enjoyed unprecedented control over which players he signed, was gone, Dein changed the parameters by which future Gunners' bosses operated. When Bruce Rioch became boss, he felt hemmed in by the restraints placed upon him. He recalls: 'It was a different situation to the one I'd been used to at Bolton. Basically, I drew up a list of names of players I wanted at Arsenal and then David Dein would take the lead in setting up negotiations. Yet once David Platt and Dennis Bergkamp arrived, the system stopped working. I'll give you an example. I was keen to sign Jason McAteer and Alan Stubbs from Bolton. We were told by Bolton that neither player was for sale, but a couple of weeks later, they signed for Liverpool and Celtic. It didn't work. By the time I was at Arsenal, he was in virtual control of the club. He was the de facto chairman, Peter Hill-Wood was just a figurehead.'

Under a *Mirror* headline of 'KEEP YOUR NOSE OUT', Rioch added: 'David Dein doesn't speak for me, he will never speak for me.' I asked Rioch if he actually uttered these words. 'It was certainly how I was feeling at the time,' he comments. Rioch's opinions on Dein are clearly affected by his knowledge that throughout his tenure at Highbury, the board was in constant contact with Arsène Wenger, Dein's friend, as Peter Hill-Wood sheepishly admitted at the 1996 shareholders' AGM. Rioch is also fully aware that upon his dismissal, Ian Wright exclusively informed the *Mirror* 'DON'T BLAME DEIN FOR ARSENAL CRISIS'. Rather ironic, considering that 'a high-profile director' had allegedly informed Wright that he was 'going nowhere' after he had slapped in a transfer request in the wake of a bust-up with Rioch. Of course, there's another side to the Rioch saga, as players from that era will confirm. The ex-Bolton boss's tendency to eyeball his players and his failure to communicate effectively with the board led many to conclude he wasn't 'big enough' for the job.

At that year's AGM, a shareholder commented that Rioch's indecision over the possible transfer of Holland's Clarence Seedorf to Highbury made Dein 'look like a c**t all over Europe'. And it was Dein, not Rioch, who was heckled during Arsenal's pre-season friendlies before the 1996–97 season. Hell hath no fury like a vice-chairman booed, apparently.

Ironically, Rioch was fired exactly a decade after Don Howe's controversial decision to resign in the wake of the board trying to lure Terry Venables to Highbury. 'Arsenal is a wonderful club, but the way my time ended there was disappointing,' Rioch claims. And does he feel that Dein was a thorn in his side, like some previous Arsenal bosses did? 'I'll leave that for you to decide,' Rioch comments, with a smirk.

In appointing Wenger, Dein finally justified the visionary hype. Dein believed Sergeant-Major Rioch's methods belonged to a bygone era, whereas Wenger's ultra-modern approach would usher Arsenal into the twenty-first century. Dein got it spot on. Whilst the internal politics that brought the Frenchman to Highbury were less than honourable, who can argue that Dein's ruthlessness didn't reap rewards in the end? Over recent years, Dein has scaled down the number of shares he holds in Arsenal. In 2000, he cut his stake in the club to 19 per cent, offloading £7.1 million worth to the club's (now) largest shareholder, Danny Fiszman. Dein has used the profits gained to invest in other business interests, further evidence that Arsenal FC has been good to him.

His profile has never been higher and he continues to be regarded as the driving force behind Arsenal. In late 2001, he was greeted by cries of 'Down with Dein. Down with the dump' from angry local residents, protesting about the proposed Ashburton Grove move. During 'Anelka-gate' and the sales of Marc Overmars and Emmanuel Petit to Barcelona in 2000, he proved himself an accomplished negotiator in tandem with Wenger, to ensure that Arsenal squeezed as much cash from the deals as possible. One almost felt sorry for Dein after Wenger left him to deal with the Anelka party alone. 'You've left me to deal with sharks,' he complained to Wenger. 'Don't worry, David,' came the reply, 'sharks always eat each other in the end.' As a member of the FA Executive, Dein was the driving force behind Sven-Göran Erikson's appointment as England manager. In late 2001, he drafted a blueprint for the future of English football, in which he advocated, amongst other things, that Rangers and Celtic should become an integral part of the English game. To the disbelief of Nationwide Clubs, he argued that Premiership clubs are not set on 'freezing out' smaller outfits. With his UEFA panel hat on, he's long been an advocate of winter breaks and a specific, globalised football calendar. Many of Dein's ideas will come to pass in the near future. You can count on that.

Yet I would argue that if David Dein is to be regarded as a revolutionary in the football world, he should encourage the Arsenal board to communicate rather more effectively with their own supporters. Dein has always been very adept at quoting sections from the Taylor Report, but he has demurred from trotting out one key phrase from the report: 'As for the clubs, in some instances, it is legitimate to wonder whether the directors are genuinely interested in the welfare of their grass-roots supporters.' Arsenal Independent Supporters' Association (AISA) founder Ian McPherson believes that due to the way the Bond Scheme was handled in the early '90s and the whopping increases in ticket prices since, up to 8,000 North Bank regulars opted not to return to Highbury.

As McPherson says: 'A fair chunk of the club's traditional fan base have been forced to spend Saturday afternoons away from Highbury over the last ten years. Of course, since the start of the Premiership, there's been thousands wanting to take their place. But what happens, say, if the dark days return? Will these fans still turn up? Probably not, because they've only known a successful Arsenal side. They have no concept of what it was like watching struggling Arsenal sides week in, week out, in the '70s and '80s. And there's no way the old terrace crew will return, because they've been priced out for good. I still believe that what happened over ten years ago could seriously affect the club in the long term.'

The board's archaic public relations skills remain for all to see.

Directors made a great show in recent years of their consultative meetings with AISA and the Official Fans Forum, where issues such as the atmosphere at Highbury, the ticket registration scheme and catering facilities were discussed. Then in 2002, when the club crest was redesigned with little prior warning, the board scored a spectacular own goal. They announced that 'a cross section of key individuals, organisations and supporters' had been consulted in advance. Not one of those people allegedly questioned have identified themselves, or been identified. Talk of the crest representing 'brand values', 'tradition with vision' and 'embracing the future' sounded more like a piece of New Labour spin than clear information given to fans. For a self-proclaimed progressive club, the crest fiasco is a clear reminder of how crass the club can be in dealing with its own supporters. In May 2003, the club set an unwanted precedent by becoming the first to dispense with the victory parade after winning the FA Cup. The decision was apparently taken after police advice. The 200,000-odd fans who had become used to the carnival-like celebrations of recent years were disgusted.

Equally as clumsy were David Dein's alleged comments about the subdued atmosphere in the Upper Tiers at Highbury on match days. At nigh on £40 a seat, the clientele is more likely to behave in a manner akin to being in a theatre. Let us not forget that the new generation, upwardly mobile Highbury-libraryites were spawned partly through the Dein-inspired gentrification of the ground. The all-seater process has created precisely the sterile, muted environment Dein is now bemoaning. He is reaping what he sowed.

David Dein is undoubtedly a passionate Arsenal fan. His 'dream Double' is to watch the youth team win in the morning, followed by a first-team success in the afternoon. As the Gunners prepare to embark on a new era at a new stadium, why shouldn't Dein take a similarly bold step and adopt ideas from other European giants in Spain and Italy, whose season-ticket holders and members actually have democratic rights in deciding the direction of the club? Through elections, fans in Southern Europe can select officials to run the club from a nominated list of candidates, and in some cases have dictated the design and even the name of a new stadium, as well as the price of seats at home games. Club directors are then genuinely accountable for their actions. Instead of trotting out old clichés about being 'guardians of your club', or simply refusing to comment on tricky issues, they can be turfed out if they are seen to be failing in their responsibilities to supporters. These ideas have been mooted amongst Arsenal fans for years. Horror of horrors, there was even talk within the AISA of badgering the club to appoint an elected representative from the forum onto the board. Such a move would be genuinely radical and inventive amongst Premiership clubs. David Dein and his fellow directors possess the clout to make it happen and, in doing so, might prevent public relations disasters like the Bond Scheme and the crest calamity occurring in the future. Don't hold your breath, though.

Together with his fellow directors, Dein is hoping that the Ashburton Grove project will turn Arsenal into a European super-club, fully justifying the Gunners' presence in the G14 group and giving them the clout to compete with Manchester United and Real Madrid in the transfer market. It's arguably the biggest decision in the club's history – greater even than Sir Henry Norris's decision to move the club out of Kent. If the move pays off, Ashburton Grove would be a shining example of Dein and co's vision. Doomsday scenario would be if the club moved to the Grove and the new ground became a monstrous white elephant, which sucked dry the transfer kitty and consigned the club to years of crippling debt. The proposals are already costing the club millions, and if serious financial strife followed, the furore which once surrounded the Bond Scheme would seem tame in comparison. As this book has shown, Arsenal's villains can turn to heroes in the blink of an eye. David Dein the Arsenal fan will surely be aware that the opposite is also true.

Bibliography

Readers who'd like to dig further into the life and times of the Arsenal players and officials detailed in this book, or delve deeper into the more controversial side of club history, should find the following useful.

BOOKS

Going Great Guns, Kenny Sansom, Macdonald Queen Anne Press, 1987.

Seventy-One Guns, David Tossell, Mainstream, 2002.

The Working Man's Ballet, Alan Hudson, Robson Books, 1997.

The Great Divide, Alex Fynn and Olivia Blair, Andre Deutsch, 2000.

Addicted, Tony Adams, Collins Willow, 1998.

Arsenal Fact File, Bruce Smith, Virgin, 2000.

Revelations Of A Football Manager, Terry Neill, Sidgwick and Jackson, 1985.

The Glory And The Grief, George Graham, Andre Deutsch, 1995.

Inside Soccer, Tony Woodcock, Queen Anne Press, 1985.

Football Emperor, Stephen Studd, Souvenir Press, 1981.

Cliff Bastin Remembers, Cliff Bastin, Etterick Press, 1950.

So Far So Good, Liam Brady, Stanley Paul, 1980.

Malcolm Macdonald: An Autobiography, Jason Tomas and Malcolm Macdonald, Arthur Baker, 1983.

The Wright Stuff, Rick Glanvill, Virgin, 1995.

Determined To Win, George Eastham, Stanley Paul, 1964.

The Book of Football Quotations, Phil Shaw, Ebury Press, 2003.

George Graham: The Wonder Years, Tony Willis and Jeff King, Virgin, 1995.

The Lad Done Bad, Denis Campbell, Pete May, Andrew Shields, Penguin, 1986.

It's All About A Ball, Alan Ball, W.H. Allen, 1978.

Arsenal: Chapman To Mee, Ralph L. Finn, Robert Hale, 1969.

Behind The Scenes In Big Football, Leslie Knighton, Stanley Paul, 1950.

Rock Bottom, Paul Merson, Bloomsbury, 1995.

Charlie Nicholas, David Stubbs, Boxtree, 1997.

Heroes And Villains, Alex Fynn and Lynton Guest, Penguin, 1991.

Ray Of Hope, The Ray Kennedy Story, Penguin 1993.

Passovotchka, David Downing, Bloomsbury, 1999.

In The Days Of Gog – The Real Arsenal Story, Alan Roper, 2003.

Plus the author's own works: *All Guns Blazing and Top Guns*.

JOURNALS

History Today, 'Stalin And His Soccer Soldiers', Robert Edelman, February 1993

History Review, 'Mysterious Muscovites', Ronald Kowalski and Dilwyn Porter, March 1999

FANZINES

The Gooner
Highbury High
One Nil Down

ANNUALS

Fab 208 Annual – 1971 – LPC Magazines Ltd